Zapotec
Struggles

Smithsonian Series in Ethnographic Inquiry

William L. Merrill and Ivan Karp, Series Editors

Ethnography as fieldwork, analysis, and literary form is the distinguishing feature of modern anthropology. Guided by the assumption that anthropological theory and ethnography are inextricably linked, this series is devoted to exploring the ethnographic enterprise.

Advisory Board

Richard Bauman (Indiana University), Gerald Berreman (University of California, Berkeley), James Boon (Princeton University), Stephen Gudeman (University of Minnesota), Shirley Lindenbaum (City University of New York), George Marcus (Rice University), David Parkin (University of London), Roy Rappaport (University of Michigan), Renato Rosaldo (Stanford University), Annette Weiner (New York University), Norman Whitten (University of Illinois), and Eric Wolf (City University of New York).

Zapotec Struggles

Histories, Politics, and Representations from Juchitán, Oaxaca

Edited by Howard Campbell, Leigh Binford,
Miguel Bartolomé, and Alicia Barabas

Poetry translated by Nathaniel Tarn

Smithsonian Institution Press
Washington and London

Copy Editor: Tom Ireland
Supervisory Editor: Duke Johns
Designer: Janice Wheeler

Library of Congress Cataloging-in-Publication Data
Zapotec struggles : histories, politics, and representations from Juchitán, Oaxaca / edited by Howard Campbell . . . [et al.] ; poetry translated by Nathaniel Tarn.
   p. cm.
   Includes bibliographical references and index.
   ISBN 1-56098-268-3. — ISBN 1-56098-293-4 (pbk.)
   1. Coalición Obrera Campesina Estudiantil del Istmo—History. 2. Zapotec Indians—Politics and government. 3. Zapotec Indians—Government relations.
4. Zapotec Indians—Social conditions. 5. Juchitán de Zaragoza (Mexico)—Politics and government. 6. Juchitán de Zaragoza (Mexico)—Social conditions.
I. Campbell, Howard, 1957– .
[F1221.Z3Z36 1993]
972'.74—dc20   92-36113

British Library Cataloguing-in-Publication Data is available

Manufactured in the United States of America
00 99 98 97 96 95 94 93 5 4 3 2 1

⊗ The paper used in this publication meets the minimum requirements of the American National Standard for Permanence of Paper for Printed Library Materials Z39.48-1984.

On the cover: *Mascara IV (Mask IV)*. Painting on turtle shell by Francisco Toledo, 1988.

For the COCEI martyrs

Contents

xi **Foreword**
Miguel Bartolomé and Alicia Barabas

xvii **Preface**

xxiii **Acknowledgments**

xxv **Abbreviations**

I **Introduction**
Leigh Binford and Howard Campbell

PART ONE
Histories of Conflict, Struggle,
and Mobilization in the Isthmus of Tehuantepec

29 **Indigenous Peoples' History (by Whom and for Whom?)**
Víctor de la Cruz

39 **The Foundation of Juchitán**
Andrés Henestrosa

41 **Ethnic Resistance: Juchitán in Mexican History**
John Tutino

63   *Song:* **A New Corrido for Che Gómez**
Tomás Ruiz

65   **Juchitán: Histories of Discord**
Adriana López Monjardin

81   **Memories of Anastasia Martínez**

87   **Irrigation, Land Tenure, and Class Struggle in Juchitán, Oaxaca**
Leigh Binford

101   **The Future of the Isthmus and the Juárez Dam**
Arturo Warman

107   *Poem:* **The One Who Rode Duarte's Horse**
Gabriel López Chiñas

PART TWO
**Representations of the Juchitecos
by Themselves and Others**

117   *Poem:* **Who Are We? What Is Our Name?**
Víctor de la Cruz

119   **A German Traveler's Observations in Juchitán**
G. F. Von Tempsky

123   **The Juchitecos as Seen by Benito Juárez**
Excerpts from a speech, July 2, 1850

125   **Juchitán Political Moments**
Macario Matus

129   **The Forms of Sexual Life in Juchitán**
Andrés Henestrosa

133   **Juchitán, a Town of Women**
Elena Poniatowska

137   **Representations of Isthmus Women: A Zapotec Woman's
Point of View**
Obdulia Ruiz Campbell

143   **Social Scientists Confronted with Juchitán (Incidents of
an Unequal Relationship)**
Víctor de la Cruz

Contents

PART THREE

COCEI: Isthmus Zapotec Political Radicalism

155 *Poem:* **My Companions Have Died**
Macario Matus

157 **COCEI against the State: A Political History of Juchitán**
Jeffrey W. Rubin

177 **Testimonies of COCEI Women**
Collected by Marta Bañuelos

183 **Inaugural Speech as Mayor of Juchitán**
Leopoldo de Gyves de la Cruz

185 **Alternatives for Struggle: The Context of the COCEI Alternative**
COCEI

191 **COCEI: Narodniks of Southern Mexico?**
Sergio Zermeño

203 *Poem:* **Naked Speech**
Macario Matus

205 *Poem:* **A Birth in the Mountains**
Alejandro Cruz

PART FOUR

Guendabiaani': **The Politics of Culture in Juchitán**

211 *Poem:* **The Zapotec Language**
Gabriel López Chiñas

213 **Class Struggle, Ethnopolitics, and Cultural Revivalism in Juchitán**
Howard Campbell

233 **Interview with Daniel López Nelio**

237 *Poem:* **Rain**
Víctor de la Cruz

239 *Poem:* **The Sun**
Enedino Jiménez

241 **Brothers or Citizens: Two Languages, Two Political Projects**
in the Isthmus
Víctor de la Cruz

249 *Cuento:* **The Bell**
Andrés Henestrosa

253 *Cuento:* **Trapped Lightning**
Recorded by Macario Matus

255 **The Tales of Moonje'**
Manuel M. Matus

259 **When Radio Became the Voice of the People**
Manuel López Mateos

263 *Poem:* **Pichancha**
Miguel Flores Ramírez

265 *Poem:* **The Third Elegy**
Víctor de la Cruz

267 **The Proud Midwives of Juchitán**
Shoshana R. Sokoloff

279 **Afterword**

285 **Appendix: Chronology of Isthmus Zapotec History
and COCEI History**

287 **Glossary**

289 **Works Cited**

303 **Source Notes**

307 **Contributors**

311 **Index**

Foreword

Miguel Bartolomé and Alicia Barabas

It should not surprise the reader that a multifaceted book like this one would also have multiple protagonists who contributed to its construction. Each one probably had distinct objectives and purposes, which is part of the plurality of the book. For our part, we should point out that we have been living and working in the interethnic regions of Mexico for twenty years, fifteen of which have been in Oaxaca. During these years, we have witnessed the ethnic drama in all of its overwhelming intensity. We have lived and we live currently with colonized people who suffer from processes that can be characterized as multiple deprivation because they entail economic, psychological, political, and social subordination. The efforts of these people to free themselves have not yet been completely successful. For the time being, the formal acceptance of cultural pluralism by the state institutions is political rhetoric lacking concrete formulation.

It is for this reason that we accepted the proposal of Charles Leslie when he asked us to collaborate with him in the realization of a book that would reflect the struggle and dynamic of the COCEI. We consider it of great importance to make known to a wider audience this successful expression of an ethnic movement. We, then, turned to our old friend, the Zapotec poet, historian, and essayist Víctor de la Cruz, director of the magazine *Guchachi' Reza*, who generously authorized the translation and publication of materials from that magazine that reflect the particular ethnopolitical and cultural perspective of

Juchitecas making tortillas. Photo by G. Iturbide.

the COCEI. With the same generosity, many people offered freely their graphic arts to illustrate the book. Among them we should not forget to make a special mention of our friend, the prestigious photographer Graciela Iturbide.

This first selection of materials was given to Professor Leslie, who enlisted the poet Nathaniel Tarn to translate the poetry, and later, the anthropologist Howard Campbell, who was working in the Isthmus, to translate the essays. Campbell's extensive work on the manuscript caused Leslie to propose Campbell as an editor and retire from the project to devote more time to his own busy research agenda. Later Campbell proposed to us the need to include Leigh Binford as editor, who, in addition to having experience in the area, was collaborating in the difficult work of translation. The new editors increased the initial selection of materials that formed the book and added their own essays. This is how this collection of documents came together. They represent a great diversity of points of view, of the compilers as well as the authors, which in themselves express the pluralism this book seeks to reflect.

This is, then, an anthropological treatment of a specific social process, but one that presupposes an important emphasis on the perspectives of the protagonists. It constitutes the conjunction of distinct discourses pronounced by different actors (indigenous people, social scientists, artists, and politicians) in an attempt to provide an image of reality that is not filtered by the exclusive eye of a single author. Here are brought together many voices that speak about the same theme but do not necessarily produce a synthesis. We do not intend to reduce a process to one of its factors, but to demonstrate the multiple facets it offers. In recent years, the so-called postmodern anthropology (of North America) has realized projects of a similar nature, although we personally do not share its theoretical postulates, which have been lucidly analyzed by Reynoso (1991). It seems to us, nonetheless, a positive effort to liberate anthropological discourse from the crushing framework of empirical fiction that proposes to achieve objectivity through extensive quantification and the supposed exclusion of the subjectivity of the author. But it should be pointed out that this represents also a late discovery (or acceptance) of what academic traditions in other countries had postulated many years ago.

All anthropologies tend to be a bit provincial, and North American anthropology is not an exception to the rule. However, it seems healthy that its representatives have accepted the influence of Foucault in relation to the arbitrariness of epistemes (paradigms and world views) and the corrosive "antiepistemic" deconstructionism of Derrida. But with this new critical arsenal, postmodernism arrived at heteroglosia, diaglosia, and polyphony as ethnographic resources, without noting its antecedents in hermeneutic anthropology, such as that of Leonhardt. Even still, the concern with breaking the monologue of the author is valid. We would also like to clarify that we value the knowledge produced by ethnography. Geertz has characterized it as a fiction. This does not mean that it is unreal, but that it is a _construction_ whose nature as such should be made explicit.

Welcome to the critique of ethnography as literature (Geertz), to experimental ethnography (Rabinow), or the creative collages of Taussig. We share the questioning of the apparently objective worlds, the relativization of authorially constructed realities. But we do not accept that reality is a fantasy, nor that it has the same ontological status as the imaginary. This type of depoliticized and depoliticizing game could be valid for First World anthropologists who continue to ignore or undervalue the human dimension of the people to whom they relate: their grandeur, misery, and struggles framed by the tragedy of colonialism. Accepting the fact that every event supposes intertextuality does not exclude recognizing that this is only another form of designing the context, and thus is susceptible to being analyzed. This is the case, for example, of an empathetic attempt to understand the collective existential anxiety that underlies social movements such as the one protagonized by the COCEI. This anxiety cannot be reduced to a literary piece, even though literature is also a legitimate resource for understanding it.

In accordance with these reflections, COCEI must be considered an ethnopolitical movement. For a little more than two decades in Latin America we have witnessed a growing process of dynamization of the struggles of the indigenous ethnic groups for their liberation and the destigmatized recovery of their cultures. These struggles, with different concrete objectives and proposals for the global transformation of the colonial realities of each country, are developing in the space of multiple federations, organizations, and movements—sometimes independent, other times allied to political parties. The varied ethnopolitical groupings compete for political space within the national states in which they are included. These are struggles not only for political autonomy, but also for the right to cultural survival and development. This contemporary emergence should not, however, confuse us. It is not a new phenomenon but the restructured expression of the long struggle that the indigenous ethnic groups have carried out, but which now is expressed through a new type of discourse and action. It is a reelaborated ethnopolitical praxis adapting to the changing circumstances that interethnic local, regional, and continental systems pass through. It is also trying to manifest itself in terms that are comprehensible within the parameters of "political rationality" imposed by the logos of the hegemonic groups. This essay is not the place where we can become aware of the numerous existing organizations in Latin America, Mexico, and Oaxaca. Nor can we digress in the singularity of the proposals and particular political styles elaborated by each of the groups that participate today in this Indian mobilization. Nonetheless, we want to emphasize the fact that the COCEI is one of the most elaborate and successful exponents of the current Indian politics, which, with great lucidity, has known how to recover the calls for freedom of earlier generations of Zapotecs and inscribe them combatively within the political and cultural arena of contemporary Mexico.

Left to right: Leopoldo de Gyves Pineda, Francisco Toledo, Eraclio Zepeda, and Víctor de la Cruz. Photo by H. Rodríguez. Courtesy of Víctor de la Cruz.

Preface

The 1970s and 1980s were characterized by indigenous resistance, revolt, and rebellion in many parts of Latin America. In Guatemala more than a half million Highland Mayans representing most of the nation's twenty-three cultural and linguistic groups fought or collaborated with guerrilla groups in a war against the Guatemalan army and police forces (Carmack 1988; Simon 1987). In Peru, Quechua speakers fought for and aided Sendero Luminoso (Shining Path) guerrillas even as others opposed the movement (Bourque and Warren 1989). In Nicaragua, the allegiance of Miskitu and Suma indigenous groups (among others) of the northern Atlantic coast province of Zelaya was a prize contested for almost ten years by the *sandinista* state and U.S.-backed counter-revolutionaries based in Honduras and Costa Rica (Bourgois 1985).

Only in El Salvador, among the nations that have experienced a major revolutionary challenge to the status quo in the last decade, have indigenous peoples not played a significant role, and that is because the Pipils, who previously populated the western provinces of the country, were mostly wiped out in a military counterstrike following the failed 1932 rebellion organized by Farabundo Martí (Anderson 1971).

In countries such as Brazil, Ecuador, and Mexico, where social conflict has been contained (for the most part) short of armed revolt against the State, indigenous minorities have also organized to defend land and natural resources and to protest assaults on their languages and cultures (Schryer 1990; Boege 1988).

This is a book about one of the most successful Latin American indigenous movements, the Worker-Peasant-Student Coalition of the Isthmus of Tehuantepec (COCEI) of Juchitán, Oaxaca (Mexico).[1] COCEI was founded in 1973 and has dominated politics in Juchitán (Oaxaca's second largest city) since 1980, controlling outright the municipal administration after winning local elections in 1981, serving as the minority party in a coalition government with the Institutional Revolutionary Party (PRI) from 1986 to 1989, and governing a coalition municipal council in Juchitán until the 1992 elections.[2] In the violent and unpredictable world of Mexican regional and local politics, COCEI has demonstrated its staying power by surviving economic boycott, repression, and efforts at cooptation by local elites and state and federal governments. As a consequence, the movement has achieved an almost legendary place in the Mexican press, vilified by the right and admired (even sanctified) by much of the left.

Despite its prominence in Mexico, COCEI is almost unknown in the United States. Thus, in addition to offering an alternative form of ethnographic presentation (which will be discussed below and in the introduction), this volume is intended to introduce an English-reading audience to an important Mexican political and cultural movement.

What does recent social science literature have to say about indigenous movements like COCEI? In general, indigenous Latin American mobilizations and rebellions took social scientists as well as government officials by surprise. The received wisdom embodied in recent social science literature held that passivity and fatalism were intrinsic features of traditional "peasant societies" and had been reinforced by hundreds of years of colonialism and a suffocating State apparatus sustained by overwhelming military force. When indigenous peoples began to speak out more forcefully and organize against elites and conservative governments, it seemed at first as though resistance and rebellion had come out of nowhere. Social scientists have responded to these events by redirecting their work, seeking out the roots of rebellion in the apparently tranquil past and plumbing the present for elements of concealed subversion (Katz 1988; Stern 1987; Scott 1985). Observing the violent reactions of power-holders to indigenous demands for self-determination, many social scientists also became spokespersons for their informants, even to the point of pleading their cases before the academy and world opinion (for examples see the numerous articles in *Cultural Survival Quarterly* and publications of the Anthropology Resource Center).

From their renegotiated position as analysts of peasant resistance (and, sometimes, advocates for indigenous movements), many social scientists now emphasize the contradictory role of culture. On one hand, culture is shaped by the ideologies of dominant classes, genders, and ethnic groups to promote compliance with institutionalized economic, political, and ideological projects. On the other hand, culture is a product of subaltern experience, and thus the medium within which class, gender, and ethnic resistance forms and through which it is expressed (Scott 1985; Ong 1987). In short, culture is an ongoing product of negotiation with multiple determinants; it is forged within a crucible of conflicting claims. And it codetermines social structure, rather than being a fully separate and independent dimension (Stoler 1984). This redirection of social scientific work has led to the revaluation of the voices of previously marginalized figures of social history as marking a new authenticity, evidence for what really happened as opposed to what "bourgeois history," with its emphasis on grand figures and epic events, says happened.

Despite the political shift associated with the search for evidence of resistance where previously there appeared to be little or none, academic approaches sustain a fundamental continuity: non-Western peoples continue to provide the raw material for theorization and interpretation by Western-oriented social scientists. Informants' opinions and views serve principally as grist for the social scientific mill and are seldom regarded as equally plausible descriptions of reality. *We* continue to explain *them,* albeit in new and more creative ways. Hence the break with the way social science used to be done has been realized by means of more fundamental methodological and epistemological continuities, which carry with them assumptions about whose knowledges count and are worth a hearing (Pinney 1989; Fabian 1983).

From the point of view of a progressive social science, an orientation toward Third World resistance as opposed to passivity is to be embraced. But insofar as this orientation is channeled discursively in such a way that the figure of Third World peoples remains unchanged, it is open to criticism. Víctor de la Cruz, an Isthmus Zapotec intellectual, states this quite clearly in his essay "Indigenous Peoples' History (by Whom and for Whom?)," which appears in Part One of this volume:

> When will we have the chance to access resources, like those who study our history supposedly for pure scientific interest? Do we not have the right to participate in the clarification of our past? Do the "indigenous peoples" not run the risk that their history is currently written in accord with the interests of foreign historians? Is it not possible that we are living another type of colonization like that of the missionaries in the sixteenth and seventeenth centuries and that historians from outside are displacing our interpretation of the facts with their own, per-

haps substituting their myths for ours? Or can we trust completely that they have no ideology and that ideology is not present in their work? Would it be definitively better for indigenous peoples' history to be analyzed and interpreted in accord with the ideological scheme of historians from outside than with our own schemes?

De la Cruz's interrogations of the historical record might equally have been directed to the contemporary anthropological record, which is produced by outsiders primarily for the edification of outsiders. In the case of social anthropology, an exchange of ideas with one's informants is an intrinsic feature of the fieldwork enterprise (Fabian 1983; Rabinow 1977), but the exchanges that dominate academic journals are those *between* professional researchers *about* their subjects. While the sharp imbalances between anthropologists and informants often prevent free and open communication, we hope in this volume to begin to break down such barriers.[3]

This book about COCEI, a radical Isthmus Zapotec movement based in Juchitán, is rooted in our belief that what others have to say about themselves and about us should be given just as much credence as what we have to say about them. With that aim in mind, we have brought together a variety of voices "internal" and "external" to COCEI and Juchitán. The volume is organized in a way that seeks to place social scientists, historians, and other non-Zapotec observers of the Isthmus in dialogue with Zapotec intellectuals, politicians, and Juchiteco townspeople. For we discovered in the course of living and working in the Isthmus of Tehuantepec that people who are self-identified as Isthmus Zapotec, and particularly those politically active in COCEI, have a great deal to say to and about both us and themselves, and that much of it has been written down in the pages of intellectual journals produced by Juchitecos from at least the 1930s. Indeed, the Zapotec intellectuals' most recent multigenre magazine, *Guchachi' Reza*[4] *(Sliced Iguana),* serves both as a model for this volume and illustrates many important issues in contemporary anthropology such as the diffusion of ethnographic authority, the dialectic of representations by "self" and "other," and the possibilities for new forms of anthropological writing. In our view, the present collection of articles, poems, songs, testimonies, and stories, many of them translated from Spanish, is an ethnography of an indigenous political and cultural movement; but it is an ethnography that, without denying our role in the selection and organization of the materials, presents Juchiteco voices in pursuit of their own projects and in opposition to the ways in which they have been represented and analyzed by Euroamerican social scientists.

The book's introduction provides the reader with basic background material on the Isthmus of Tehuantepec, Juchitán, and COCEI. We situate the remainder of the book in the context of discussions of new ethnographic writing and the "new social movements" literature. The articles, poems, and testimony in Part One, "Histories of Conflict, Struggle, and Mobilization in the Isthmus of Tehuantepec," portray the changing historical role of the Isthmus and of the Isthmus Zapotecs in general, and Juchitecos in particular, in their relationships with Aztecs, Spaniards, the French, and representatives of the Mexican State. Part Two, "Representations of the Juchitecos by Themselves and Others," consists of selected portrayals of the Juchitecos by Isthmus visitors and other outsiders, Juchiteco self-portrayals, and critical representations of visitors to the region by Isthmus Zapotec writers. Part Three, "COCEI: Isthmus Zapotec Political Radicalism," contains articles, poems, testimony, and speeches recalling, analyzing, and representing political developments and struggles in Juchitán as they are remembered, currently understood, and projected toward the future. The articles, poems, and *cuentos* (folklore) in Part Four, "*Guendabiaani':* The Politics of Culture in Juchitán," discuss and illustrate the critical role that culture has played in COCEI political mobilization and exemplify some significant Juchiteco cultural productions. The photographs and reproductions of art work contained throughout this volume are further testimony to the color, passion, and creativity of the Juchiteco intellectual movement and should be examined and studied in conjunction with the other materials of the book.

It is our hope that this volume will serve both as an introduction to Isthmus Zapotec culture and history *and* make a contribution to the analysis and understanding of indigenous peasant-based social movements in Mexico and elsewhere. We also hope that it will encourage multigenre, polyvocal, and experimental styles of ethnographic presentation and, in the process, lead its readers to question the privilege extended to social science in arriving at truths about others and to reassess the implications for knowledge production of their own social and historical positioning.

NOTES

1. Coalición Obrera Campesina Estudiantil del Istmo.
2. The movement was founded under the name of Coalición Campesina Estudiantil de Juchitán in 1973, and adopted the name COCEI in 1974. After work on this book's manuscript was completed, COCEI won the 1992 Juchitán municipal elections and currently governs the town.
3. By this statement we do not mean to imply that all informants' views, any more than all anthropologists' views, are equally valuable, enlightening, or accurate. Nor are we attempting to deny the role of anthropologists in the selection and choice of

ethnographic materials for presentation (such as in this book). We do argue, however, that the distance between "anthropologist" and "informant" may be reduced
and that one possible avenue for narrowing the gap is the creation of multivocal
volumes, such as we have attempted here. One could also imagine such a volume
designed and edited by indigenous people themselves (in fact, COCEI has already
produced books along these lines). We feel that such volumes are a substantial improvement over monographs in which a single Western observer claims to accurately represent a group of people and their way of life.
4. The apostrophe after several Zapotec words used in the text indicates that the
   vowel so marked is pronounced with a glottal stop.

Acknowledgments

The creation of this volume has indeed been a collective project. The initial idea for such a book came from Charles Leslie. Charles, a student of Robert Redfield, carried out his dissertation fieldwork in the Zapotec town of Mitla, Oaxaca, in the 1950s. He later shifted his focus to India, and Asia generally, and became a noted specialist in medical anthropology.

In spring 1988, while enjoying a sabbatical in Oaxaca, Charles came across the Isthmus Zapotec cultural magazine *Guchachi' Reza* and other publications of the Juchitán intellectuals. He decided to assemble an anthology of essays, poems, and other materials about Juchitán and the COCEI loosely mirroring the multigenre format of *Guchachi' Reza*. Charles invited the anthropologists Miguel Bartolomé and Alicia Barabas of the Oaxaca branch of the Instituto Nacional de Antropología e Historia to collaborate with him as editors of the volume. He asked them to make a selection of scientific articles, essays, poetry, and photographic and graphic art that would include Zapotec collaborators as well as foreigners who have produced texts and artistic work concerned with Isthmus Zapotec culture and the COCEI. He also solicited the help of his long-time friend and colleague, Nathaniel Tarn, to translate the poetry.

As time passed, Charles's other professional commitments prevented him from continuing work on the Juchitán volume. He asked Campbell to take his place as editor along with Bartolomé and Barabas. Campbell, busy writing his dissertation on Zapotec intellectuals and COCEI, also recruited Leigh Binford to join them as an editor. Campbell carried out most of the Spanish-English translation and played an important role in increasing the initial selection. The foreword was written by Bartolomé and Barabas. The preface, introduction, subintroductions, and afterword were written collaboratively by Binford and Campbell and went through so many drafts that it has become difficult to recall who wrote what. Needless to say, our collaboration has been an exceedingly pleasurable experience.

Leslie's plan was to divide the book into two parts: an internal discourse section by Zapotec intellectuals and an external discourse section by outside observers of Juchitán like ourselves. But as we read the essays and poems, it seemed to us that a more fruitful approach would be to interweave the various perspectives and graphic materials rather than to separate them. The original idea of presenting the reader with a multiplicity of discourses produced by different social actors was maintained, but the materials were reorganized into the various sections that make up the book. The end result is a polyvocal volume based on the contributions of many different people.

In particular, we would like to mention Obdulia Ruiz Campbell, who proofread and commented on many aspects of the book, sharing her insights into life in the Isthmus of Tehuantepec. Miguel Bartolomé and Alicia Barabas obtained without cost the photographs of their friend Graciela Iturbide as well as photographs by Emilio López and reproductions of artwork by Israel Vicente.

Víctor de la Cruz and Graciela Toledo also helped obtain photographs and artwork. The Juchiteco artists, Francisco Toledo and Miguel Angel Toledo, graciously granted permission to reproduce photographs of their paintings. David Flores of the University of Texas at El Paso prepared the photographs for publication. Howard Campbell, Charles Leslie, and Jeff Rubin provided financial support to obtain art work for the volume. Special thanks are due to Víctor de la Cruz for giving permission to use many pieces originally published in *Guchachi' Reza*.

We would also like to thank the leaders of the COCEI (Héctor Sánchez, Daniel López Nelio, and Pólin de Gyves) and the former director of the Casa de la Cultura of Juchitán, Macario Matus, for allowing us to pry into their affairs and ask many questions about Juchitán and the COCEI. Oscar Cruz, Manuel López Mateos, and Julio Bustillo made fieldwork in Juchitán a pleasure. Chris Gjording provided us with a detailed critique of our contribution and helped us clean up a great deal of messy writing. James Faris read and commented on early drafts of our subintroductions. The University of Texas at El Paso Graduate School and the Julian Samora Research Institute of Michigan State University provided support for the preparation of the manuscript. Finally, Daniel Goodwin of the Smithsonian Institution Press was always friendly and supportive.

Abbreviations

AMAR	Archives of the Ministry of Agrarian Reform
ANOCP	Asamblea Nacional de Obreros y Campesinos Popular (National Peasant Worker Assembly)
BANCRISA	Banco de Credito Rural del Istmo, Sociedad Anónima (Rural Credit Bank of the Isthmus, Incorporated)
CNC	Confederación Nacional Campesina (National Peasant Confederation)
CNIA	Confederación Nacional de la Industria Azucarera (National Sugarcane Industry Confederation)
CNPA	Coordinadora Nacional Plan de Ayala (National Plan of Ayala Coordinating Committee)
CNTE	Coordinadora Nacional de Trabajadores de la Educación (National Coordinating Committee of Education Workers)
COCEI	Coalición Obrera Campesina Estudiantil del Istmo (Worker-Peasant-Student Coalition of the Isthmus of Tehuantepec)
CTI	Central de Trabajadores del Istmo (Union of Workers of the Isthmus)
DAAC	Departamento de Asuntos Agrarios y Colonización (Department of Agrarian Affairs and Colonization)
DFS	Dirección Federal de Seguridad (Federal Directorate of Security)
FNCR	Frente Nacional Contra la Represión (National Front against Repression)
IMF	International Monetary Fund
INBA	Instituto Nacional de Bellas Artes (National Fine Arts Institute)
PCM	Partido Comunista de México (Mexican Communist Party)
PEMEX	Petróleos Mexicanos (Mexican Petroleum)

Abbreviations

PMS	Partido Mexicano Socialista (Mexican Socialist Party)
PPS	Partido Popular Socialista (Popular Socialist Party)
PRD	Partido de la Revolución Democrática (Party of the Democratic Revolution)
PRI	Partido Revolucionario Institucional (Institutional Revolutionary Party)
PRT	Partido Revolucionario de los Trabajadores (Revolutionary Workers' Party)
PSUM	Partido Socialista Unificado de México (Unified Socialist Party of Mexico)
RAP	Radio Ayuntamiento Popular (Popular Municipal Radio)
SARH	Secretaría de Agricultura y Recursos Hidráulicos (Ministry of Agriculture and Water Resources)
SEDUE	Secretaría de Desarrollo Urbano y Ecología (Ministry of Urban Development and Ecology)
SNTE	Sindicato Nacional de Trabajadores de la Educación (National Union of Education Workers)
UNAM	Universidad Nacional Autónoma de México (National Autonomous University of Mexico)

Zapotec
Struggles

Introduction

Leigh Binford and Howard Campbell

In 1981 in Juchitán, Oaxaca, the Worker-Peasant-Student Coalition of the Isthmus of Tehuantepec (COCEI), in electoral alliance with the Mexican Communist Party, defeated the entrenched government party, the Institutional Revolutionary Party (PRI), in Juchitán's municipal elections.[1] Following the victory, a COCEI administration governed this important regional city until it was impeached by the Oaxaca State Legislature in August 1983 and then forcibly removed from the municipal buildings four months later by the army and police.

COCEI is certainly not the only local movement to challenge PRI political control in recent years. But it is the first leftist organization to inflict a major urban loss upon PRI since the government party was formed in 1929. Equally significant, this loss was inflicted by Isthmus Zapotec people, representatives of Mexico's indigenous minorities, rather than mestizo bearers of the dominant national culture.

Following their removal from office in 1983, COCEI leaders and militants were pursued by the police, military, courts, and right-wing paramilitary squads. Despite harassment and persecution, which swelled the ranks of COCEI martyrs, the organization survived, sustained by its deep roots in the community and region. COCEI bounced back to contest the 1986 Juchitán municipal elections and eventually entered into a coalition government with the local PRI between 1986 and 1989. During this period the election of a

Leigh Binford and Howard Campbell

Photo by G. Iturbide.

liberal Oaxaca state governor (1986), internal dissension within PRI, and an unexpectedly strong presidential challenge mounted by dissident ex-*priísta* (PRI member) Cuauhtémoc Cárdenas (1988) created a new political opening in rural Mexico (Cornelius et al. 1989a). COCEI took advantage of this opening in 1989 and once again won municipal elections. As the dominant force in a mixed administration—PRI held a minority of city council seats— COCEI controlled Juchitán through summer 1992. In November 1992, COCEI marched to victory again and will control the municipality until at least 1995.

COCEI was formed in 1973 as a class-based Zapotec opposition organization with roots both in the Mexican student movement of the late 1960s and Juchiteco groups opposed to the local PRI hierarchy. For more than five years, COCEI's militants and supporters engaged in political activity: invading land;

blocking highways; organizing peasants and workers; and circulating demands for municipal self-determination, solution of the region's agrarian problems, and honest municipal government. These activities attracted little attention outside the state of Oaxaca until COCEI's surprising 1981 electoral victory and controversial impeachment two years later. During that turbulent period, national and foreign journalists, intellectuals, and students were drawn to Juchitán like flies to honey to observe directly the first leftist organization to defeat PRI in urban elections and to investigate an unusually successful movement of indigenous peoples. In ensuing years, COCEI was intensely scrutinized in the state and national press and major periodicals, becoming the subject of academic analyses in books, articles, and theses in Mexico and, to a lesser extent, the United States, Japan, and Europe.

The journalists and social scientists writing on COCEI have generally focused on the movement's place in Mexican national politics, or its history and ideology. They have paid relatively little attention to COCEI's grounding in Isthmus Zapotec culture and thus seldom analyzed the way that COCEI draws creatively on Zapotec language and culture to promote its alternative political project. Speeches are delivered in Zapotec as well as Spanish; marches and demonstrations are modeled on local fiestas and ceremonial processions; and COCEI interpretations of Isthmus history emphasize the continuity of Zapotec resistance to Aztec, Spanish, and French invaders, gringo outsiders, and representatives of the Mexican State (see the articles by Víctor de la Cruz and Howard Campbell in Part Four).

COCEI politics are thereby creatively interwoven with indigenous culture and draw on a long Zapotec tradition of self-presentation through ethnography, history, song, poetry, painting, and drawing by artists and writers like Andrés Henestrosa, Gabriel López Chiñas, Víctor de la Cruz, Macario Matus, and others, many of whom are represented in this collection. Few Mesoamerican indigenous groups have produced such an elaborate local intellectual movement. Long before the formation of COCEI, Juchitecos expressed themselves at home, work, and play through song, poetry, *cuentos* (folklore), and in the pages of homegrown periodicals such as *Neza* in the 1930s and *Neza Cubi* in the 1960s. *Guchachi' Reza* (*Iguana Rajada,* or *Sliced Iguana*), the latest and most sophisticated Juchiteco journal, was started by COCEI intellectuals in 1975 and has become one of the most provocative cultural publications to emerge from rural Latin America. Finally, Francisco Toledo, one of Mexico's foremost contemporary painters and a native Juchiteco, has spread images of COCEI and the Isthmus Zapotecs to the cultural capitals of Europe, the United States, and Japan through his colorful and provocative work.

COCEI, then, is a sophisticated Isthmus Zapotec political and cultural movement whose members are conscious of their historical roles, proud of their indigenous roots, and creative in their handling of the raw materials of Isthmus history. COCEI supporters are the antithesis of stereotypically shy, ignorant, culturally impoverished Indians who require interlocutors and mediators (anthropologists, journalists, politicians) to represent their interests. On the contrary, they have demonstrated that they are able to represent themselves concretely through political mobilizations, election campaigns, and literacy programs; and intellectually and artistically through paintings, poetry, and in the pages of *Guchachi' Reza* and COCEI's official publications.

The present volume provides a sampling of outsiders' representations of Juchitán and COCEI, among which are writings by social scientists, such as ourselves, who have visited or resided in the Isthmus, become acquainted with Isthmus Zapotec peoples and customs, and researched Isthmus economy, culture, and politics. The book also contains Juchiteco and COCEI self-representations and offers some Zapotec representations of non-Istmeño "others" including tourists, travelers, and agents of the Mexican government bureaucracy.

In the following sections we introduce the Isthmus of Tehuantepec, Juchitán, and COCEI, and then attempt to relate the movement and this work about it to current thinking on ethnographic writing and new social movements in Latin America.

THE ISTHMUS ZAPOTECS AND THE ISTHMUS OF TEHUANTEPEC

Population, Geography, and Natural Resources

In recent years COCEI has developed substantial influence in a number of Isthmus Zapotec communities and among some non-Zapotec ethnic groups. Yet it has always been based in Juchitán, Oaxaca, a sprawling, overgrown peasant-dominated city of approximately 80,000 inhabitants, located in the center of the Pacific coastal plain of the Isthmus of Tehuantepec, five miles inland from the Pacific Ocean (see map).[2] The Isthmus is one of eight regions in Oaxaca, a poor, ethnically diverse southern Mexican state. Of Oaxaca's 2.5 million people, about 900,000 speak one (or more) of fifteen indigenous languages (Bartolomé and Barabas 1986:20–21). This makes Oaxaca the most culturally and linguistically diverse state in Mexico. Within Oaxaca, Zapotec is second to Spanish in the number of speakers.[3]

The Isthmus region encompasses the districts (similar to U.S. counties) of

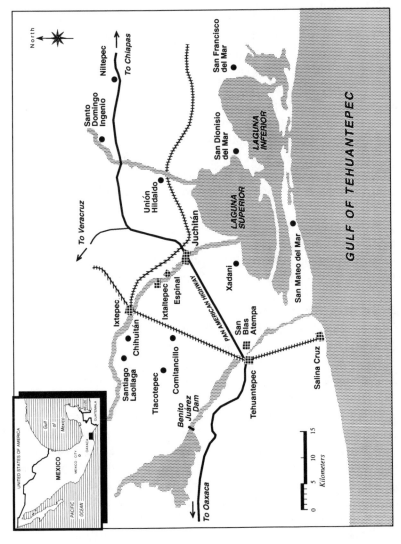

The southern isthmus of Tehuantepec.

Leigh Binford and Howard Campbell

Juchitán and Tehuantepec. It stretches from the state of Veracruz in the north to the Pacific Ocean in the south and is bounded by the Sierra Madre del Sur on the west and by the state of Chiapas on the east.[4] More than 350,000 Istmeños live in 375 named localities grouped into forty-one municipalities. Sixty percent of the named localities contain fewer than 300 persons, and only nineteen of them have more than 3,000. The three major Isthmus cities are Juchitán, Tehuantepec, and Salina Cruz. Much of the Isthmus is mountainous and sparsely settled, transportation and communication are ill-developed, and the majority of the inhabitants are poor by general rural Mexican standards (Gobierno del Estado de Oaxaca 1980:87–88, 91–92).

Juchitán and other communities in the narrow Pacific coastal plain stand apart from the remainder of the Isthmus, as they have since before the Spanish conquest. Flat topography, a large expanse of cultivable terrain, rivers and springs, and a deep-water harbor at Salina Cruz contributed to make the area within the rough triangle formed by Tehuantepec, Tapanatepec, and Matías Romero one of the most important agricultural and fishing regions in the state. At one time or another it has been a major regional site for the production of cochineal and indigo dyes, sugar, sesame seed, rice, beef, salt, cloth, fish and shrimp, and other sea products. More recently, extractive and transformative industries have been introduced into the Isthmus in the form of plants producing lime, cement, and refined petroleum.[5]

Historical Background

It is not clear exactly when Zapotec people first occupied the Isthmus, nor are the circumstances of that occupation well understood. It is most likely, however, that the Zapotecs migrated from the highland Oaxaca Valley sometime in the mid-fourteenth century and displaced the Huaves, Zoques, Mixes, and Chontals from the prime agricultural land and living sites of the region. Soon after the Spaniards conquered the Aztecs in 1521, expeditions were sent south to expand the borders of the new colony. Cortés quickly seized on the promise of the Isthmus and established a mammoth cattle hacienda there, part of the Marquesado del Valle, which survived for approximately three hundred years. Despite political domination by Spanish overlords, the Zapotecs sustained a vigorous local economy based on the production and trade of locally made cloth, salt, fish, and other products and clung steadfastly to their language and distinct ethnic identity. In this way the Zapotecs remained the dominant indigenous ethnic group in the Isthmus of Tehuantepec throughout the colonial and postcolonial periods to the present.

Early contacts between the Zapotecs and Spaniards were nonviolent, as the

Zapotecs sought alliances to strengthen their position against the Aztecs. But when the Spanish-imposed colonial authorities forced the indigenous inhabitants to provide burdensome tribute and seized large tracts of Isthmus land, the Zapotecs protested vigorously. Isthmus colonial history was marked by periodic Zapotec armed rebellions waged against the invaders, the most prominent those of 1550, 1660, and 1715 (Tutino, Part One, this volume).

After Mexican independence from Spain in 1810, Juchitán became the center of armed rebellions against the Oaxaca state government authorities. In 1827 and again in 1847–51 (Tutino, this volume), the Juchitecos attempted to secede from the state of Oaxaca. In 1866 local struggles for self-determination reached a high point when Juchitecos allied with inhabitants of San Blas Atempa to defeat a battalion of French Interventionists in armed combat.[6]

Juchiteco independence sentiments were rekindled once again in 1911 by the Che Gómez revolt, the second largest regional insurrection (after *zapatismo*) in Mexico at the time. Although many Juchitecos fought in the Mexican Revolution (1910–20), most of the local spoils of the period were controlled by General Heliodoro Charis, a poor Zapotec peasant who rose to prominence in the Mexican military and became a close collaborator of General and later President Alvaro Obregón. After an incipient movement for local autonomy was crushed in Juchitán in 1931, "social peace," albeit dominated by the Charis *cacicazgo,* reigned until the 1960s. Charis helped bring schools, hospitals, the Pan American Highway, and other modern amenities to the Isthmus, but he did not resolve the poverty and agrarian problems of the Zapotec peasants who were the bulk of the population (López Monjardin, Part One, this volume).[7]

In the late 1950s and early 1960s, the government financed the construction of the Benito Juárez Dam and Federal Irrigation District No. 19. However, the coming of modern agricultural infrastructure was accompanied by land speculation and land grabbing, which increased the disparities in access to cultivable soil. Bungling government attempts to ameliorate the problem backfired, provoking extreme hostility among Isthmus peasants (Binford, Warman, Part One, this volume). With Charis out of power and his suffocating control relegated to the archives, disenfranchised Juchitecos sought a greater voice in community affairs. This was the explosive political and economic backdrop for the emergence in the early 1970s of COCEI.

Several anti-PRI opposition movements of the 1960s faltered, but in 1971 Manuel Musalem (Tarú), a charismatic politician, successfully led the Popular Socialist Party (PPS) to victory in Juchitán (Royce 1975). When Tarú's administration collapsed, a group of radical students (veterans of the 1968 Mexican protest movement), workers, and peasants calling themselves the

Leigh Binford and Howard Campbell

Worker-Peasant-Student Coalition of the Isthmus of Tehuantepec (COCEI) became the sole opposition force in Juchitán and continued a political trajectory leading to COCEI's electoral victory in Juchitán in 1981.

Juchitán and the Isthmus Zapotecs

The economic and political importance of the Isthmus of Tehuantepec has increased in recent years as a result of the construction of the Pan American Highway (1950s); the dam and irrigation project (1960s); and the nation's largest Pacific Coast petroleum refinery, in Salina Cruz (operating from 1979). The region also occupies a strategic position as a result of its proximity to the war-torn Central American republics. Within the Isthmus, Juchitán is the center of Isthmus Zapotec culture and political influence. For all these economic, political, and strategic reasons, control of Juchitán by a radical leftist, antigovernment organization is treated by PRI as a regional threat rather than a merely local threat.

Despite its economic and political importance, the Isthmus region has not been as heavily studied as Highland Chiapas, Morelos, the Oaxaca Valley, and other Mexican anthropological meccas. A punishing climate, the decrepit highway system, lack of "modern" facilities, and a reputation for violence have combined in various ways to warn both gringo and Mexican anthropologists away from the Isthmus and other Oaxacan regions, such as the southern sierra and the Mixtec coast (La Costa Chica).[8]

For most of the year the Isthmus is stiflingly hot and dry. Even during the summer rainy season (May to October), droughts frequently result in disastrous crop losses. During the winter, when temperatures drop slightly, ferocious northern winds pummel the gritty, unpaved streets of Isthmus towns, raising up stinging clouds of sand and dirt that invade the eyes and penetrate every corner of houses and patios. Conjunctivitis ("pinkeye") is common during this time of year, as are colds and other throat and nasal ailments. During the summer, torrential rains, frequently of monsoon dimension in August and September, turn the streets into fields of mud, small ponds, and dangerous chuckholes, which make pedestrian and vehicular travel an adventure at best and, at worst, a stodgy, mucky waste of time.

Chronic bouts with amoebic dysentery and a variety of parasitic infections would be greatly diminished if Istmeños enjoyed refrigeration facilities and waste disposal service in the towns and did not allow pigs, chickens, and turkeys to range freely during the day. Many Istmeños also suffer from diabetes (related to high sugar and alcohol consumption) and alcoholism; the region is reputed to have the highest per capita beer consumption in Mexico. If this is not enough, *la quebradora* (dengue or breakbone fever), a mosquito-borne viral infection characterized by high, spiking fevers and excruciating joint pains, reached Mexico from Jamaica in the late 1970s and has become epidemic during the Isthmus rainy season.

Isthmus social and health problems are typical of indigenous areas of rural southern Mexico, which have historically received little help from federal and state governments.[9] Within Oaxaca, most state investment has gone disproportionately to the maintenance, restoration, and improvement of Oaxaca City, the state's financial and tourist capital. More recently, federal and state governments have poured funds into the Pacific resort of Huatulco, which is being touted as a new international tourist attraction, eventually to rival Cancún.

Substandard education, high rates of unemployment and underemployment, and the lack of health and sanitation facilities lead many locally born people to leave the Isthmus each year (cf. Binford 1983). Their numbers, however, are more than made up by Mexicans who migrate from even more depressed areas to seek formal and informal employment in Salina Cruz's burgeoning refinery-based economy (Rodríguez 1984) or in large market towns such as Tehuantepec and Juchitán. Also, the Isthmus is home (or way station) to many Guatemalans and Salvadorans fleeing civil wars and economic depression in their own countries. Rapid population increase, especially in Salina Cruz, Tehuantepec, and Juchitán—the region's industrial, commercial, and political centers—has exacerbated many of the problems mentioned above.

Alongside the poverty and misery, visitors and local people alike observe that there is much beauty in the Isthmus, whether in the brightly colored bougainvilleas, frangipani flowers, and jasmine; the luxuriant, multicolored velvet *huipiles* (sleeveless blouses) of Isthmus women, embroidered with geometric designs and floral patterns; the rugged high-roofed adobe and wood-beamed homes (increasingly being replaced by angular one- and two-story homes of cement block walls and poured concrete roofs); or the tropical vistas of lush mango trees and coconut palms swaying in the wind in well-watered and wind-sheltered areas. Also, the Isthmus Zapotecs have a rich and expressive language and have developed a lively musical and literary tradition. Through their own creative efforts they have elaborated a profusion of beliefs and practices that, as Zapotec people are quick to point out to the newcomer, provide them with substantial satisfaction. The indomitable spirit of the Juchitecos has been extolled even by outsiders. For instance, Miguel Covarrubias (1946:299), a well-known Mexican painter and ethnographer who visited the region in the 1930s and 1940s, remarked that the Juchiteco's "pride of race expresses itself in an acute love and loyalty to their hometown, a sort of provincial nationalism."

Leigh Binford and Howard Campbell

ETHNOGRAPHIC AUTHORITY AND
INDIGENOUS SELF-REPRESENTATION

The selection of materials for this book was made initially by Bartolomé and Barabas and later by Campbell and Binford, who obtained various new texts and reorganized the contents. The majority of the materials came from the Zapotec magazine *Guchachi' Reza*. The book has also been shaped in part by our desire to contribute to the current debate over ethnographic authority and cultural representation within the field of anthropology. Without losing sight of the variety of positions and their differences, it can be said that the debate pairs off anthropologists influenced to various degrees by the new wave of poststructuralist and deconstructionist philosophical and literary theory, skeptical of anthropology's epistemological claims (Clifford and Marcus 1986; Clifford 1988; Tyler 1987a), with defenders of anthropology's grounding in scientific method, ethnographic realism, and objective representation (Sangren 1988).[10]

The former group, which we will refer to as "postmodernists," maintain that the field of anthropology has entered into a crisis resulting from philosophical and literary challenges to its traditional methods of knowledge production.[11] Putting aside the nuances of the different arguments, most anthropologists in the postmodern school argue that the partial, fragmentary, and multisubjective nature of fieldwork is disregarded in the unitary, homogeneous, thematically secure, and authoritative texts that issue forth from the hand of the ethnographic writer. "How, precisely," Clifford (1988:25) asks, "is a garrulous, over-determined cross-cultural encounter shot through with power relations and personal cross-purposes circumscribed as an adequate version of a more or less discrete 'other world' composed by an individual author?" In response to this question Clifford and others suggest that anthropologists establish the authority—and thus encourage readers to accept the truth—of their descriptions through a variety of literary techniques. They write in the present tense, invoke known and widely accepted terms ("kinship," "myth," "culture"), employ allegorical and pastoral narrative modes familiar to Western readers, and bolster their claims as competent witnesses through descriptions of their first difficult days of fieldwork (Clifford 1983; Crapanzano 1986; Rosaldo 1986).

These techniques help to make the descriptions and analyses of other cultures more acceptable and "real" to readers who did not share the author's field experience. But in the process, ethnographic writing often reinforces, albeit unintentionally, deeply embedded Western notions about non-Western peoples that many contemporary anthropologists would reject if expressed openly (Fabian 1983; Pinney 1989). For postmodernists, therefore, purportedly "scientific" anthropology is saturated with unscientific ideology.

It can be argued that the postmodern critique of anthropology applies anthropological principles to the discipline itself—an "anthropology of anthropology," so to speak. Social anthropologists have long explained cross-cultural misunderstandings in terms of differential socialization; but because practitioners have sought recognition as scientists rather than humanitarians, they have also maintained that they possess techniques that neutralize the effects upon their analyses of their own culture, history, and ideologies and establish the basis for understanding what the beliefs and practices of others *really* mean, as opposed to what others say they mean.[12] As McGrane (1989:125) has noted: "Anthropology lives by seeing and interpreting everything as culture-bound . . . everything but itself."

We are in agreement with the postmodernist position that all claims about truth are ultimately founded on propositional assertions that cannot themselves be proven (Rorty 1980). Once such claims are deprived of their hard, "scientific" edges, then anthropologists' supposition that they possess a window on the real that is not available to those who have not shared the same history and training loses its power (Fabian 1983). As possessors of knowledge and interpreters of the world, cultural insiders would then have to be taken just as seriously as their anthropological interlocutors (Faris 1990; Faris and Walters 1991; Spivak 1990).[13]

Few anthropologists have yet to make such a radical break with anthropology's historic practice. Perhaps because anthropology's very existence rests upon its status as neutral (or at the least, privileged) arbiter of other people's worlds, even "postmodern" alternatives to traditional ethnography are based on dialogical and polyvocal methods of presentation, which only peripherally challenge the discipline's foundational assumptions (Clifford 1983; Marcus and Fischer 1986).[14]

Many professional anthropologists and students eschew the postmodern approach because they believe that a critical deconstruction of anthropology as science is nihilistic, tearing down the discipline without providing the basis for an alternative. For instance, Polier and Roseberry (1989:260) referred to postmodernism as a way "of living with crisis without seriously thinking about it." In our view the strength of postmodern writing is that it has focused attention on the real power discrepancies involved in the field situation and in a few cases linked them to global power differences that determine who represents whom and whose representations count. But many postmodernists have committed the error of believing that joint authorship, polyvocality, or open-ended texts can in some way compensate for these local, national, and global imbalances of power. But is it not just as likely that an exaggerated concern with literary experimentation will result in subtler and even more pernicious forms of authority if readers accept the results as evidence of the author's evenhandedness, rather than the product of politically informed choices?

There is no simple and unambiguous way out of this impasse, no "politically correct" strategy that can set the anthropological conscience to rest. Anthropology was, as Lévi-Strauss once noted, a child of imperialism, and imperialism—having diversified its forms—is still with us. The fact that we in the First World can choose to represent others whose power of refusal or reply is limited by their position in the global social economy signifies the problem.[15] As long as anthropology remains a practice dedicated to producing knowledge of those others, the inescapable fact of that choice will be with us—postmodernists or not.

On what basis are such choices to be made if the criterion of truth is no longer acceptable? What are we to write if we can no longer be confident that our ethnographic work constitutes accurate representations of other peoples' lives? We believe that anthropologists must assume the responsibility of deciding whose beliefs and actions to represent and how much weight to give them, and that these decisions should be politically informed.[16] But this approach to representation requires taking seriously the beliefs of others. Indeed, "Only an explicit political critique can take seriously the truths of indigenous discourses" (Faris and Walters 1991:11). From this perspective, postmodern cultural projects need not degenerate into narcissistic extolments of individual anthropologist's writing skills. Nor is postmodernism, by definition, aloof or removed from the concrete fields of power in which ethnographic knowledge is created or disseminated. As the COCEI case illustrates, a cultural project concerned with genres of representation by self and other can be directly linked to and grounded in a class and/or ethnic movement promoting political change. Indeed the very process of challenging denigratory representations and promoting positive self-representation is often an integral part of the political praxis of grassroots movements like COCEI.

In short, we feel that postmodernism does not necessarily have to be naive about politics or politically regressive. It may be employed as a valuable tool for the production of knowledge and ideas by and about oppressed groups rather than a set of signposts resulting in esoteric literary works or knowledge for consumption by the powerful. Rather than being ahistorical or ignoring social totalities, a politically motivated postmodern cultural project could be the vehicle for a critique of history and encompassing social structures, and of efforts to change them.

Guchachi' Reza provides one example of such a project. First, as a multigenre expression of Isthmus Zapotec people, it embodies many of the experimental techniques now finding increasing favor in anthropology. In the pages of *Guchachi' Reza* one encounters history, ethnology, myth, personal testimony, interviews, songs, poetry, and art produced by and about Juchitecos and the Isthmus Zapotecs. Most articles appear in Spanish, although Zapotec-language materials are common. Local intellectuals are prominent contributors to the historical and ethnographic pieces, and so are Mexican nationals and foreigners.

However, the editors of *Guchachi' Reza* differ in one very important way from many postmodern ethnographic writers: They are consciously pro-COCEI and are informed by a critical, leftist political project in the selection and organization of materials that appear in the publication. This does not mean that *Guchachi' Reza* is either one-sided or dogmatic, for it does include articles translated or republished from other journals that are critical of COCEI and its views of Isthmus Zapotec history and culture. The editors record their points of agreement and disagreement in a preface or introduction. In this way *Guchachi' Reza* is both a vehicle for Isthmus Zapotec self-representation and a means of disseminating knowledge of others' representations of Isthmus Zapotec history and culture while commenting upon them.

Like *Guchachi' Reza,* this book does not represent all Juchitecos in equal measure or with equal favor. Even if we sought to represent everyone, it would not be possible, for there are too many distinct actors, and not all have the opportunity to speak with equal force, even locally. Like every people, the Isthmus Zapotecs are characterized by an existing distribution of power relations that privilege certain voices over others, so that even anthropologists who might wish to represent marginal groups would find their access limited. The Isthmus Zapotecs are divided along lines of class, status, gender, and age, anthropological and historical characterizations to the contrary (Chiñas 1973; Royce 1975). For instance, men dominate political decisions that largely determine who gets what and how much. Even *Guchachi' Reza* is a largely male project, and the COCEI Political Commission is exclusively male (de la Cruz, Poniatowska, Ruiz Campbell, Part Two, this volume).[17]

In this book, we have deliberately sought to listen to poor Zapotec women and local critics of the social status quo, but powerful local merchants, large landowners, middle-class professionals, and the leaders of the Juchitán PRI—all of whom have ample access to the Mexican media—are not represented here. In our approach, we have included a variety of materials that are generally supportive, and sometimes critical, of COCEI. This, of course, is a reflection of our politics and the way in which those politics have been shaped, among other things, by experiences with representatives of the Mexican State, peasants, workers, and COCEI supporters and leaders. Since our politically mediated experience of the Isthmus has exposed us to the social inequality, discrimination against indigenous customs, corruption, and antidemocratic government policies confronting Zapotec people, we are very sympathetic to COCEI's calls for land and resource distribution, higher wages for workers, clean government, and defense and promotion of indigenous culture.[18] In presenting the views of *coceístas* and Zapotec intellectuals, juxtaposed with analyses of Juchitán by outsiders in a multigenre format modeled on *Guchachi' Reza,* we hope to demonstrate the usefulness of politically engaged, postmodern forms of ethnographic representation.

COCEI: A "NEW SOCIAL MOVEMENT" IN JUCHITÁN?

A current trend in Latin American sociology and anthropology focuses on the analysis of "new social movements," which, according to many scholars, are a categorically new social phenomenon in the region. Indigenous organizations, peasant unions, feminists, slum dwellers, greens, and others have grown out of what Cockcroft (1989:3) refers to as "the long dark night" of dictatorship and heavy-handed State repression. Although there is still no consensus about precisely what kinds of groups "new social movements" refers to, the term has been adopted by many Mexican and foreign researchers investigating popular organizations and political alternatives to PRI (Street 1989). But the purported "newness" of such movements and their potential to provoke national-level and grassroots political change in Latin America remain hotly debated issues.

In what sense, one might ask, is COCEI a "new social movement," and in what sense is it a continuation or a permutation of earlier Isthmus Zapotec organizations resisting encroachment by the State? How do COCEI's organization, strategy, and goals compare with those of other "new social movements"? We do not propose to resolve the many issues raised by the "new social movements" literature, but we do think that analysis of Isthmus Zapotecs and COCEI can make an important contribution to it.

In Mexico, "new social movements" generally refer to contemporary anti-government organizations outside the organized left, which remains weak and has only shallow roots among the working classes and the peasantry (Carr 1986; Semo 1986).[19] Apart from the sudden and unexpectedly successful rise of *neocardenismo* (Carr 1989:370–71), the most dynamic developments during the 1980s were the formation of independence movements within government-controlled unions; the mobilization of rural and urban dwellers in opposition to State-imposed austerity policies; and the creation of broad fronts incorporating disparate organizations against repression and for the promotion of human rights (e.g., the National Front against Repression, FNCR), the continuation of agrarian reform (the National Plan of Ayala Coordinating Committee, CNPA), and greater democracy (the National Peasant Worker Assembly) (Carr 1986; A. M. Prieto 1986).[20]

In Knight's (1989) view, the "newness" of such social movements rests on three claims made about them: They represent a renewed opposition to PRI and the State in comparison to the 1940–65 period of PRI's absolute hegemony (although Foweraker [1989:117] disagrees); their demands differ from those of the earlier movements due to the emphasis on democracy and respect for human rights, and a reduced concern with economic matters; they constitute subjects in new ways—as women, gays, or neighborhood residents rather than merely as workers. Knight presents evidence to support his rejection of all three claims and argues that the social movements' literature is more a product of social science discourse than of changes in reality. For Knight, a close look at Mexican history reveals few authentically new protest movements:

> We should perhaps see the social protests of recent years chiefly as replications of earlier movements, now rendered more extensive and (perhaps) more radical by harsh economic circumstances. The majority of "new" social movements would not, therefore, be considered strictly new, but rather as developed examples of historically familiar phenomena. (1989:19)

Against Knight's view that contemporary social movements in Mexico manifest, in many respects, "continuity-within-change," we suggest that COCEI represents a new social phenomenon for Juchitán and may prove so for other areas of rural Mexico as well. We can best clarify our position by briefly discussing Juchitán's recent history in the context of some of the issues that Knight raises.

As noted above, the Isthmus experienced recurring cycles of protest and rebellion from the early colonial period through the revolutionary era. Struggles for control of land, water, salt pans, and political autonomy repeatedly moved peasants to revolt against local and regional elites. The enemies of the Juchiteco peasantry were primarily Tehuantepec and Oaxaca Valley political bosses, and usurers in a merchant-dominated economy. Thus, if there was a continuity of rebellion and protest over the long haul, there was also a persistence locally of a relatively egalitarian indigenous social structure and of essentially noncapitalist production relations dominated in the sphere of circulation by local businessmen, often of European descent.

This set of circumstances changed markedly after the Second World War with the construction of the Benito Juárez dam and irrigation project, the Pan

American and Trans-Isthmian highways, and the Salina Cruz PEMEX oil re-finery. Agrarian capitalism, followed by modern industrial capitalism, pene-trated the hitherto merchant-dominated economy as the government sought to convert the Isthmus into a full-blown development pole. The results were in-tense social polarization, class differentiation, and pauperization of sections of the peasantry; the emergence of a small but growing agrarian bourgeoisie; and a rise in the number of middle- class professionals and technicians. COCEI emerged out of this divisive and conflictive milieu.

Not only did capitalist development create new socioeconomic conditions in the Isthmus but it transformed the local political environment as well. Prior to the construction of the highway, dam, and refinery, Juchitán was a medium-sized town that epitomized in many respects Wolf's (1957) closed-corporate community. Political conflicts primarily pitted Juchitecos against non-Zapotec outsiders (Aztec, Spanish, French, Huave, Mixe, etc.) or residents of nearby communities such as Tehuantepec, Espinal, or Ixtepec. The changes brought by agrarian and industrial capitalism internally divided the Zapotec population of Juchitán, as many peasants lost their land and the growing merchant/ professional/political class expanded its economic endeavors. Because it effec-tively defended the interests of the Zapotec poor against indigenous upper classes, COCEI—while overtly an Isthmus Zapotec political movement—was not a movement of a united Juchitán against non-Zapotecs as in the glory days of the defeat of the French or Meléndez's battles with Juárez (Tutino, Part One, this volume). Rather, COCEI represented the interests of peasants and workers in a Zapotec community rent by internal class divisions to a degree never seen in the past. In this sense, COCEI—an organization that aggressively con-fronted Zapotec peasants against Zapotec elites—was a new form of protest movement in formerly ethnically unified Juchitán.

But more generally, COCEI was a singular phenomenon in Mexican rural politics because the movement combined a provincial, ethnic, even xenophobic collective identity and locally focused grassroots political program with an eclectic, internationally informed political and ideological project. During the COCEI "people's government" (1981–83), Juchitán not only became the cul-tural center of the Isthmus Zapotec region but also drew many urban Mexican and foreign intellectuals and leftists to the community. Juchitecos learned from these interactions and encounters with outsiders and incorporated what they learned into new projects and activities. During the two years that COCEI gov-erned Juchitán, the city became a kind of laboratory of political experiments and innovative ideas. Like Berkeley, California, or Madison, Wisconsin, during the 1960s and early 1970s, Juchitán was a *city* with a foreign policy, a commu-nity that sought political kinship less with national and elected officials than with the revolutionary regimes of Cuba and Nicaragua. Between 1981 and 1983, COCEI brought a Cuban band (at great cost) to play for the traditional *vela* festivities, carried out a Paolo Freire-style literacy campaign similar to that in Nicaragua, and sponsored the showing of films documenting the military overthrow of Allende's Chile. COCEI leaders participated in hunger strikes in solidarity with foreign causes, and COCEI women protested human rights abuses with signs in English (for the benefit of tourists and the mass media) in front of Oaxaca's famous Santo Domingo Cathedral.

In the cultural realm, *coceístas* established a radio station (López Matus, Part Four, this volume) that not only broadcast in Zapotec, but played classical music and read international newscasts to its largely indigenous peasant audience. Unlike the parochial, inward-focused Isthmus Zapotec journal of the 1930s, *Neza,* the COCEI-linked *Guchachi' Reza* published Zapotec translations of Brecht and Neruda and juxtaposed theoretical analyses of Isthmus society by outside academics with old photos, paintings by young Juchiteco artists, and local poetry. In Francisco Toledo's art, images and symbolism from Zapotec folklore and mythology and Isthmus flora and fauna are blended with avant-garde artistic techniques and ideas to form original creations, combining local motifs with contemporary style.

There is a clear continuity between COCEI and earlier movements for control of land and municipal offices, but there are important discontinuities as well. COCEI has creatively and successfully combined ethnic pride with class-based politics, a regional orientation with an openness to learn from struggles waged by workers and peasants elsewhere in Mexico as well as in other nations. And, not surprisingly, COCEI joined and has participated actively in the National Plan of Ayala Coordinating Committee, hosting its national meeting in Juchitán in 1981, and the National Front against Repression. Thus COCEI transcends many of the dichotomies often used to categorize social movements: ethnic vs. class-oriented, Marxist vs. *indigenista,* rural indigenous vs. urban Westernized, parochial vs. international. If its features are examined and compared individually with those of earlier movements, it may be easy to find precedents for COCEI in Mexico's past. Yet it is the unique combination of elements—the linking of indigenous cultural forms to avant-garde radical chic, grassroots mobilization with modern media-conscious politics, and extreme localism with socialist internationalism—that make of COCEI something new and different on the Mexican scene.

COCEI is not without contradictions and limitations (see critiques of COCEI by Zermeño, Part Three; Campbell, Part Four; and in the afterword, this volume), but it has shown that it is possible for indigenous people to maintain a distinct ethnic identity and culture while adopting a radical political program aimed at transforming existing social and economic conditions. Finally, *coceístas* demonstrate that rural indigenous people are not only capable of representing themselves in political and intellectual forums and media, but that they are able to do so in ways that are both highly creative and challenge the existing representations of themselves by powerful outsiders.

NOTES

1. The nomenclature of the Mexican left has undergone many changes since government electoral reform (the LOPPE law) led to formal legal registration for selected left parties in 1977. In 1981, soon after its electoral alliance with COCEI, the Mexican Communist Party (PCM) combined with four smaller leftist parties to form the Unified Socialist Party of Mexico (PSUM). In 1988 the PSUM dissolved into the Mexican Socialist Party (PMS) by combining with the Mexican Workers Party and other parties, and nominated Heberto Castillo as its 1988 presidential candidate. Shortly before the elections, Castillo dropped his candidacy so that PMS could unite with several small parties to support Cuauhtémoc Cárdenas. Eventually Cárdenas's supporters formed the *cardenista* front (PRD). Only with the sponsorship of an officially recognized party is a local group, such as COCEI, permitted to contest elections and exercise the rights—to representation on local electoral committees, poll watchers, and so on—that reduce the likelihood of fraud on the part of PRI.

2. Estimates of the Juchitán population vary widely. In his article in Part Three of this volume, Zermeño estimates the population at 60,000, while Rubin (Part Two, this volume) claims 72,000. In our view, Juchitán residents have been seriously undercounted by official (and unofficial) sources, such as the 1990 Mexican census, which recorded 66,525 Juchitecos in its preliminary report (INEGI 1990). Juchitán's current population likely approaches 80,000, if not more.

3. Almost 80 percent of the 350,000 Zapotec speakers recorded in the 1980 census also speak Spanish (Bartolomé and Barabas 1986:20–21). Zapotec is less a language than a language family containing nine or more mutually unintelligible languages, of which Isthmus Zapotec is one.

4. The Isthmus is territorially the largest of the Oaxacan subregions, according to the 1980–86 state development plan. Other subregions are the Cañada, the Coast, the Mixteca, the Northern Sierra, the Southern Sierra, the Papaloapan, and the Central Valleys. This regionalization was first proposed in the 1968 *Plan Oaxaca,* a study of natural resources sponsored by the United Nations in the late 1960s (Moguel 1979). "Tehuantepec" and "Juchitán" refer to districts composed of numerous municipalities as well as the major urban centers within those respective districts.

5. Raw materials for lime and cement factories are of local origin; the crude oil processed in Salina Cruz enters the region via the trans-Isthmus oil pipeline.

6. San Blas was at the time a barrio of Tehuantepec, an important regional colonial governmental center. In the French intervention, many Tehuanos sided with the French, a fact well known to contemporary Juchitecos. Following the French defeat, the Blaseños separated from Tehuantepec and obtained status as a free municipality (Dorsett 1975:103). Fraternal relations between inhabitants of Juchitán and San Blas are rooted in this shared history and in the barely concealed disdain that many residents of both communities continue to manifest toward the Tehuanos, who are generally regarded as conservatives or even traitors. The Tehuanos, in turn, view Blaseños and Juchitecos as Indians and rebels.

7. On Charis see de la Cruz (1989).

8. Historically, anthropological work in Oaxaca has predominantly focused upon the temperate Central Valleys region in the vicinity of the state capital. Secondary foci of anthropological interest are the Mixteca and the northern sierra. Until the COCEI arrived on the scene, the only significant ethnographic work in the Isthmus was that of Royce (1975) on culture and politics in Juchitán; Chiñas (1973) on women of San Blas; Covarrubias (1946) on Isthmus Zapotec culture and history (with emphases on Juchitán and Tehuantepec); and Dorsett (1975) on ecology, economy, and language in Juchitán and Tehuantepec. Also, Warman (1972) wrote an insightful article on the sociology of Irrigation District No. 19. Since COCEI's electoral victory in 1981, the number of theses, dissertations, books, and articles, most of them dealing with Juchitán and COCEI, have become too numerous to mention. Few of these works adequately address Isthmus Zapotec culture in its complex relationship to COCEI politics, although virtually all acknowledge the indigenous identity of the movement.

9. In 1970 Oaxaca had the lowest annual per capita income in the country (764 pesos), only about one-sixth that of the Federal District, the area of highest income (Hernández and Córdoba 1982:25). On the basis of a comparison of 1970 and 1980 census data, Bartolomé and Barabas (1986:47) concluded that with a few exceptions, Oaxaca's productive structure was entropic, or "in a permanent and progressive retrocession."

10. Defenders of the status quo mounted a concerted attack on the "post-modernists" in a session organized by Marvin Harris at the 1989 annual meeting of the American Anthropological Association.

11. We use the word with trepidation, aware that Stephen Tyler is one of the few contemporary anthropologists who really fits the bill. Other terms that might have been substituted, such as "interpretationists," "experimentalists," or "anti-epistemologists," are also problematic. Our goal is not to mark out two well-defined and antagonistic camps; these do not exist. Rather, we wish to distinguish those anthropologists who view anthropology's truth claims as standing on increasingly tenuous grounds from those, such as Marvin Harris, who continue to defend its scientific status as producer of accurate representations and explanations of other peoples' worlds. Those in the latter group believe that with appropriate methods of data gathering and analysis, anthropologists can obtain a window upon the

real; those in the former group study the discourses that have escaped examination by anthropologists confident in their truth mission.

12. Anthropologists accept the contextual legitimacy of these meanings. However, most also argue that because they are immersed in local meanings, informants have but limited potential to understand the larger social and cultural significance of their beliefs and practices. The *real* meaning, not available to culture-bound informants, becomes apparent when anthropologists work over the raw material of informants' beliefs and practices through anthropological method and theory (functionalism, cultural ecology, Marxism, etc.). In this way, Western, scientific, "culturally neutral" modes of analysis are held to be superior.

13. Speaking of Navaho accounts of the past and non-Navaho historiography, Faris and Walters (1991:1) state: "These latter accounts are often at odds with Navaho views (most archaeological orthodoxy, for example, places the Navaho in the American Southwest just about the time of, or a short period before the arrival of the Spanish to the area). We are not concerned with these accounts, nor is the interest here to reconcile the Navaho accounts with non-Navaho accounts, nor indeed to reconcile the many Navaho accounts with each other, nor to dispute them, nor to seek any single accurate chronicle of the past and the way things came to be. Given that each account is coherent and meets its own goals, each may be regarded as equally true."

14. Clifford (1988) surveys the historical forms of ethnographic authority from the experiential and interpretive approaches to more recent dialogical and polyvocal forms. All are critiqued for their shortcomings, but the latter two are favorably compared with the former. This, combined with Clifford's claim that ethnography produces "partial truths," suggests a progressive improvement of ethnographic writing, to which more strictly postmodern anthropologists like Tyler (1987a, 1987b) are opposed.

15. That anthropologists in the Third and Fourth Worlds do the same to their have-nots is not sufficient to reject this statement. In effect, Third World anthropologists are First World people; they are among the "First World in the Third World" that Trinh T. Minh-ha (1987) speaks of, while the homeless, the poor, and ethnic minorities in the United States and elsewhere, her "Third World in the First World," are prime subjects of the anthropological gaze.

16. Given the ingrained political and ideological assumptions with which anthropologists, like others, operate, such choices are frequently unconscious. They are part and parcel of the discourses, the conceptual systems, through which our experience of the world is structured. Such choices are also affected by extant power relations in the society under examination, which determine to whom anthropologists are allowed to speak and what can and cannot be said (see the introduction to Part Two).

17. It is worth noting that Mascia-Lees et al. (1989) suggest that postmodern anthropology is also a male project with the goal of preserving male intellectual authority. They point out that this male challenge to representational authority arose at

the same time that previously silenced women, minorities, and Third World peoples were assuming for the first time the right to represent themselves in Western intellectual forums. They claim that by critiquing all representations, postmodernists seek to undermine these previously silenced voices and to preserve for themselves the right to arbitrate knowledge.

However, it is equally legitimate to interpret the postmodern project as undermining the foundation of all claims to male privilege and as shifting disagreement over gender to strictly political terrain. Moreover, feminists have long experience in deconstructing discourses of male dominance. In exposing the political agendas of representation projects, postmodernism could open the way for previously silenced groups to counter prejudicial representations of themselves by white, male, intellectual authorities or others, or more successfully promote their own versions of history, worldview, or knowledge. In itself, postmodernism is neither politically progressive nor politically reactionary.

18. Admittedly, where we have "seen" evidence for exploitation and discrimination, other commentators have "seen" only laziness and racial inferiority. While for us COCEI is an important multiclass and ethnic organization struggling to change an oppressive social system, others see only a communist-inspired threat to social peace. We do not claim either scientific or political neutrality as guideposts.

19. The independent left suffered a decline in its vote totals from 1985 to 1988, furthering a trend that began in 1976 (Carr 1989:375).

20. The National Plan of Ayala Coordinating Committee was named after Zapata's Plan de Ayala. The National Peasant Worker Assembly (ANOCP) was formed in June 1983 from the combination of the National Committee in Defense of the Popular Economy and the National Front in Defense of Wages against Austerity and the Cost of Living. ANOCP organized a civic strike in October 1983 in which an estimated 1.5–2 million Mexicans participated (Carr 1986).

P A R T   O N E

Histories of Conflict, Struggle, and Mobilization in the Isthmus of Tehuantepec

Until recently many intellectuals viewed history as a singular series of nonrepeatable events subject to a "best" or "correct" interpretation. Western academics believed that their knowledge of methods of information selection, organization, and interpretation authorized them to write histories of the West as well as the Rest. Immersed in the immediacy of events, lacking a "neutral" position, and often illiterate and/or unacquainted with social science methodology, the subjects of these histories were not considered to be competent and capable of producing "accurate" accounts of their own lives. Thus anthropologists, historians, and others assigned indigenous intellectual productions to the (nonhistorical) categories of "oral history," "myth," "anecdote," or "folktale," none of which carried as much epistemological weight as academic "history" (Clifford 1988; Vansina 1985).

The title of Part One is intended to suggest that *our* version of history and what was previously denominated *their* myth now coexist in definite tension with one another. The once singular concept of "history" is being increasingly pluralized by recognition that accounts of the past are inexorably shaped by writers' social, cultural, political, and gender positionings. This suggests, in concert with the philosophical crisis of epistemology as the basis for accurate knowledge production (Rorty 1980), that there is no fail-safe way to select a best among competing accounts. *All* visions of the past—particularly Western, colonial-inspired discourses on others—are ideologically suspect and politically weighted (Said 1978; Fabian 1983; Pinney 1989; Gordon 1988). This chapter presents accounts of the Isthmus Zapotec past derived from different intellectual and political projects of Mexican and North American academics, Juchiteco intellectuals, and individuals whose lived experience of the past informs their accounts of it.

In the lead article Víctor de la Cruz poses the key question: "Indigenous Peoples' History (by Whom and for Whom?)" He observes that it has been to the advantage of the West to acknowledge indigenous peoples as artists, to benefit from the exchange value of their artistic productions, but that the same acknowledgement does not extend to the case of history, which continues to be written by the West about others. He is skeptical of Western historians' claims to scientific neutrality and wonders whether contemporary Western histories of indigenous peoples might not serve the same purposes of domination as did those produced by churchmen in the colonial period. De la Cruz also rejects the claim that the precolonial Zapotecs produced only mythology and not history; in his view, contemporary historians are simply unfamiliar with the Zapotecs' metaphorical use of language. What historians treat as creative exaggeration might also be understood as the "creative-religious framework" of Zapotec history:

> They [ancestors of contemporary Zapotecs] knew how to distinguish the real facts within this religious scheme . . . . Thus not everything was a "lie" or fable as the colonizing friars maintained. Our ancestors knew how to distinguish the exaggerated, invented narrations from the words that they related and recorded in their books about the real events of autochthonous people.

The next piece is Andrés Henestrosa's rich narrative, "The Foundation of Juchitán." According to Henestrosa, Saint Vincent Ferrer, ordered by God to found a city in the Isthmus, rejected the well-watered, fertile Tehuantepec plain in favor of the dusty, arid region around Juchitán. Adversity, Saint Vincent thought, would develop children who are "hard-working and strong" rather than "indolent and dispirited." This charter suggests that Juchitecos formed themselves through the grueling toil required to wrest a living from an inhospitable (windy, rainy, scorching) physical environment and that Juchitecos value their valiant and tough self-image (see Part Two). COCEI also depicts contemporary Zapotec society and character as the product of a continuous history of social struggle stretching from the pre-Columbian period to the present. In its numerous publications, excerpts from which are presented throughout this volume, the organization draws on oral and written accounts to construct a millenarian vision of Isthmus history that differs substantially from that held by national politicians, bureaucrats, and most Mexican and foreign intellectuals. According to COCEI, an essential feature of Zapotec people is the long and continuous struggle that they have waged against domestic and foreign interference in Isthmus affairs.

At least three important Isthmus rebellions are inscribed in Juchiteco consciousness today in addition to their defeat of a foreign battalion on September 5, 1866, during the French Intervention. The first is the 1660 Tehuantepec Rebellion, discussed by John Tutino in his "Ethnic Resistance: Juchitán in Mexican History." The second was led by Gregorio Meléndez in the 1840s. According to Tutino, peasant leader Meléndez sought to recover Juchiteco control over marine salt resources, which Oaxacan government officials had parceled out for exploitation by members of the non-Juchiteco, mestizo elite from Tehuantepec. Tutino's examination of these rebellions and other aspects of Juchitán's history lead him to conclude that Juchitecos are unique among modern Mexican indigenous communities for their intense ethnic pride, economic prosperity, and tenacity of opposition to the State. He attributes Juchitán's distinctiveness to its historically constituted culture of resistance and Juchitecos' ability to successfully adapt to and, at times, profit from social and economic changes.

The third rebellion took place in 1911, shortly after the outbreak of the Mexican Revolution, and was led by Che Gómez, a Juchiteco lawyer who served in government posts in different parts of the country before he returned to Juchitán to become its mayor and lead the southern revolt against the Porfirio Díaz dictatorship. Like Meléndez, Gómez defended Juchitán's material resources against despoliation by the central government and was an advocate for municipal sovereignty. The turmoil of the revolutionary period, during which Gómez was murdered by government officials, lives in Juchiteco consciousness through the remembrances of people like Anastasia Martínez, whose testimony is reproduced here.

After the Mexican Revolution, Juchitán passed through a thirty-year period of relative political stability and slow economic growth when "nothing happened," or at least nothing of social or political significance, according to Adriana López Monjardin. General Heliodoro Charis, a revolutionary war hero turned *cacique,* exercised iron control by a judicious combination of calculated benevolence, political maneuvering, and violence. He is, not surprisingly, a controversial figure in Juchitán's history. López Monjardin relates how "El Rojo" Altamirano, a conservative *cacique,* identified himself with the Charis legacy with the object of attracting peasants and workers to support local PRI candidates and the party's "modernization" project during 1983 elections. But just as PRI's development plans are contested by COCEI, so is its view of the past. Without rejecting Charis, who befriended many peasants, COCEI seeks the essence of *lo juchiteco* in more remote periods, remembered principally for the struggles for self-determination and defense of communal resources that Zapotecs waged against the onslaughts of Spanish colonialists, French invaders, and the Oaxacan state government. Among the major COCEI heroes, therefore, are Meléndez and Gómez.

The last two articles, by Leigh Binford and Arturo Warman, provide similar perspectives on recent agrarian history, marked off here by the construction of the Benito Juárez Dam, located near Jalapa del Marqués at the confluence of the Tehuantepec and Tequisistlán rivers, and Federal Irrigation Project No. 19. Both authors argue that irrigation of thousands of hectares of Juchitán's land prompted rampant land speculation leading to the dispossession of hundreds of peasant agriculturalists. They differ, however, in their understanding of the relationship of this period to the *longue durée* as well as its contemporary political significance.

Binford suggests that agricultural land was plentiful and free for the taking prior to the development of the irrigation project and that COCEI represents a new form of mobilization and resistance made possible by changes in regional class structure that accompanied capital intensive investment. He also argues that many peasants within the irrigation district preferred that the State grant private land titles rather than legitimize communal control or incorporate the land into *ejidos* (State land). Binford concludes that current confusions over the tenure status of land in Juchitán owe as much to errors and ambiguities of past presidential administrations as to local struggles between COCEI and its largely bourgeois opposition.

Finally, Warman, one of Mexico's foremost anthropologists and ex-director of the Instituto Nacional Indigenista (National Indigenist Institute), recounts how amazed he was to discover when he worked in the Isthmus during the late 1960s that State officials failed either to inform affected Istmeños about the irrigation project or to seek their input and advice. He, too, analyzes the intricate maneuvers surrounding the conversion of communal land to private property and suggests, along with Binford, that such conversion was illegal.

The careful reader will note that although the two articles on Isthmus land

and economy exhibit nuanced differences, they converge in their critique of the role of the Mexican State and in the acknowledgment that class struggle over material resources is a prime motive factor in recent Isthmus history. Isthmus history can be, and has been, written differently, as, for instance, the product of elite mediation in which upper-class Zapotecs play the role of Juchitán's defenders against assaults from the outside, rather than local opponents of peasants and workers, as in the views of Binford and Warman (Royce 1975; Zeitlin 1989). In a single volume it is not possible to provide space for all voices, but then, even within the smallest social and cultural system, there are those voices that are customarily silenced or that speak in whispers (Keesing 1987; Polier and Roseberry 1989). By presenting a variety of views, however, we seek to open up rather than limit or shut down debate over the past, present, and future of Juchitán, specifically, and rural Mexico, more generally. For in Juchitán, as these articles illustrate, the lessons of the Isthmus Zapotec past are always central to the struggles of the present and the possible futures.

Indigenous Peoples' History (by Whom and for Whom?)

Víctor de la Cruz

The idea that indigenous peoples have history is now a scandal. It would appear that with this recognition, their past might come out of the shadowy and mysterious regions of fable and pass along the intricate paths of mythology, until it reaches the illuminating light of historical science. But does this recognition not imply more risks and challenges for the poor indigenous people of America, who can hardly acquire the indispensable minimum to subsist, and now have to parade naked or dressed in rags before the gaze of the historians? Eurocentrism relegated the indigenous peoples' past to the distant and poetic zone of myth, while the West ascended to the apex of wisdom to show humanity the road that all earthly peoples must follow in order to enter the channel of universal history, where civilized nations march within the rapid and irreversible currents of progress.

The accusation that weighs upon the work of conserving the past of the peoples outside the Mediterranean and European area is that one is dealing with a confused mix of myths or sacred texts and real data, a quasi-history, on the one hand, and privileged science restricted to the West, on the other:

> What were the steps and the stages through which the modern European idea of history passed in order to come into being? In my view not one of these stages occurred outside the Mediterranean region, that is to say, outside Europe and the Near East, from the Mediterranean to Mesopotamia and the northern coasts of

Major Leopoldo de Gyves Pineda, long-time Juchiteco political leader. Photo by G. Iturbide.

Africa. I have nothing to say about historical thought in China or in any other part of the world, save the region that I have mentioned. (R. G. Collingwood, cited in Léon-Portilla 1980:55)

But if the accusation is that indigenous peoples outside the mentioned regions enclosed the conservation of their past in a religious scheme of myths and legends, is Europe perhaps free of this sin in the exercise of science in general and of history in particular? In spite of Western positivism—and still in the middle of this century—Bertrand Russell dedicated a chapter of his book, *The Scientific Perspective,* to combating the religious contamination caused by eminent physicists and biologists, whom he accused of adopting an imprudent and unscientific attitude when they "supported traditional religious beliefs," and who "in their condition of being good citizens, anxious to defend virtue and property" gave through their declarations, approved and spread by theologians, the "impression that physics confirmed practically the totality of the Book of Genesis," which is to say Christian myths about the creation of the earth and man (Russell 1971:84).

And currently can we now consider North America, the model of Western society, free of the sin imputed to the indigenous peoples, who wrap up their studies and records of reality in a religious context in order to justify ostentation and the exercise of power by the dominant class? Is the power of the dominant class in that model of civilized society, the North American, not perchance founded upon the force of the Judeo-Christian myths contained in the Bible? Are we not now confronted with a theocracy when we see the president of the United States, the country in which science is most advanced, place his hand on a sacred Bible when he takes an oath to fulfill his duty. Power has invoked the hand of religion, myth, ceremony, and history in order to legitimize its origin and justify its actions. That which is myth and fable for the "primitive peoples" is religion for the "civilized nations," although one is dealing with the same thing: myths, sacred texts in which the dominant classes base their ideological control of society. However, few of those scientists of Western positivism have had the valor and the courage of Bertrand Russell to confess their atheism and denounce the ideological manipulation of science either by those who show off their power or that of their colleagues, who are disguised believers in religion.

If the West now acknowledges, not without resistance, indigenous peoples as creators of works of art in the past—that is to say, that there were artists outside the ambit of the Mediterranean and its frontiers, that the indigenous peoples of other regions had and it is possible that they still have artists—does this not signify that, since they are now acknowledging us as peoples with history, it might also be possible that we have historians? Not necessarily. The existence of art presupposes the existence of its creators; but that we might have history, a record of the past, does not necessarily presuppose the presence of historians in indigenous communities. Because historiographic work, the analysis and criticism of the memories of the indigenous past, can be carried out very well by nonindigenous historians for their own interests. Moreover, for the criollo bourgeoisie, oppressors of the peoples called Indians, the absence of indigenous historians or their nullification is the necessary condition so that they can expropriate with impunity the prestigious past of the defeated for the benefit of the dominant classes.[1]

So that sculptures and paintings made by peoples outside the West might be considered art, and so enter into capitalist commercial circuits, it was necessary for their authors to be considered artists, though anonymous, and not simply artisans. In this way the works attained a high exchange value. But, as mentioned above, neither the same thing nor anything similar appears to have occurred in the terrain of history. It is fine that we might have artists, creators of art works for the capitalist market and capitalist museums; but it is not deemed suitable that there be indigenous historians, who could, in a near or distant future, learn to make use of their critical capacities in order to separate those ideas invented by the criollo bourgeoisie for its benefit from the real facts; to reclaim their expropriated past and attempt to relate it with the present of the exploited, all of which becomes dangerous because subversive in the long or the short run. It is better that they continue reading history in the official texts, where the heroes are bearded white men who knew how to guide the indigenous masses.

The missionaries' colonizing work was to invalidate the record that the indigenous people kept of their past by characterizing it as foolishness, lies, and nonsense that the devil had put in their heads. At the same time they inoculated the defeated with new myths brought from the Judeo-Christian religious tradition, instilled as true accounts of the creation of the earth and men. Friar Francisco Burgoa exemplifies quite well the work of negating and deforming the indigenous past at the same time that he burdens us with long and boring accounts of the new myths brought by the colonizers. In the two weighty volumes of his *Geográfica Descripción,* all that he says of the ancestors of the *binizá* or Zapotecs, that is to say, of the *binnigula'sa',* is the following:

> . . . and with this gentleman being so absolute, and feared, even by the monarch Montezuma, as will be seen in due course, neither his origin nor his ancestry are known, nor is the epoch in which he took possession of this valley because there is so much nonsense in their histories and paintings instilled in them by the devil

that it is indecent to refer to them. Neither the Egyptians nor the Chaldaics were so blind in their vanities as them. Priding themselves valiant, they made themselves children of lions and wild beasts—great, old gentlemen, brought forth from shady, towering trees, invincible and persistent, full of pride that they were born from rocks and boulders; and as their language was so metaphorical, like that of the Palestinians, they spoke in parables when they sought to persuade, and their historians formed characters of that which they said. (Burgoa 1934, 1:412)

It seemed obscene to Burgoa to give an account of the myths of the *binnigula'sa'*. He did not understand the metaphorical use of *didxazá* [the Zapotec language] and the parables used to narrate the myths. Yet he did not think it indecent to dedicate long, dry paragraphs to the narration of the fables that he brought and inculcated in the defeated. Conscious of being in the presence of a figurative use of language and that the indigenous historians knew how to form characters referring to their past, he refused to transmit to us those that he heard. True, when the *binizá* wanted to say that they were valiant, they said that they were children of lions and wild beasts, and when they wanted to say that they were great gentlemen, they called themselves descendants of "towering and shady trees." To speak of their invincibility and persistence in struggle they considered themselves the offspring of rocks and boulders. They were using their language metaphorically and not in the strict sense. They established "the theoretical-religious framework" of their history, but they knew how to distinguish the real facts within this religious scheme.

Nor did Burgoa, our chronicler and source for Zapotec studies, work in an early period as did Friar Bernadino Sahagún with respect to the Nahuatl culture, since his work proceeds from the second half of the seventeenth century. But a friar, philological colonizer, author of an art of the Zapotec language and a complete lexicographic work with which he integrated a monumental vocabulary of the language, in the sixteenth century, records the following (Córdova 1942): The ancient Zapotecs or *binnigula'sa'* designated the action of "composing lies or putting into the head or inventing" in two ways: *tozaaxihuijaíchaxihuij* and *tíchahuenilá chi*. Translated into contemporary Isthmus Zapotec, it gives us the following forms: *ruza'xhihuí diidxá xhihuí,* which means "to compose exaggeratedly" or "exaggerated words," and *diidxá binnihuala'dxi,* "words of the aboriginal people," which is to say that the first usage that Córdova gives would serve to name narrations invented by the human mind, in other words "lies," "myths"; while the second form would serve to designate past acts of autochthonous people, that is, history. And the books where their historians record those acts are called *quíchi tijacolaca,* "papers with words by or about the old people," in order to distinguish them from another type of book, such as those of stories, for example. Thus not everything was a "lie" or fable as the colonizing friars maintained. Our ancestors knew how to distinguish the exaggerated, invented narrations from the words that they related and recorded in their books about the real events of autochthonous people.

The *binnigula'sa'*, our ancestors, appeared in books of "Indian figures," according to Córdova, or with the "characters" that the historians formed, in Burgoa's words. In my opinion, the accounts that Córdoba called in his *Vocabulary diidxa' binnihualadxi* were the ancient Zapotecs' history. But how many of those books containing accounts of real events were conserved? The case of the Zapotecs was not like that of the Mixtecs or the Nahuas, of whom were preserved a good quantity of those documents known as codices. I say a good quantity not because they might be enough to know the history of those ethnic groups, but because among our ancestors, the *binnigula'sa'*, those documents are rare. I personally know only of one, on which I have worked following the labor of two eminent and knowledgeable foreigners, Edward Seler and John Paddock, criticizing them where I think that they are not right. This document is the *Lienzo de Guevea* (the bottom half of which contains the genealogy of the lords of Zaachila), which I think is an account of the military chiefs who founded the town of Guevea. Although it was painted at the beginning of the colonization, it surely represents the last document of a long indigenous Zapotec tradition of making books with painted figures. How many of those documents were lost, were destroyed by the colonizers, or are found in the libraries of foreigners? That I became acquainted with a copy of this document might be considered good luck, because the majority of the members of the peoples called "Indians" lack even the minimal awareness of the grounds on which they might search for their past.

When will we have the chance to access resources, like those who study our history supposedly for pure scientific interest? Do we not have the right to participate in the clarification of our past? Do the "indigenous peoples" not run the risk that their history is currently written in accord with the interests of foreign historians? Is it not possible that we are living another type of colonization like that of the missionaries in the sixteenth and seventeenth centuries and that historians from outside are displacing our interpretation of the facts with their own, perhaps substituting their myths for ours? Or can we trust completely that they have no ideology and that ideology is not present in their work? Would it be definitively better for indigenous peoples' history to be analyzed and interpreted in accord with the ideological scheme of historians from outside rather than with our own schemes? Is it not possible that we might

have reached these heights by developing a critical capacity like that supposedly possessed by European historians? Have they purged history's original
sin, derived from its birth in the service of the power of the dominant class,
while the indigenous peoples still have not? Many are the questions put forth
in this brief space, but many are the doubts that I have with respect to the
neglected state of our indigenous peoples as regards participation in the task
of analysis and interpretation of their past.

Let us examine an example of how a myth brought by the colonizers substi-
tutes for our myths in the epoch of the Spanish colonization. With this I mean
that a strange form of interpretation of our history can currently displace our
own interpretations of the past, without the myth—the interpretation carried
from outside—being necessarily better than ours.

The metaphoric use of language by the Zapotecs was observed not only by
Burgoa, nor was it restricted to myths. Deeds were also explained in this manner. We must not dismiss the possibility that they applied it in recording historical acts, apart from reasons of state security or for the sake of elegant speech.
The codex Vaticano-Ríos (engraving 87) gives us an example of this:

> These people [referring to the Zapotecs] were such friends of metaphors in both
> words and works that in order to convey a man's age they painted a mountain,
> and placed a child at the foot as if he were about to begin to climb. Because they
> said that a man up to twenty years old was like one who climbs to the top of a
> high hill, cuts flowers, and delights himself with his vices and sins. From twenty
> to forty it's as though he is on top of the mountain, now in repose; at that age he
> is skilled in combat and able to walk wherever he wants, and to offend and de-
> fend. But from forty to sixty years he begins to descend from the mountain and
> starts to stoop, to the point that he has to look for a cane in order to support him-
> self, returning like a child to the first age.

Well then, knowing this, Burgoa did not want to understand the form in which
they recounted to him that they descended from tigers and forest beasts, from
shady, towering trees, from rocks and large stones; he wrote that these beliefs
were only crazy foolish things of which the devil had persuaded them. Edward
Seler still succeeded in hearing, or he read some place about this metaphorical
form of speaking, in which they referred to themselves as lightning or the rain:
"Ti-api nica, tiapi laa o tiapa que la quiepaa, ticoo laa quiepaa": "Water falls,
fire falls; precious stones fall (with the water) and fire falls." Who can assure
us that the historians concerned with indigenous peoples' history have Seler's
sensibility and understand this form of speaking metaphorically of the lightning or rain and that our speakers of *didxazá* called themselves, as we know,

nisa guie, which is to say, "stone water"? Do we not continue to say *siadó guie,* "morning in flower," for morning; *cayaba gui guidxilayú,* "fire falls on the people of the earth," for midday; or *huadxi dxita,* "afternoon turned into bone," to refer to late afternoon?

My fear is that the interpretations of historians foreign to our peoples may not be better and may displace those of our own historians, as occurred in the case of the Christian myths that fused together with the indigenous myths or totally displaced them. Let us examine an example of this phenomenon of syncretism, attained after more than four hundred years of colonization, in the case of the myth of man's creation. I heard it in Zapotec as a child, and soon thereafter I succeeded in reconstructing it in Spanish:

> God created man on various occasions before attaining the results that exist today. The creator began his work various times, until it came out well. The first men he made were of wood. Those men grew and multiplied without end. They grew and grew, but they did not worship the god who had made them for they had no feelings toward anyone. They felt nothing because they were made of wood. They did nothing but grow and multiply.
>
> One day the creator came down to earth and they ignored him. Furious, the creator rose to the sky once again and hurled fire down upon them until the men were petrified. After that he sent water upon the earth for forty days and forty nights, so that all might drown and none might be saved. It is those men who have been found made of stone under the earth. They are called the *binnigula'sa'*. And it is their implements, toys, and gods that our children play with when we find them in furrows during the sowing of the fields or at the edge of the roads of our communities in the rainy season or *guciguié.*

It can be noted in this reconstructed myth how the elements of the colonizer's culture have deformed the origin myth of the *binnigula'sa',* displacing original elements. Apart from other elements that mythologists can identify, there appears the image of a Christian god who punishes people with the deluge. This image functions to further the religious ends of the conquest. We do not know, from the point of view of the literary text, if the syncretic version of the creation myth is better than the original Zapotec and Christian versions; but from the ideological point of view it is clear that elements of the autochthonous religion have been erased and substituted by those of Christianity. Simply put, this is called colonization or ideological conquest. Are we not running similar risks when historians from outside write the history of our peoples? Is it certain that the current studies of our past have now abandoned the eurocentrism that characterized the missionaries of the Spanish conquest?

If there are real and great risks in leaving the study of indigenous peoples' history in the hands of nonindigenous interests, how will intellectuals from indigenous communities respond to the challenge of studying their own past? Will their good will and political enthusiasm suffice? Who will support this work of indigenous peoples? Will it be these same peoples, who live in misery? Will it be the official institutions? The foreign foundations? How and when will indigenous peoples be enabled to have their own intellectuals who study their past from the perspective of those peoples?

NOTE

1. Enrique Florescano in his work *El indígena en la historia de México* (1977) has analyzed some aspects of this process of expropriation-appropriation.

The Foundation of Juchitán

Andrés Henestrosa

The little wild ducks called *pijijes,* which we hear singing at night as they pass by on the eve of *guciguié* [summer or rainy season], had spread the news of the death of Saint Teresa. Now that her soul was back in heaven, God restored her to his breast. But the city in which he wanted to bring together the dispersed men had not yet been constructed, so the Lord persisted in his plan. He ordered his emissaries to call Vincent Ferrer, who despite his youth was already a saint.

God told him: "Go down to earth and erect the city which Saint Teresa could not construct and keep there the men whom kindness saved from the catastrophe of the ocean."

Without showing his joy, the saint returned to earth to carry out the celestial order. In that place where he landed, the air was fine and clear, as if it had been hung out to be whitened by the sun, the land was fertile, and water was close at hand. The rain lived on high but docilely came when it was called. The jungle closed in tightly, beckoning with its arms full of fruit.

"This will not be the place for my city," concluded Saint Vincent, "for the residents would have no obstacles or dangers, and they would become indolent and dispirited; I want children who are hardworking and swift."

He abandoned that region, which the following morning became Tehuantepec, and wandered around the district looking for an area where the air was thick and dirty, the land arid, the water deep, the rain unruly, and where the jungle extended from the foot of the horizon. When he found it, relief came over his heart.

That same day, he gathered the first men, built the first house, and dug the first well, whose waters did not flow until it was seven fathoms deep. In time, the other wells and houses that form the city of brave men gathered around the first well and house. To make a living, they must go to the jungle, which extends from the foot of the horizon. There they fight with the wild beasts for construction materials and hear, mixed with their own footsteps and the sounds of the wind, the passing of a tall, thin figure with two gigantic gray wings whom only the mute and newborn can see because they cannot tell anyone about it. The city is for hardworking men who live next to the dead river. To quench their thirst, they have to dig wells seven fathoms deep and have to rip the chest of the earth after scarce rains to obtain its fruits.

The bravery, uproar, and misfortune of its first settlers are repeated in all the movements of its current inhabitants.

Ethnic Resistance:
Juchitán
in
Mexican History

John Tutino

Juchitecos—the Zapotecs of Juchitán, Oaxaca—stand staunchly against the mainstream of modern Mexican history. They maintain a community that is proudly Zapotec, from local elites to the working majority; they continue to resist with remarkable tenacity and notable successes the encroaching powers of the centralizing Mexican State and the national culture it promotes; and they maintain a relatively prosperous provincial economy in which peasant subsistence production survives while commercial activities thrive—and in which women are important, publicly visible economic and social actors (Whitecotton 1984; Royce 1975; Campbell 1989).

The contrast with most Mexican communities is striking. "Being Indian" in modern Mexico is usually a negation. Survivals of indigenous languages and cultural traditions generally are linked with poverty, illiteracy, and lack of economic opportunity (Friedlander 1975). Opposition to Mexico's centralizing State usually is blocked by the overwhelming power and resources of that State. Provincial agrarian economies are almost always impoverished, and the women in them usually face very restricted roles—or become economically important only in situations of extreme desperation (e.g., Finkler 1974). In contrast, the uniqueness of Juchitán—proudly Zapotec, not Indian; persistently resistant to the State; and prosperous while offering women economically important roles—is blatant.

This essay seeks a historical understanding of the uniqueness of Juchitán.

Why have Juchitecos of all classes clung to the Zapotec tongue and to an adamant pride in Zapotec culture? How have Juchitecos built and maintained a
historical tradition of local autonomy and resistance to encroaching outsiders?[1]
What follows, then, is a historical interpretation seeking to explain Juchiteco
traditions of ethnic and cultural pride and political resistance. I focus on developments during the centuries just before the Spanish conquest, the complex
transformations of the colonial era, and on the decades from independence to
the liberal reforms of the mid-nineteenth century—by which time Juchitán had
emerged as a center of adamant resistance to state power, the role it maintains
to this day. As a caution, I must emphasize that this interpretation is based
on currently available, historical information. The essential, deeply researched
history of Juchitán and the Isthmus of Tehuantepec in Mexican history—a
history that will reveal much more about regional development, cultural traditions, and gender relations—awaits its historian.

PREHISPANIC ORIGINS

At the time of the Spanish conquest, Zapotecs were powerful newcomers to
the Isthmus of Tehuantepec.[2] Zapotec political and cultural traditions dated
back nearly two millennia but were rooted in the central valley of Oaxaca in
the interior highlands. The most prominent Zapotec center was Monte Albán,
holding sway from a mountain top just outside the modern city of Oaxaca.
Monte Albán was one of the major political and ceremonial centers of
Mesoamerica's classic age, ruling the Valley of Oaxaca and surrounding regions from about A.D. 200 to 900, while Teotihuacán dominated central Mexico and Tikal flourished in the Yucatán. Zapotec Monte Albán was a classic
Mesoamerican city, imperial capital, and religious center. It was ruled by an
elite of warlords and priests and sustained by the surrounding peasantry. Monte
Albán's priests organized the worship of Cocijo (Lightning and Rain) and Pitao
Cozipi (Maize and Sustenance): forces of obvious importance to the cultivators
who sustained the city, while subject to its rule. Warlords worked to expand the
power of the Zapotec elite, fend off competing rulers, and ensure that subject
peasants remained subjects who provided the material base to maintain the city
and its military and religious powers.

The Zapotec majority of the classic era lived as classic Mesoamerican peasants. Families lived in communities engaged primarily in cultivating the
land—raising the maize, beans, chile, and other things essential to family sustenance. They made cloth and pottery for family and community needs. Most
families and communities worked to maximize basic economic autonomy,
while exchanging small surpluses in local and regional markets. And peasant

families and communities sustained beliefs and rituals that addressed the forces essential to agriculture, protected their families, and simultaneously integrated community life. Typical of societies in which a peasant majority maintains ample subsistence autonomy, power in classic Zapotec civilization was exercised primarily through coercion that was organized by warlords and justified by linking that coercion to the deified forces of nature that were so unpredictable, yet so fundamental to the subsistence production essential to the lives of the majority.

The available evidence indicates that during the classic age of Monte Albán the peoples of the Isthmus of Tehuantepec were not Zapotec. They were likely the ancestors of the Zoque and Huave peoples who would later share the region with Zapotecs. But there are indications of contacts between the powerful highland Zapotecs and these Isthmus communities, probably driven by the highlanders' desires for salt, cotton, and other products of the coastal lowlands. Whether those early contacts were based on exchange, coerced extraction, or some combination of the two is not known.

Sometime around A.D. 900, the powers that sustained the regional dominance of Monte Albán disintegrated. As happened across Mesoamerica after the collapse of the classic imperial centers, Oaxaca moved into a long era of conflictive competition among numerous smaller city-states. Peasants continued to produce, trade, and negotiate with the forces of nature, and to provide sustenance and soldiers to those who fought to rule. Now, however, there were many more warlord-religious elites engaged in constant conflict, bringing a long era of violence and insecurity.

During those times of conflict, the Zapotecs of the Valley of Oaxaca began to face mounting pressures from increasingly powerful Mixtec peoples based in the rugged highlands to the north. And as Mixtecs pressed against the Zapotec city-states of the Valley of Oaxaca, the Zapotecs began to push their power southeast toward the Isthmus. Sometime in the fourteenth century, the Zapotec center of Zaachila sent expeditions to Tehuantepec, seeking tributes in salt, cotton, and other produce of the coastal lowlands. The peoples of the Isthmus, the inland Zoques, coastal Huaves, and perhaps some Chontal Mayans to the east began to pay tributes to the Zapotec lords of Zaachila. They also had to make room at the Isthmus for Zapotec colonial settlements centered at Guiengola, a hilltop fortress near the modern town of Tehuantepec, and several outlying villages, including Juchitán.

When in the fifteenth century Zaachila was defeated by Mixtec foes, the lords of Tehuantepec emerged as the most powerful rulers of Zapotec culture. Zapotecs remaining in the Valley of Oaxaca began to pay tributes to the lords of the Isthmus. Thus, as Mixtec power rose in the Valley of Oaxaca, Zapotec power shifted toward Tehuantepec. Mitla, in the southeastern extension of the Valley of Oaxaca, remained the center of Zapotec religion.

With Zapotec lords facing the Mixtec challenge and working to consolidate their new center at Tehuantepec, in the late fifteenth century they also confronted more powerful warlords from farther north. The Mexicas (Aztecs) of Tenochtitlán then sent expeditions of conquest and trade toward Oaxaca and the Isthmus. Aztec imperialism sought political sovereignty and the power to demand tributes from subjugated peoples. Their interest in the Isthmus also included securing the trade route to Soconusco and beyond, the source of treasured cacao.

In their dealings with the Mexicas, Isthmus Zapotecs exhibited an astute combination of resistance and negotiation. They fought staunch battles against the Mexicas, never fully "defeating" their armies, but making it clear that Isthmus Zapotecs would not be transformed easily into subject tributaries. In these battles, Sahagún reports the participation of Xuchilán as a fierce opponent of Mexican power (Sahagún 1979:490). After having demonstrated their power of resistance, the lords of Tehuantepec negotiated a dynastic union between the paramount lord of Guiengola and a Mexican noblewoman, creating an alliance of unequals that allowed the Mexicas free passage across the Isthmus while preserving Zapotec lordship over the peoples of the region in exchange for recognition of ultimate Mexican lordship.

The Isthmus Zapotecs lived a complex history during the centuries before the Spanish conquest. They had come to Tehuantepec as conquerors and colonists, subordinating and exploiting the Zoques and Huaves to reinforce the power of Zaachila in the Valley of Oaxaca. As Zaachila weakened, Tehuantepec emerged as the center of Zapotec power. Colonial settlers in a "foreign" territory, Isthmus Zapotecs clung to their cultural traditions. And soon after settling the Isthmus and claiming power there, the Zapotecs had to grapple with the intrusion of the expansionist Mexicas. The lords of the Isthmus then demonstrated an ability to use a nuanced combination of armed resistance and diplomatic negotiation to prevent a collapse into simple subordination to the Aztec empire.

This pre-Hispanic history would orient the responses of Isthmus Zapotecs to the Spanish conquest and colonialism that began in the early sixteenth century. During the decades and centuries that followed, the powers of social and cultural resistance developed in indigenous power struggles would be tested under extreme pressures. Again they would lead to remarkable adaptations.

CONQUEST, COLONIALISM, AND
RESISTANT ADAPTATION

Spaniards bent on power arrived at Tehuantepec in 1522, soon after the fall of the Aztec capital of Tenochtitlán. Rather than risk war against the triumphant conquerors of the Mexicas, Cosijopi, the last Zapotec lord of Tehuantepec, negotiated a new alliance—a relationship the Spaniards viewed as mere submission. Cosijopi remained lord of the Isthmus Zapotecs. He accepted Christian baptism, took the symbolic name of Don Juan Cortés, and struggled to learn quickly how to deal with the new means of power rapidly encroaching on life at the Isthmus. The last independent lord of the Zapotecs became the first colonial broker between European rulers and the peoples of Tehuantepec.[3]

Don Hernando Cortés early on saw the Isthmus as the ideal base for several enterprises: There he would mine gold; there he would graze herds of livestock imported from Europe; there he would establish shipyards and a port to begin exploration and trade in the Pacific. The leader of the Spanish conquest of Mexico thus claimed personal sovereignty over the southern Isthmus and its peoples as part of his massive domain, the Marquesado del Valle de Oaxaca.

To provide the core of permanent workers for his Isthmus enterprises, Cortés sent several hundred Mexicans enslaved in the conflicts of conquest. They panned for gold and built ships, often supervised by a small core of enslaved Africans. The indigenous peoples of the Isthmus were then required, through the Spanish institution of the *encomienda,* to sustain the population permanently working in Cortés's enterprises. Cosijopi, now Don Juan Cortés, and other surviving native lords became colonial intermediaries, collecting tributes from the Isthmus peasantry to sustain the commercial activities of the conqueror Cortés. Early colonial tributes included not only traditional Isthmus products such as maize, cloth, and shellfish, but also European impositions from gold to chickens to the timbers used in shipbuilding.[4] Isthmus Zapotecs, Zoques, and Huaves had to incorporate these products into their household and community economies, deliver them to Cortés's enterprises, and periodically provide the conqueror with supplemental labor in rotating shifts.

From the conquest through the 1540s, the Isthmus Zapotecs and their neighbors faced intense Spanish demands. Yet these pressures came at a time when Isthmus communities retained strong links with their indigenous past: Native lords still ruled locally, the subsistence economy persisted, and the languages and cultures of pre-Hispanic times were alive in a population that in large part had lived in those times. Among the Zapotecs, staunchly oriented to preserve maximum political and cultural autonomy, these early impositions necessitated rapid learning about Spaniards, their power, and their culture. Isthmus Zapotecs began then to adapt for their own purposes what they found useful in Spanish ways, while they learned to resist Spanish impositions.

The early Spanish incursion also brought destructive pressures. Most obviously, the indigenous population of Tehuantepec plummeted from about 24,000 tributary heads of household at the time of conquest to just over 6,000 by 1550—a devastating loss of 75 percent.[5] As elsewhere in Mexico, this catastrophe resulted from the devastation wrought by Old World diseases on a population without immunities, simultaneously weakened by postconquest economic demands and cultural disruptions.

Also during the early colonial decades, the peoples of Tehuantepec began to face Dominican friars who pressed them to adopt Christianity. We know of Cosijopi's rapid, public conversion, but we know little of the Zapotec majority's evolving response to missionary pressures and the Christian religion. Indigenous religion as preached by Zapotec elites had justified and reinforced political sovereignty. The collapse of that sovereignty was evident in the early Spanish presence and power at the Isthmus, despite the survival of indigenous lords as intermediaries. Beliefs linked to temporal powers that had collapsed became open to question and challenge. Meanwhile, missionaries preached a religion that proposed to explain and justify the emerging powers of Spaniards. And despite emphasizing the inevitability of worldly inequity and exploitation, Christian missionaries also preached a religion of equality in salvation after death. The message, at a time of mass dying, helped to gain a hearing for Christianity.

Growing numbers of Isthmus Zapotecs began to call themselves Christians. They began to honor the all-powerful Christian God, whose force was perhaps the only available explanation for the sudden coming of Spanish power, yet whose compassion offered hope in the face of death. Yet the majority of Isthmus Zapotecs knew that they must continue to negotiate with the Forces of Nature that ruled their agriculture, their fertility, and their health. They thus created during the colonial era (the precise timing and content remain invisible) what might be called Zapotec Christianity: a religion Christian in its vision of cosmic questions of creation and salvation, and perhaps also in its claims to justify Spanish sovereignty, while insistently Zapotec in the continuing emphasis on the powers that ruled and regulated daily life in an agrarian society. Zapotec Christianity became dominant in the annual cycle of community rituals that integrated life in Tehuantepec communities in the colonial era and beyond.

The early colonial decades thus brought a period of intense Spanish-Zapotec interaction. The results were demographic destruction, pressures toward religious conversion, and intense involvement in the emerging commercial economy, all at a time when Zapotec political traditions endured and Zapotec culture remained strong. Later developments suggest that these early colonial interactions served to entrench Zapotec identity as a cultural defense against Spanish impositions. Surviving Zapotecs surely blamed the conquest and colonialism for the period of death, economic demands, and cultural uncertainties they faced from the 1520s through the 1540s.

Then the 1550s saw the rapid waning of the Spanish presence and pressures at the Isthmus. Following the death of the conqueror Cortés, and the troubles brought upon his son Martín by his alleged involvement in a conspiracy against the colonial State, the seigneurial domain of the Marquesado del Valle de Oaxaca was shrunken at the Isthmus, and what remained to the Cortés family was embargoed for decades. Tribute demands were restricted to traditional goods, mostly maize and cloth, plus small amounts of colonial coin. Diseases continued their destruction. Tributary counts fell from just over 6,000 in 1550 to under 4,000 by 1580, though the rate of demographic decline began to slow. In the early 1560s, colonial officials accused Cosijopi of conspiring with Zapotec religious leaders at Mitla in an attempt to revive traditional beliefs. If true, the accusations reveal the eventual displeasure of Cosijopi with his early decision to collaborate with the Spaniards and accept Christianity. Had he become disillusioned with becoming Don Juan Cortés?

The years from the 1550s to the 1580s, then, brought a recession of Spanish power and a respite to Zapotec society that apparently allowed a new consolidation of Zapotec colonial culture. In 1580 there remained at Tehuantepec only an *alcalde mayor* (the colonial justice), several Dominicans, and a Spanish community of but twenty-five families (Torres de Laguna 1928). After a brief time at the center of Cortés's vision of the New World, the Isthmus had taken its place at the far southern margin of a colonial society being entrenched by a State based in distant Mexico City and driven economically by the booming silver mines even farther to the north.

The late 1580s and especially the 1590s brought a resurgence of Spanish interest in the Isthmus, however.[6] This second colonial incursion proved very different from the first. The postconquest decades ruled by the conqueror Cortés had placed intense demands for produce and labor on a declining peasant population. The late sixteenth-century incursion, in contrast, focused on claiming much of the land vacated by the dying Isthmus peasantry—only 2,800 tributaries would remain in the 1620s. Spaniards began to use the lands to build extensive estates for grazing livestock. The Cortés family, now entrenched among the Castilian nobility, recovered its Isthmus estates (but not its seigneurial jurisdiction) and rapidly expanded livestock production across the interior uplands of the Isthmus, consolidating what would come to be known as the

Haciendas Marquesanas. The Oaxacan Dominicans also built several grazing estates at the Isthmus, as did numerous colonial Spaniards based in Oaxaca or the town of Tehuantepec. Vast areas of Isthmus land were awarded to Spaniards through titles issued by the colonial State, with activity feverish in the 1590s.

Livestock, hides, and salted beef from the estates' cattle herds, along with hides and wool from sheep, went to markets in Oaxaca, central Mexico, and even Spain. With the commercial livestock boom came an increased Hispanic presence and revived commercial activity at the Isthmus. By the 1620s there were about a hundred Hispanic families, mostly in the town of Tehuantepec. They operated vessels that traded with ports from Acapulco through Central America to Peru. They also traded overland with the Valley of Oaxaca, Chiapas, and Highland Guatemala. Much of the trade depended on Isthmus salt deposits. Raw salt along with salted beef and seafood were among the traders' primary products. The economic boomlet of the early seventeenth century is confirmed by the 600-peso price assigned the post of *alcalde mayor* of Tehuantepec. In Oaxaca, only the city of Oaxaca was valued so highly by those who sold and bought official positions based upon the expectations of commercial profit.

This second colonial incursion brought outsiders and their commercial ways to the Isthmus. Yet it did not prove deeply destructive of Zapotec life and culture. There were numerous conflicts over favored lands, along with suits over the damages caused by Spaniards' livestock trampling peasant crops. Those conflicts reveal both Spanish impositions and a staunch Zapotec will to resist. There were also creative adaptations among the Zapotecs to the colonial livestock economy. Local elites often went to the colonial State to claim a Spanish title to grazing lands and then joined the commercial livestock economy on a modest scale. Several Isthmus communities did the same collectively. Meanwhile, peasant control of the region's subsistence economy persisted. Zapotec families raised maize and other food crops, often on communally held irrigated fields. The region's haciendas generally lacked irrigation and thus remained dependent on maize obtained from peasants to provide basic food rations to their permanent workers. Many of the peasant families at the Isthmus still made cloth. Zapotecs and Huaves along the southern lagoons kept control of salt production. And the coastal Huaves ruled both fishing and shellfish collection.

Retaining a monopoly over basic foodstuffs while also controlling the production of elements essential to the local commercial economy, the Isthmus Zapotecs did not—and probably would not—serve as the core of permanent, dependent workers on the region's livestock estates. As a result, the major grazers had to invest in expensive slave laborers, now primarily Africans. During the late sixteenth and early seventeenth centuries, they were forced to come in sufficient numbers to introduce a third cultural tradition to Isthmus life.

The decades of respite that followed the first colonial incursions had allowed the Isthmus Zapotecs to adapt and consolidate a colonial culture of resistance, adamantly Zapotec, that enabled them to face the livestock and commercial developments of the decades around 1600 with some strength, despite declining numbers. Zapotec elites joined the colonial commercial economy, while the Isthmus peasantry maintained a solid subsistence base, joining too in the commercial economy when it served their interests.

Then, from the 1630s, the Isthmus livestock economy began a long and steady decline. The waning of the first Mexican silver boom shrank market activities across Mexico. As the livestock region farthest from the colonial centers of mining and commerce, Tehuantepec was progressively excluded from shrinking markets. Grazing estates remained at the Isthmus, but their production and profitability declined substantially through the seventeenth century.

As profits waned, Isthmus estates no longer purchased African slaves. By the second quarter of the seventeenth century, permanent estate workers were increasingly listed as free mulattoes. They were the offspring of the earlier generation of African slaves joining primarily with Zapotec women, given the small numbers of Hispanic and African women in the region. As the free children of Zapotec mothers, many Isthmus mulattoes may have lived culturally as Zapotecs, infusing an African component into the historically changing cultural complex we call Zapotec. And the emergence of a free Afro-Zapotec population, children of slave fathers and Zapotec mothers, may have reinforced the cultural will toward resistance so characteristic of Isthmus culture.

In 1660 it became clear that the tradition of resistance had not been weakened during over a century of creative adaptation to colonial rule. In that year a revolt was triggered by the demands of a newly appointed colonial justice (Rojas 1964; Iturribarría 1955:101–3). Don Juan de Avellán believed that the people of Tehuantepec were taxed too little, and he quickly doubled tribute demands. Local Zapotec elites were expected to collect the suddenly increased taxes, and they were quick to protest. They were flogged, and the protest escalated into riot. The local Dominicans could not pacify the irate Zapotecs. Avellán was killed. That left rebellious Zapotec leaders in control of the Isthmus region. They remained in revolt for a year and sent emissaries to recruit allies among Zapotec communities in the Oaxacan highlands. They thus began to recreate—or perhaps they revealed the subterranean persistence of—the pre-Hispanic relations linking Tehuantepec lords to highland Zapotecs.

Knowing that they could not oppose the full force of the colonial regime, rebel leaders wrote the viceroy in Mexico City insisting that they had not risen against the colonial order, but only against the greed and injustice of one corrupt official. No viceroy could accept such pleading. A colonial official had been killed by rebellious subjects under indigenous leadership. Thus, in 1661, a force assembled under the bishop of Oaxaca occupied Tehuantepec and captured the leaders of the rebellion. Several were executed to discourage continued resistance. The larger Zapotec populace of the Isthmus was then pardoned—a response typical of colonial justice in Mexico. Subsequent investigation by the colonial regime concluded that Avellán was right about the low level of tribute collections at the Isthmus. Yet the investigators cautioned against any immediate attempt to raise collections to levels common elsewhere in Mexico. The revolt convinced the colonial State that the Isthmus Zapotecs had their own definition of bearable colonial demands, along with a clear willingness to defend their view.

Through the decades following the revolt and its suppression, the Isthmus all but fades from the historical record. That indicates that the region remained neither economically important to the colonial order nor a challenge to the colonial State. The commercial economy of the Isthmus continued its decline into the early eighteenth century. Tribute data indicate that the population classified as Indian for tax purposes finally stopped its decline and began a slow rise: to 3,500 tributaries in 1735 and 3,800 by 1743. In the latter year, the nearly 4,000 indigenous households included about 13,000 people. They were joined in the Tehuantepec jurisdiction by about 1,300 persons classed as Spaniards and mulattoes, mostly concentrated in the town of Tehuantepec, which had a population of about 5,000. In the 1740s, the Isthmus was reported as producing maize, salt, and fish—the core of the indigenous economy—along with cattle, the legacy of earlier Spanish development. Newly reported were cochineal and sugar, early signs of a third wave of commercial expansion during the late colonial decades (Gerhard 1962:25).

Also under way during the century after the revolt of 1660 was a pivotal change that remains invisible in the available sources, yet is evident in later developments. The revolt was the last major act of resistance, the last vehement defense of local autonomy and Zapotec culture, led by the colonial descendants of the lords of Guiengola. The defeat of the uprising and the execution of most of a generation of resistant leaders, combined with the long-term effects of the presence in the town of Tehuantepec of the regions' Spanish community, brought a tendency toward hispanization among Tehuantepec elites and increasing accommodation and collaboration with colonial authorities. When Isthmus resistance emerged again, adamantly, in the early nineteenth century, it would be led by the still proudly Zapotec elite of the town of Juchitán.

Thus, after 1660 and before 1800, the center of Zapotec political power and cultural resistance shifted again. From its classic center at Monte Albán to its postclassic bases at Mitla and Zaachila (all in the highland Valley of Oaxaca), the center of Zapotec power and culture had shifted to Guiengola-Tehuantepec in the face of late pre-Hispanic pressures from the Mixtecs. Juchitán began in the late preconquest era as an outpost subject to Guiengola. The heirs to the lords of Guiengola remained the leaders of Zapotec life through the first half of the colonial era. But when their defeat in rebellion was followed by a subsequent tendency to adopt Hispanic colonial ways, their orientation toward resistance and thus their ability to lead Isthmus Zapotecs were steadily diminished. In that context, Juchitán would emerge during the late colonial era as the new center of Zapotec power, led by a local elite that remained insistently Zapotec and oriented toward resistance.

While Juchitán was thus developing outside the vision of those who compiled most colonial records, the second half of the eighteenth century brought a third colonial wave of commercial development to the Isthmus. The eighteenth-century silver boom stimulated commercial production across Mexico. Specifically, however, the resurgence of commercial production at Tehuantepec after 1750 responded to the rapid expansion of textile production in Europe. Mixtecs of the Oaxacan highlands had long produced cochineal, insects that when crushed produced a fine red dye, and exported modest amounts to Europe. The eighteenth-century textile boom that would culminate in the industrial revolution brought escalating demand for colonial dyes. The Isthmus began to raise both cochineal and indigo for export.

Simultaneously, the Isthmus experienced a period of sustained population growth. The jurisdiction of Tehuantepec, with but 14,000 inhabitants in 1742, reported nearly 22,000 in a census of 1793: 2,226 Spaniards, 3,316 mulattoes, and 16,189 Indians. Periods that combine export expansion with population growth have often proven destructive of both the welfare and culture of indigenous peoples in Mexico. Yet that did not happen in late colonial Tehuantepec, due in part to the goods produced for export and in part to the Zapotecs' capacity for resistant adaptation to colonial pressures.

Cochineal production was so labor intensive that it rarely became an estate crop. It was usually raised by the women of peasant families. They placed a few insects on the abundant nopal cactus, awaited their multiplication, and then painstakingly brushed the insects off. Dried and crushed into dye, the cochineal was then delivered to a local merchant, usually the local justice, who doubled as the agent of a Mexico City commercial house. At Tehuantepec, the justice joined the trade near the middle of the eighteenth century. Many Isthmus Zapotecs then took up cochineal production as a supplement to the subsistence-oriented family economies. Cochineal did not disrupt established economic or social relations and offered a bit of additional income to peasant families facing population growth (Hamnett 1971a).

Indigo, in contrast, was primarily grown on Spaniards' estates. The grass-like crop is sown extensively and demands a large but mostly seasonal work force to mow the crop and process it in vats into dye. A crop demanding extensive lands and much labor might have threatened peasant family economies at the Isthmus. But indigo was raised primarily on lands long held by old live-stock estates. The core of permanent estate workers was recruited, still, among the mulatto descendants of the early colonial African slaves. Many Zapotec villagers were hired as seasonal hands to cut and process indigo. That work, too, was organized to serve as a supplement to subsistence production, providing another source of additional income to peasants grappling with population growth.[7]

Typical of their responses to colonialism, some among the Zapotec elite grew indigo on a modest scale. Many peasant families raised cochineal, and many labored seasonally for wages at the indigo estates. Yet all this Zapotec involvement in the export economy was supplemental to an enduring peasant subsistence economy. At Tehuantepec, commerce had to adapt to Zapotec society and culture, thus limiting export development and preserving the foundations of peasant community life.

Three late colonial reports reveal much about Isthmus life on the eve of national independence. A 1792 survey of industries reports only two indigo estates operating at Tehuantepec. The land was said to grow fine indigo, but limited water supplies restricted any expansion of Isthmus production (Florescano and Gil 1973:57). The limits on available water are explained by a survey done six years earlier, seeking information on maize production in the wake of the great famine of 1785 and 1786 in central Mexico. The justice at Tehuantepec reported that no commercial estates raised maize at the Isthmus, where it was harvested entirely by small holders, mostly indigenous peasants, who fed themselves and also supplied local town dwellers and estate residents. The report goes on to note that in the hot, coastal climate of the Isthmus, maize did not keep long. But that difficulty was compensated by the peasants' ability to harvest two, even three, crops per year (Florescano 1981:571). Irrigation was essential to such year-round cropping. Clearly, the water resources of the Isthmus region remained devoted to peasant subsistence production. The limit to indigo at Tehuantepec was not an absolute lack of water. It was the Zapotecs' control of that critical resource and their insistence that maize came first.

The third report, a survey of textile production in 1793, reveals that Juchitán was then the only Isthmus community with substantial cloth production. And Juchiteco merchants traded locally produced cloth in both Highland Oaxaca and Highland Guatemala.[8] Here is a glimpse of the late colonial emergence of Juchitán as the center of Zapotec power, based on creative and resistant accommodations to Spanish colonialism.

After three centuries of colonial rule and three waves of commercial incursion, and after a catastrophic depopulation followed by a slow demographic recovery, Isthmus Zapotecs maintained a cultural tradition built upon a history of creative adaptation to colonialism and resistance to what they defined as colonial excesses. And by the late colonial era, the center of Zapotec culture and resistance was clearly shifting from Tehuantepec to Juchitán.

INDEPENDENCE, CONFLICT, AND INSURRECTION

The political and social conflicts that led to Mexican independence in 1821 developed far from Tehuantepec. The consequences of independence, however, brought fundamental change and escalating conflict to life at the Isthmus. The region's export economy all but collapsed. Always limited by lack of access to the region's water, dye production also depended on long and difficult transportation to the port of Veracruz. When he visited the Isthmus around 1800, Alexander von Humboldt emphasized that high transportation costs left the Tehuantepec dye trade easily subject to collapse should high prices fall (Humboldt 1966:9–10, 170–71, 469–70). After 1821, the Mexican economy struggled to adjust to its sudden extraction from the Spanish imperial system, just as the production of both cochineal and indigo expanded rapidly elsewhere. Cochineal, long a Oaxacan monopoly, suddenly boomed in newly independent Guatemala—it was that rare export that could be raised in an economy still based on peasant family households. Meanwhile, the British promoted indigo in India, as did the Dutch in Indonesia and the French in North Africa (Heers 1961:11–16). Long before the invention of chemical dyes, rising competition among colonial and newly independent producers drove world production up and prices down, causing the collapse of the dye industry at the Isthmus of Tehuantepec. The heirs to the Cortés family patrimony found economic prospects at the Isthmus so limited that they looked to sell the Haciendas Marquesanas.

Yet the postindependence collapse of the export economy did not lead to another era of Isthmus marginality. Independence brought a new orientation to state power in Mexico. The national State, including its provincial substates such as Oaxaca, increasingly functioned as the agent of aspiring economic elites. In the city of Oaxaca, the Spanish merchants who had ruled colonial commerce were replaced by a clique of European newcomers, including French, Milanese, British, and German entrepreneurs, who had come to profit from the opening of Mexico, long fabled for its wealth.[9] The rise of these postindependence immigrant entrepreneurs in Mexico and Oaxaca coincided with the emergence of politicians who aimed to use the developing powers of state to implement a vision they called "liberal." They envisioned a society ruled by private property and commercial production, and they demanded the separation of church and state. Thus they pursued a program that challenged both the remnants of the Spanish colonial order and the community cultures adapted under that order by indigenous peasants such as the Isthmus Zapotecs.

Despite the difficulties that plagued the export economy (or perhaps because of them), the immigrant entrepreneurs of postindependence Oaxaca began an assault on Isthmus resources. Often, they were backed by the powers of state in the hands of liberal politicians. Immigrants bought the best Isthmus estates and took control of the region's trade. A partnership of a Frenchman, José Joaquin Guergue, and a Milanese, Esteban Maqueo, bought the Haciendas Marquesanas in the 1830s. Investing in vast properties in a time of economic decline, these immigrant entrepreneurs pushed for every source of profit. Increasingly, they claimed exclusive use of lands that had long been available to the Isthmus Zapotecs. And their land claims came while the peasant population continued to grow. The Tehuantepec jurisdiction increased from just under 22,000 people in 1793 to more than 27,000 by 1827. Zapotec peasants' need for land was increasing just as a new elite aimed to deny them access to lands they had customarily used.

The haciendas began to sequester villagers' livestock found grazing on disputed lands. Villagers retaliated by taking estate livestock. Postindependence land disputes at the Isthmus began in the 1820s and culminated in the 1840s. By then, conflict was heightened by parallel disputes over salt, trade, and taxes. By the late 1840s, Isthmus Zapotecs were ready to deny the rule of the state of Oaxaca—and the state would go to war against the Isthmus Zapotecs.[10]

It was in the course of these mounting postindependence conflicts that Juchitán clearly claimed the leadership of Zapotec resistance. Zapotec remained the language of Juchitán. Zapotec surnames appear repeatedly on the lists of rebel leaders. And Juchitecos remained committed to an economy that first preserved the subsistence base of the peasant majority, while local notables worked to profit from active and independent participation in available commercial opportunities.

The persistence of creative and resistant adaptations to changing economic and political pressures is revealed by the Juchitecos' response to the postindependence challenge of imported, industrially produced textiles. The mass importation of British cloth undermined textile production in Juchitán, as it did elsewhere in Mexico and Latin America. Juchiteco merchants' trade in cloth with Guatemala was also threatened. But turning crisis to profit, at least for themselves, Juchiteco leaders began to ship Isthmus salt, along with some dye, to Guatemala, and returned with imported British cloth, which they sold in the Isthmus. For Juchiteco elites, this was creative adaptation. If imported cloth now ruled the market, they would claim a part of the trade. But their trade went through Guatemala. To the Mexican State, Juchiteco creativity was mere contraband. The same trade also challenged the immigrant entrepreneurs of Oaxaca, who aimed to monopolize Isthmus commerce.

Juchiteco trade became the second focus of escalating conflict. The State prohibited that commerce with Guatemala but lacked the police power to enforce the ban. The subprefect at Juchitán became a focus of Zapotec discontent. His repeated attempts to enforce the trade prohibition appeared to be blatant support for the immigrant entrepreneurs based in the state capital, and an attack on Juchiteco traders. The same official sided with the estates in most land disputes. And Juchitecos also discovered that they paid far higher taxes than did the rival town of Tehuantepec, the regional seat of the state government and the base of Isthmus trade for the Oaxacan immigrant elite.

As conflicts over land, trade, and taxes escalated, the state of Oaxaca in alliance with aspiring entrepreneurs pressed another policy that threatened the foundation of the Isthmus Zapotec economy. The salt beds of the lagoons along the Pacific shore had long been a key to the prosperity of Isthmus peoples. Salt was essential to the Mesoamerican diet and an important food preservative. As it was not widely available, salt was a pivotal asset to those who produced it. Salt had attracted the first Zapotecs who came to the Isthmus in the preconquest era. It was basic to both Zapotec and Spanish economies during the colonial era. And salt was essential to Juchiteco trade with Guatemala after independence. Since time immemorial, the Isthmus salt beds had belonged to no person, no community. Villagers had claimed sectors for their residents' primary use, and there were sporadic disputes over boundaries. But historically, Isthmus residents had access to whatever salt they worked to extract.

The postindependence alliance of liberal politicians and aspiring entrepreneurs had a different vision. A law of 1825 called for a state-granted monopoly of Isthmus salt production. The monopolist would more profitably—and more taxably—exploit the lagoons' natural Isthmus salt. A chosen entrepreneur and the Oaxacan treasury would benefit, while Isthmus Zapotecs and Huaves would lose their customary access to salt for both consumption and trade. By the 1840s, the monopoly was held by one Francisco Javier Echeverría, who was struggling to enforce his state-granted claims while facing escalating resistance.

This array of mounting conflicts led to what Oaxacan authorities defined as rebellion, beginning in 1842 and culminating in the late 1840s and early 1850s. The Juchitecos and the Isthmus Zapotecs they led, however, never planned an insurrection. Rather, they were continuing the local tradition of creative and resistant adaptation to encroaching powers. They struggled in the courts and in the fields to maintain a society that served their interests. Zapotec violence was limited, directed specifically against local officials seen as betraying community values, or at the representatives of exploitative outsiders. Far greater violence would be directed by the state against Juchitán and its allies. It was the state, struggling to make its laws into realities, that saw coercion as its primary means of effective power.

Land disputes that had begun in the 1820s came to a head in 1842 when a few local officials at Juchitán offered to sell title to disputed areas to the immigrant *hacendados.* This collaboration provoked an increasingly large and organized opposition. The offending officials were ousted and the property transfer blocked, despite its legal sanction by the state. The government sent an armed squadron to enforce its will, and two years of resistance followed. State troops won most direct battles, but Juchiteco resistance proved tenacious. In 1845, the state offered to negotiate and to recognize at least some of the Zapotec land claims. The national government, however, refused to offer amnesty to the resistance leaders (Reina 1980:231–34).

Among those leaders was José Gregorio Meléndez. Owner of a *rancho,* a modest landed property, Meléndez was a prosperous Juchiteco who participated in the commercial economy and was active in state and national politics. Yet he maintained his base in Zapotec culture and the peasant society of Juchitán. He emerged as the paramount leader of Juchiteco resistance through the 1840s and into the 1850s.

The conflict that began in 1842 subsided with the negotiations of 1845, but the underlying issues remained unresolved. When in 1846 the military forces of both the Mexican nation and the state of Oaxaca were suddenly occupied by the war provoked by the United States, the people of Juchitán and surrounding communities took the opportunity to resume their customary use both of disputed lands and of the salt beds. For nearly two years, Isthmus Zapotecs enjoyed another brief era at the margins of power, with its resulting local autonomy.

When the international war ended late in 1847, however, the state of Oaxaca quickly turned to imposing its norms on the Isthmus peoples. The new governor was Benito Juárez, a highland Zapotec by birth but a lawyer by education, a liberal in ideology, and an aspiring politician by vocation. Taking office when state powers across Mexico were weak, Juárez saw only chaos at the Isthmus.

His liberal vision, along with his need for support from the economic elite of Oaxacan entrepreneurs, led him to demand a return to the rule of state law in both property rights and salt extraction. To enforce his demands, Juárez took a risk. He appointed José Gregorio Meléndez to lead the militia forces charged with enforcing state power at the Isthmus.

Juárez's gamble failed. Meléndez not only refused to become the agent of the Oaxacan state; he declared the separation of the Isthmus from that state. When forces from the rival town of Tehuantepec blocked that secession, Meléndez in 1848 joined in the ongoing raids on the salt beds, in defiance of the state monopoly. The state saw only theft. In May of 1848, the rebels raided the Juchitán jail, freeing allies held there. Then they sent a message to Juárez declaring that they acted only to redress injustices and now desired only peace. Juchitecos then turned their attention to raising maize through the summer rainy season. The peasant base of the movement took precedence.

After the harvest, in the fall of 1848, the Juchitecos returned to active salt mining. The monopolist Echeverría demanded that the state enforce his claims. Meanwhile, the *hacendados* Guergue and Maqueo demanded enforcement of their land titles. Governor Juárez responded by sending a small force of troops to Juchitán in the spring of 1849. The Juchitecos greeted the troops cordially and avoided any confrontation. Another summer approached, and the Isthmus peasantry turned again to its first concern—subsistence cultivation.

But in the fall of 1849, with another crop in, hostilities resumed and escalated. Juchiteco rebels jailed the local official they held most responsible for the early "sale" of community lands to the Haciendas Marquesanas, and took 500 pesos from him as recompense. State officials based in nearby Tehuantepec forcibly freed that captive and jailed several dissident leaders. In response, Meléndez organized a large force of angry Juchitecos and others, drove out the Tehuantepec garrison, and took full control of Juchitán, surrounding villages, and much of the countryside. The state received reports of a thousand armed rebels, mostly Juchitecos, supported by others from Huilotepec, San Gerónimo, Ixtaltepec, and the San Blas barrio of Tehuantepec.

In control of the Isthmus, except for the town of Tehuantepec, the rebels sent the state another proclamation of peace as the 1850 summer growing season approached. Juárez now refused to negotiate. He acted as the liberal governor he was and sent a force of four hundred troops and light artillery to enforce the state's claim to monopolies of coercion, the determination of property rights, and the resolution of disputes at the Isthmus. For Juárez it was time to make the state the effective power at Tehuantepec. The resulting battle for Juchitán proved bloody and destructive for Juchitecos. The state commander reported seventy dead rebels and presumed many more casualties among those carried off the field of battle. Fire set off during the fighting destroyed a third of Juchitán as flames quickly devoured homes of wood and thatch.

Yet the destructive battle and fire only strengthened the Juchitecos' resolve. Meléndez led his surviving forces east across the Isthmus toward Chiapas. Oaxacan troops could not enter the neighboring state without permission. While that was negotiated, Meléndez used his local knowledge to lead his rebel force back across the Isthmus to Juchitán. Along the way, several haciendas were sacked and one estate administrator killed. The rebels then marched past Juchitán and assaulted Tehuantepec. They sacked and burned the properties of several hated merchants. Then Meléndez led a return to Juchitán. He found the town center controlled by the subprefect and a modest force. Meléndez would not provoke another battle in Juchitán. Instead, he and his men remained in the area, sustained and hidden by the sympathetic populace.

Then cholera struck. It apparently devastated most severely the state troops sent from the cool highlands to the hot Isthmus. The army collapsed, and Meléndez again claimed control of Juchitán, killing the subprefect. Another raid on Tehuantepec, destructive mostly of property, followed. Then through the remainder of 1850 and into 1851, Meléndez and the Juchitecos ruled themselves.

In the spring of 1851, however, Governor Juárez assembled an army large enough to gain the immediate surrender of most Juchitecos. Meléndez and a core of rebel leaders fled into the back country, holding out as symbols of Juchiteco resistance. That autumn, Juárez came to Juchitán. He pardoned all who swore submission to state authority. He installed a new municipal council loyal to the state and ready to collaborate with Oaxacan elites. And Juárez agreed to pay a state salary to the new subprefect—an implicit admission that state justice at Juchitán had been for sale to the highest bidders.

With an overwhelming show of force and one limited concession, Juárez and the liberal state apparently won. The Juchitecos and their Isthmus Zapotec allies faced subordination. Appearances deceived. The conflicts of 1842 to 1851 resulted in a short-term triumph for the state. But that decade of conflict also renewed and entrenched the revived tradition of Isthmus Zapotec resistance—a tradition that endures.

ETHNIC RESISTANCE: A JUCHITECO TRADITION

The culture of Zapotec resistance to state power and other encroaching outsiders was fully established and rooted at Juchitán by the 1840s. There was already in place a local elite that remained proudly Zapotec, demanded local

autonomy, and looked to profit from local commerce. Some among these Juchiteco notables were tempted to collaborate with powerful outsiders. But
when outside powerholders became too intrusive and threatened the preeminence of the Juchiteco elite, Zapotec notables repeatedly turned to building
support among the Isthmus peasantry. To mobilize that populace, Juchiteco
leaders remained committed to the peasants' vision that land and water were
community resources available to all. Notables might hold more land than
most, some owned modest private properties, and many profited by trading in
peasant produce. But the notables' ability to mobilize mass peasant support
depended on their defense of the Zapotec peasant vision of shared access to resources.

Zapotec culture cemented this relationship. The details of the beliefs and
rituals of Isthmus communities during the nineteenth century are not provided
in the available sources. But it is clear that being Zapotec, speaking Zapotec,
and participating in a community life expressed in Zapotec were cultural media that integrated the interests of locally powerful notables and the peasant
majority at the Isthmus. Zapotec culture compromised the goals of Juchiteco
notables focused on profit and local power with the values of a peasant majority insistent on subsistence autonomy. Zapotec peasants joined in commercial
production—as long as it built upon subsistence production. And Juchiteco
notables understood, at least implicitly, that the price of peasant support for
their political agenda of local autonomy was a reciprocal support for the peasants' right to subsistence autonomy. Shared Zapotec culture negotiated that
evolving relationship, while defining for all the critical category of outsider.
Zapotec notables were often bicultural. It was essential that some among them
be conversant in both Zapotec and Mexican national culture. Meléndez is the
obvious example. But the sociocultural complex of ethnic resistance at Juchitán also mandated that local elites remain staunchly Zapotec.

Elements of this relationship have been common across Mexico. Yet the
culture of resistance of the Isthmus Zapotecs is unique. Peasant insistence on
subsistence autonomy is widespread. Local elites seeking power and profit appear everywhere. But in most of Mexico, indigenously rooted ethnic identities
have tended to become primarily peasant identities—cultures of the agrarian
poor. Most local elites have steadily adopted Spanish-speaking, Mexican national culture to better rule and profit in a State-ruled, commercial society.[11]

The absence among Isthmus Zapotecs of the cultural division so prominent
elsewhere in Mexico demands explanation. The historical sketch offered here
suggests two primary, interwoven threads of explanation. First, the Isthmus
Zapotecs were a pre-Hispanic colonial outpost of the classic civilization of
Highland Oaxaca—colonists who in the fifteenth century found themselves

the last defenders of a besieged political and cultural tradition. From those origins developed the Isthmus Zapotecs' deep cultural pride and orientation to resistance, which were repeatedly mobilized in the face of Spanish colonialism. Second, the history of the Isthmus under Spanish colonialism and Mexican national rule was characterized by neither marginal isolation nor overwhelming subjugation. Instead the periodic incursions and subsequent recessions of state power and commercial economy allowed Isthmus Zapotecs to learn to adapt, accommodate, and even profit from those developments without being crushed by them. The cultural tradition we call Isthmus Zapotec could thus change to endure. The result was a regional society that historically compromised the visions of provincial elites and a peasant majority, while all remained insistently Zapotec and ready to defend with force, when necessary, their vision of Zapotec life.

The culture of ethnic resistance, consolidated at Juchitán by the 1840s, persisted and adapted, defining the local history of the Isthmus Zapotecs and their relations with the national State and the international economy through the rest of the nineteenth and twentieth centuries. In the 1850s, Juchitecos, led for the last time by Meléndez, could ally with Mexican conservatives in exchange for promises of local autonomy. In the 1860s, they could fight beside liberals, led by Benito Juárez, against French imperialists. Yet later that decade they would turn against the same liberals over their cherished goal of Isthmus independence. A Juchiteco, Rosendo Pineda, could be a leading *científico* advisor to President Porfirio Díaz, also a Oaxacan. Yet with the beginnings of a national revolution against Díaz in 1910, Juchitecos quickly joined the conflict in pursuit of their cherished autonomy. And from the Revolution emerged General Heliodoro Charis, a Juchiteco who consolidated wealth and power as Isthmus strongman while claiming lands for the Isthmus peasantry through postrevolutionary agrarian reform programs.

Through the middle decades of the twentieth century, Juchitecos led the Isthmus Zapotecs in continuing the tradition of resistant accommodation to the increasingly powerful encroachments of the national State and the Mexican segment of the world capitalist economy. When, in the 1980s, those encroachments became too much to accept, COCEI emerged to take up the Juchiteco tradition of more adamant resistance. Its power may rise and recede. Its ability to claim the attention of the Mexican State proves that the Juchiteco tradition of ethnic resistance endures.

NOTES

1. Unfortunately, the historical origins of women's prominence at Juchitán cannot now be traced. The available historical information has been generated by the

state or those focused on economic issues. Thus we know little about family relations and gender roles. I presume that the Juchiteco tradition of active women is linked to the traditions of Zapotec pride and political resistance. But I cannot now trace their historical interactions.

2. This interpretation of pre-Hispanic society is based on Whitecotton (1984), Spores (1965), and Zeitlin (1989).
3. For the early colonial period, I depend on Zeitlin (1989), Moorhead (1949), Berthe (1958), Torres de Laguna (1928), and García Martínez (1969).
4. See Archivo General de la Nación (1952), *El libro de las tasaciones de pueblos de la Nueva España: Siglo XVI.*
5. Population figures cited in this essay are from materials in Tutino (1978).
6. On the cattle boom and its impact, see Brockington (1989), Thompson (1958), Burgoa (1934, 2:394, 396), and Vázquez de Espinosa (1966:287).
7. On indigo, see Smith (1959) and Browning (1971).
8. Archivo General de la Nación, Ramo de Alcabalas, vol. 37, May 7, 1793.
9. On the elite of postindependence Oaxaca, see Tutino (1978) and Berry (1981).
10. This discussion of the conflicts in the 1840s and 1850s, unless otherwise noted, is derived from Tutino (1978).
11. For a perceptive analysis of such development, see Warman (1976).

A New
Corrido
for
Che Gómez

Tomás Ruiz

I am going to sing you the life of Licenciado Che Gómez
his parents were Gregorio and Doña Rosalía López;
he was born in 1858, gentlemen,
in my barrio of Cheguigo in Juchitán the well-beflowered.
A Thursday second of November nineteen eleven
at about two in the afternoon they cried, "Long Live Che Gómez!"

A group of Juchitecos took up positions all around
the Carlos Pacheco barracks, armed with great courage.
"Democracy and Justice for a sovereign people!"
cried the *chegomistas* to the five hundred soldiers.
Then the commander in chief, who was Colonel Sosaya,
ordered Cándido Aguilar to answer with machine guns.

Seventy-two hours into it the soldiers surrendered
but thirty days later they murdered Che Gómez.
Dead by the hand of Ventura Cano on a fifth of December,
his remains were buried in the atrium of St. Vincent.
Farewell, my beloved city, which is Juchitán the well-beflowered;
Farewell, my barrio of Cheguigo and farewell, farewell Che Gómez.

Juchitán:
Histories
of
Discord

Adriana López Monjardin

We defeated the French here: they all died, they all died . . . Che Gómez is like the
Zapata of the Isthmus . . . it's just that the Tehuantepec people have always been traitors . . . there were two parties: the greens and the reds . . . a land baron owned these
lands. The peasants bought them in the times of Obregón and paid for them in
kind . . . things were better in the past, but it wasn't long before we were assaulted by
those who were interested in the land.

These are the voices of the Juchitecos. They fill their discourses; they are beginning to appear in journals, essays, and some books. But above all, oral tradition is the calling card they wield when in the presence of strangers who
question them. Perhaps it is necessary to situate the Juchitecos in the present,
explaining their activities in their own terms. But when their answers continue
to be full of the past, one begins to discover that for them there is no dichotomy
between the then and the now, and that the history that speaks of yesterday is
simultaneously alive and their own.

Juchitán opens up an extraordinary space for reflection about the past, one
that mediates between national education, which tends to destructure the historical memory configured in regional processes, and local conscience, whose
alterity endures because it has not been tested by the nation and modernity. It
is impossible to encounter the pure extremes represented by these options in

Adriana López Monjardin

social reality; it is easier to identify and to emphasize those cases where one or the other predominates. In Juchitán, however, the two discourses coexist interwoven with one another, although they are decidedly differentiated. What marks the regional discourse is the interaction between memories of past acts and current and daily preoccupations. There exists a collective memory in continuous activity, a selective going and coming toward the wide array of histories that exact meaning at every moment of the confrontation.

A point-by-point comparison would demonstrate the exact similarities and divergences between national history and local history, but it would aid us only a little to understand the logic that organizes Juchiteco discourse. This discourse makes sense in its unity and in its functionality and cannot endure the schism between form and content.

Beyond what each history says, the complex way in which it is said reveals two distinct logics. National history is taught in schools; it deals with unknown and illustrious persons. No one knows who made it; it arrived petrified in paper and ink, as if to affirm, "That's the way it was, whether you like it or not, it can no longer be changed." Regional history, on the other hand, speaks of the ancestors and is discussed in Zapotec; it has bridges that connect it with the hopes of today. This history doesn't deal with the dead but with "we, the living." Therefore, nostalgias and questions emerge when one's own history begins to be written:

> Why write on paper at all
> instead of on the ground?
> Earth is huge,
> broad, extensive.
> Why don't we write below the sky's surface
> everything our minds speak out,
> everything born in our hearts?
> Why don't we write on the green leaves,
> on clouds, on water,
> on the palm of the hand?
> Why on paper?
> Where was paper born
> that was born white
> and imprisons our own speech,
> the word our fathers sculpted among flowers.[1]

Despite their profound differences, the two historical discourses are neither necessarily antagonistic nor exclusive. Collective memory emphasizes the participation of the Juchitecos in the great moments of national life and profiles their presence in the construction of Mexico. The Juchitecos are convinced of their rebelliousness in the face of oppression, and they know that other peoples fought against the same enemies as they did: the Spaniards during the colonial period, the French during the Intervention, and the latifundists and political bosses during the Porfiriato.

The Juchitecos also shared the peasants' grand aspirations at the dawn of the twentieth century: respect for the community's agrarian rights and for the free municipality. Years later, a bit of development came to them; schools were constructed, roads passed through the Isthmus, and a dam provided water to irrigate their lands. They conserved some autonomy within the municipality and began to engage in politics in wider spheres, within the Institutional Revolutionary Party (PRI). Juchitán's downtown was urbanized. Streets were named, with the result that José F. Gómez Avenue could be parallel to Morelos or perpendicular to Hidalgo. May Fifth Street started from the monument commemorating the Battle of September Fifth, in which the Zapotecs (and not the Zacapoaxtlas) defeated the French in the Isthmus (and not in Puebla). In Revolution Park a statue of General Heliodoro Charis, a Juchiteco military leader allied with Obregón, was erected.

In the postrevolutionary period Juchitán's history coincided with that of the nation in many ways. Even so, all was not harmonious, not even during the best moments. The textbooks say that Benito Juárez is one of Mexico's greatest heroes, but this does not stop the Juchitecos "from stringing together memories of old struggles rooted in centuries of injustice" (de la Cruz 1983c:5), with which they judge Juárez harshly. Thus a Juchiteco intellectual states that in 1847, Juárez

> assumed his role as representative of the enemies of the Indians. . . . As he felt more certain of his control over the government, he began to take the initiative to recover control of the department of Tehuantepec, to complete the dispossession of lands and salt flats to the detriment of the Indians, and to repress the Juchitán Zapotecs and their leaders, who headed the movement for the restitution of communal lands. (de la Cruz 1983c:13)

It might seem that the Juchitecos were bent upon feeding old grudges, were it not for the fact that during the 136 years that followed the rebellion crushed by Juárez, they had reasons to spare for challenging state and national governments. When the conflicts did finally sharpen, it was important for them to be able to appeal to a spirit of rebelliousness anchored solidly in the social conscience.

"THE LIGHT LEFT FOR ANOTHER PART
OF THE DAY"[2]

What are the possible readings of history for a people who have sustained intense political combats during the last fifteen years? First, it is clear that there are quite a range of wrongheaded readings—those presided over by harmony and by an indiscriminate unity. It is clear also that all possible readings will be permeated by social conflicts, which the readings will have to account for, even if the explanation of them occurs behind the backs of those who evoke the past. For at every moment regional historical discourse is marked off by two coordinates: first and foremost, by Juchiteco ethnic identity, and more generally by Isthmus Zapotec identity (here questions about "what were we like" are inseparable from reflections about "who are we and what do we want," which are projected toward the future); second, by the forms in which the Juchitecos understand their role within the nation and conceptualize their relations with the outside world.

Contemporary Juchitán cannot be characterized as a "marginalized" community or as a "refuge region" of Zapotec Indians who fled the attacks of capitalism, if for no other reason than its privileged geographical location at the intersection of important commercial routes in use even in the prehispanic period. Moreover, accumulation began to open a breach in Juchitán from the end of the eighteenth century, when the production of vegetable dyes destined for the European textile industry was extended to the Isthmus. Nor are we dealing with an internally homogeneous community. Social differentiation, which began to crystallize when the colonial administration backed an Indian leader charged with collecting tributes, later favored an unequal distribution of the benefits that the community retained from dye production. It is possible to trace throughout the nineteenth century the trajectory of local groups of merchants who dealt in textiles and salt produced in the region and in coarse cotton fabric _(manta)_ introduced from Guatemala. The postrevolutionary period saw the consolidation of a bourgeoisie of Zapotec origin, whose activities were basically commercial.

The Juchitecos did not submit docilely to this capitalist expansion. For almost a century after the uprising that they carried out in the middle of the nineteenth century, they found themselves involved in conflicts and rebellions that intensified during the heat of the Mexican Revolution and the combats that lasted until the 1930s. Those disturbances did not oppose a monolithic Zapotec community against an external offensive. Rather, internal fractures occurred, and alliances, more or less feeble, were developed with diverse belligerent national forces.

This long and agitated stage led to a period of relative stability that lasted around thirty years (from the end of the 1930s until the end of the 1960s). During this period development led to visible changes but did not thereby undermine the fundamental conditions that the majority of the inhabitants required to reproduce themselves. These conditions included access to land and the combination of agricultural and fishing activities with the production of salt and craft goods, all of which favored an intense interchange within the community and permitted the retention of surpluses by those who might have been deprived of them under a different set of circumstances. The introduction of schools, health services, and communications contributed to the general well-being and stimulated a commercial circulation that involved in different degrees broad masses of merchants. A leading local faction mediated relations with the exterior. Their dominion was based as much on the exercise of municipal power and the gradual development of a monopoly over certain commercial activities as on internal consensus, and could be sustained as long as it contributed to guarantee the internal reproduction of the whole community. From the point of view of national elites, this ascendant bourgeoisie had won its place in the bosom of the "revolutionary family."

The preceding gives only an abbreviated idea of how the ethnic identity of contemporary Juchitecos has been formed through a conflictive and intense process of interaction with dominant classes and national states, in the midst of various assaults from capitalism that succeeded in becoming interiorized within the community as social differentiation deepened. It was to be expected that a new stage of capitalist expansion, that which accompanied the projects undertaken at the end of the 1960s for the modernization of the Isthmus of Tehuantepec, would be received with reticence and resistance. But if during the last fifteen years there has been a sharpening up and polarization of forces in the region, with little possibility of reconciling the people with the initiatives of the dominant classes, it is because these classes have assaulted the most elemental conditions of reproduction by dispossessing the community of its land.

The confrontation unfolding during this last period is not entirely without precedent in Juchitán. It does not simply represent the opposition of a traditional community against development, capitalist accumulation, and the rise of the bourgeoisie, for modernization has been opposed and assimilated before without leading to the disarticulation of ethnic identity. Anyway, the only really "traditional" aspect of the Juchitecos is their rebelliousness in the face of oppression and their flexibility in adapting to change, while conserving and refining their specificity.[3]

Neither should recent struggles be seen, as they are from the other extreme,

Adriana López Monjardin

as the immediate and logical continuation of a combative past, for they imply profound ruptures with the pact that founded the earlier stability. They bring Juchiteco identity, now rent with irreconcilable divergences, into question, and they open up a debate around the parameters that govern the ties of the Juchitecos to the nation, because the nation shows the Juchitecos its most aggressive face.

After the Benito Juárez Dam led to Irrigation District No. 19, inaugurated in 1964, the State's compulsive preoccupation with recuperating the construction costs and its consequent efforts to orient agricultural production toward immediate profitability began to limit many peasants' access to land or to marginalize them when it came to making decisions about cultivation. The local bourgeoisie hastily intensified its monopoly over land ownership, and its greed increased, fed by growing expectations generated by irrigation and official credit. It resolutely slid along, turning more and more into a gang opposed to the popular majority (Warman 1972, 1983).

When the people developed hostility to virtually every project pursued by the State, then each additional step taken by the dominant factions added a new link to the long chain of offenses weighing upon the populace. The concentration of huge extensions of land in a few hands was sanctioned by the expedition of private property titles and, later, by the application of the Idle Lands Law.[4] Usury or entrepreneurial criteria have predominated in the handling of credit, and this translates into the exclusion of poor farmers or the dispossession of indebted peasants. The installation of the López Portillo sugar mill was plagued by technical errors and characterized by the imposition of a rigid control over sugar cane growers.[5] Simultaneous with the expansion of salaried work in the fields and in Juchitán's urban zone, efforts were made to deprive the workers of each and every one of their legal rights. The growth of Salina Cruz restricted irrigated agriculture by privileging industrial water use. *Caciques* and large landholders exercised municipal power for their own benefits and were sustained in this exercise by the support of the official party and the official repressive forces over the course of four municipal administrations, crushing those groups of people that fought, beginning in 1968, for a democratic municipal government. Nor do prospects appear encouraging for the near future: the operation of a modern interoceanic railway will have the effect of binding the Isthmus more closely to North American geopolitics.

Once again the Juchiteco community readies for struggle. At this time one becomes aware of the wisdom of those who have not forgotten the Juchitecos' legacy of struggle, because it will be necessary for them to activate their traditions and revive their memories of struggle in order to confront the new threats represented by their powerful opponents. Only thus will life come to be organized for resistance.

"WORDS UNSHEATH WORDS"[6]

The long period of combat sustained in Juchitán has led to the constitution of two great social blocs, regionally identified with the PRI and COCEI, respectively. Though not without contradictions, the former has been dominated by local *caciques* and large landholders. As part of the official party, the bloc composed of *caciques* and landholders has been converted into the bearer of modernization initiatives for the Isthmus. The latter (COCEI) has attracted a broad contingent of people seeking to defend agrarian, worker, and political rights. At the same time that these organizations define two distinct projects and marshal support for them, they go about constructing the discourses that establish their legitimacy. In these discourses ethnic culture and historical memory are once again made coherent and functional. Insofar as the integrants of both blocs want to participate in the construction of the future, they have to prefigure it in a utopia, and if they want the utopia to strengthen the movement it has to synthesize experiences and aspirations and conquer its legitimacy in opposition to enemy projects, convincingly demonstrating them to be antinatural and illegitimate.

In order for a project to mobilize wills and incite agreement it is not enough to sum up oppositions and enlist hopes, because the collective experiences that will make people believe in the viability of the project are located in the past. This imposes the need, therefore, to draw from history the strength that sustained the arduous combats of the past. Each contending group claims itself to be the depository of a "continuity" articulated from opposed interests, which permits it to characterize the opposing factions as contravening that continuity.

For the bloc represented by PRI, it is enough to search out the permanence of "progress" and appeal to that development stage comprising the period between 1940 and 1970, during which it exercised a practically undisputed hegemony over the entire population. PRI calls insistently for the harmony and social peace that guided those times. The fact that the character of the leading faction directing this bloc might have changed in recent years, simultaneous with the transformation of the conditions of life and work of the broad masses, is relegated to a second plane. The pact's bases have been eroded, but PRI demands its maintenance in the name of continuity. Whatever departs from that pact is called by many more or less equivalent names: disorder, insecurity, vandalism, guerrilla, violence, illegality, and even Soviet imperialism.

The future proposed by the dominant classes signifies new and fiercer forms of repression against Juchitán's people. The pact that organized the recent past is fractured. For the popular masses to uphold it would be to put their own survival at risk; to appeal to it would imply that they accept the perpetuation of the state of things that they currently oppose. This obliges the people to search for a continuity in a more distant past, in a past extraordinarily rich in episodes of struggle.

In choosing its complicities and treacheries, memory keeps faithful company with resistance. This explains why so many peasants remember and converse enthusiastically about the French defeat and painfully about the death of Che Gómez, but fail to revive the events of the 1950s with the same clarity. From their point of view, "nothing happened" before the offensive to take away their lands, or rather, very little happened in the social realm. In a COCEI document edited in 1977, the early social uprisings [Che Gómez, etc.] were extensively discussed, followed by "a long period of calm" that requires no more commentary (COCEI 1977). If the movement is to account for the present, then history is the history of struggle, or there is no history, nothing to recount. If Juchitecos admit that there has been progress and well-being, it is because these are viewed as the results of previous victories that are now in danger of being reversed; they are not viewed as the gradual result of several decades of stability. Because one cannot build if the land is not cleared of obstacles that grew during those years when "nothing happened." Because the right to see into the future will have to be conquered by interrogating the past.

Since the popular project did not encounter a favorable terrain in which to take root during those years preceding the rise of discontent, its continuity has to be constructed in more complex and remote spaces. The land monopolists managed to obtain the surrender of agrarian private property titles at the end of the 1960s from President Díaz Ordaz and the agrarian authorities, thanks to which they accelerated its concentration. However, the primordial titles of the community, once put on the table, demonstrated that these lands had always been communal, that their privatization could only be illegitimate, and that it will be rejected, as were the repeated attempts to take their land during the nineteenth century. If a small group of Juchitecos currently control great extensions of land, this means that they have turned away from the people and that they have placed themselves in the camp of the foreign latifundists Guergue and Maqueo and of the monopolist Francisco Javier Echeverría, who wanted to usurp Juchitán's lands and salt flats around 1840.

The local *caciques* received broad support from state and federal governments; but the peasants knew that they should not trust the *"vallistocracia"* that has governed Oaxaca for the benefit of the bourgeoisie and the Central Valley region and marginalized and oppressed the Isthmus population. Yet the dominant faction within PRI abandons the interests of the majority in order to impose the interests of the *vallistos* (inhabitants of the Valley of Oaxaca), who are reincarnated as enemies dressed in blue: the Oaxaca state police.

At the beginning of the 1960s, the people's trust in their leaders was put to the test: Manuel Musalém Santiago, "Tarú," became mayor with the support of the peasants and then betrayed them from the mayor's office when he associated with a group of *caciques* who had controlled power. Nonetheless, there is historical evidence that Juchitecos have known how to produce faithful leaders. Therefore, during the last repressive assault, in September 1983, some peasants warned their leaders against dining with their enemies because Che Gorio Melendre was poisoned to death in one of these dinners in 1853. Others insisted that the deposed president of the popular government not travel alone, because this was how Che Gómez had been assassinated in 1911. The warnings conjured up dangers and were also acts of faith. Yesterday's enemies reappear in the images and likenesses of the current ones.

Numerous Zapotec intellectuals have been sensitive to the search undertaken by their people. Like Andrés Henestrosa, new generations of artists have found their own images and traditions to be sources of inspiration. But in Henestrosa's times it was possible to believe that the community and the nation could live with one another and that local culture might contribute to the enrichment of all Mexicans. . . .

Years later Juchiteco intellectuals and artists began to develop an awareness of the discomfort and confusion that were entrapping the peasants. In 1967 a group of them united around a small publication: *Neza Cubi (New Road)*.[7] It was a young generation, "revolutionary and in struggle for justice," that undertook "the revalorization of Zapotec culture." In a classic move to "return to their roots,"[8] and in the terrains of poetry, journalism, and literature, they began to strip away the veils that folklore extended over the oppression of the masses. Many of those who proceeded upon this road began to associate with popular struggles. From the relative cultural localism of this stage they learned the historical lessons of defense that served them in the future. When they wrote the history of their countrymen, they expanded on these tales of combat.

"AND NOT BECAUSE YOU WISH TO ARE YOU GOING TO STAY"[9]

The change of municipal authorities in Juchitán proclaimed itself, from the first months of 1983, as a particularly turbulent conjuncture. So it has passed and will now have to be disentangled within the complex context of modern Mexico: where political reform and suffrage coexist with electoral fraud; where attachment to institutional life is by no means foreign to the manipulation of the law (used to dismiss the popular government elected in 1981); where the traditional red bandannas of COCEI peasants shine under the same sun as the high-powered arms of Teodoro "Rojo" Altamirano, the PRI candidate for deputy who introduced into the community some important advances in war technology. But none of the above points prevents the development of an intense struggle over historical patrimony.

This battle was waged basically around the figure of Heliodoro Charis, an important Juchiteco revolutionary general affiliated with Obregón. We will not restrict ourselves to what a few books might say about Charis. It suffices to note his close collaboration in the construction of the modern State, his participation in the war against the Cristeros, and his fictive kin ties *(compradrazgo)* with Obregón. Among his countrymen he stood out for his contribution to the social welfare, without thereby forgetting about his own welfare. He founded the "Alvaro Obregón" colony in some lands close to Juchitán, one part of which was expropriated from the land baron Maqueo and another bought by the peasants, who paid for them with cattle and loads of corn. The colony is currently a political dependency *(agencia)* of Juchitán.

It is of greater interest here to reconstruct the trajectory of Charis developed by the protagonists in the current struggle. If regional history always speaks of the ancestors, it is in this case dealing with a much nearer ancestor: Charis was the father of the candidate for deputy alternate of the COCEI-PSUM alliance [Javier Charis, today a prominent COCEI politician] and father-in-law of the PRI candidate. Rojo Altamirano married the general's legitimate daughter, thereby converting himself into Charis's descendant. Apart from the metaphorical and ideological meaning that such a legacy might have had, Rojo benefited directly from Charis's wealth and lands.

As local leader of PRI, Rojo Altamirano had gained notoriety for his belligerence in the fight against COCEI. Later he demonstrated that he was also familiar with the art of radical discourse. On April 26, 1983, he organized a public affair in Revolution Park: Some six hundred persons congregated in front of the statue of General Charis to commemorate the anniversary of his death. Together with some surviving *charista* soldiers, Rojo exalted the figure of his father-in-law, comparing him to Mexican heroes such as Benito Juárez and Alvaro Obregón. Reviving the fatherland's history, he declared himself energetically opposed to foreign-introduced leaders and ideas, making the well-known reference to their character as "alien to our idiosyncrasy." The homage might have passed more or less unperceived by the majority of the population had it not been for the attendance of Oaxaca's governor, Pedro Vásquez Colmenares, and by the ample deployment of state police. A little later the official party named Rojo Altamirano its candidate for deputy.

The April 26 concentration established the guidelines that governed the whole electoral campaign. PRI sought its central points of support in the nation and used this as a watershed to exclude the opposing faction. If COCEI leaders did not represent the fatherland, they could only be accomplices of the "Central American guerrillas" or agents of "Soviet imperialism." When PRI took refuge under the legitimacy embodied by the state governor, they impugned other options as clear demonstrations of disorder and violence.

In traversing that road, the *priístas* set themselves apart from the memory of the peasants, for whom history cannot be a straight and uninterrupted line that leads from Juchitán to Vásquez Colmenares; they lost track of the coordinates of Juchiteco identity, according to which the alien and the "foreign-introduced" are not identified with scarcely known countries but with those who oppress them from the state capital [Oaxaca].

Rojo Altamirano appealed to the figure of Heliodoro Charis to anchor himself more thoroughly in Juchitán. Charis was a figure near to hand because of the kinship relationship. The fact of kinship, however, did not suffice to convert kinship into a political argument. Rather, Rojo tried to emphasize that from his perspective the general was an image of harmony, as much in the interior of the community as between the community and state and national governments. Charis had participated actively in the battles that occurred during the first decades of the twentieth century, inaugurating and stabilizing the following stage of social peace that the inhabitants of the region lived through for more than thirty years. Rojo settled into the task of synthesizing the desired continuity and evoking at the same time a leader who reckoned with popular sympathy.

"BUT LOOK WITH WHOM THEY ASSOCIATE!"[10]

If Charis can be a model of concord, Che Gómez evokes the regime's treachery and revives battles that admit of no shady deals. Even though both were contemporaries, the relatively mundane success of the first and the early assassination of the second separate them. Being, moreover, very popular and respected in Juchitán, José F. Gómez was converted into the central figure of *coceísta* continuity. Heliodoro Charis only appeared occasionally in this discourse. Most of the time he was relegated to the tower of those memories that were not needed daily.

On the other hand, the heritage of Charis occupied a role of the first order in the life of peasants in Alvaro Obregón colony. On May 10, 1983, during the celebration commemorating the fifteenth anniversary of the founding of Ejido Emiliano Zapata in lands largely disputed since Charis's death, *coceísta colonos* and *ejidatarios* and their leaders surveyed the history of their struggles stored up in the collective memory, the *corridos,* the narration of anecdotes lived in common, their happiness over the victory and the obstacles overcome, and the guarded affection that they pledge to the construction of their future.

Adriana López Monjardin

When Charis was alive, the *colonos* obtained access to enough land within the area that had been expropriated from the land baron Maqueo to provide for their needs. The remainder of the land of what had been a huge *latifundio* that the peasants had bought—some five thousand hectares—remained in reserve as a hedge against future needs. From that point in time the figure of the general came under dispute. Some say that he aided the peasants a great deal with land transactions and by giving loans to needy families, and that the people followed him without questioning his authority. But, anyhow, there are rumors. They say that Rosalino Matus, a peasant who opposed him, was killed on his order. In reality the problems began when the general was already very old, at which time his wife and daughter [Lugarda Charis, spouse of Rojo Altamirano] made all the decisions. When he died, things got worse because the lands that the *colonos* had paid for were in his name; the family took advantage of this, snatching them away from the peasants and selling them to Federico Rasgado, who also succeeded in appropriating the nearby salt flats.

During those times—at the beginning of the 1960s—life was very hard. An *ejidatario* [interviewed by the author] who was subcommander of the municipal police in the popular government recreated this period with narratives and songs, at times in Spanish, or translating fragments of the conversation into Zapotec. At the age of thirteen he had to leave to pick cotton in Tapachula; he didn't know how to speak Spanish, nor did he know how to read, nor did he have land or anything else. He taught himself little by little and had to do a bit of everything: He was an agricultural day worker, a barber, he learned to write, and he took up the struggle for land and for the municipal government, to the point that they named him police subcommander to "care for the community."

A few people even came close to standing up to Charis, but Federico Rasgado did not have such luck. Unlike the general, he had very few points in his favor, at a time when the need for land was becoming more pressing every day. The agrarian movement was initiated even before COCEI emerged. The *ejidatarios,* decidedly *coceístas,* refer to those early years with a mix of the pride (of precursors of the movement) and doubt (of isolated combatants who eventually dissolved into the Coalition): "Ask whoever you want, ask Polín de Gyves [COCEI mayor of the popular government from 1981 to 1983], who is the pillar of the Coalition." They can say this because the struggle, now seen from the vantage point of COCEI, was vigorous and successful. On various occasions the army entered the community. "Choca," a local leader and member of the *ejido*'s vigilance council, told of one such case. The soldiers arrived and surrounded them. He approached them and they threatened him, but just like Spartacus, Choca discovered the ancient password: I will return and I will be millions. "I told them that if they wanted to they could kill me, but that I was going to return, I was going to be born again. They didn't understand what I meant, that I would return in the people, in the community."

In the end those peasants recuperated the lands that their fathers and their grandfathers had paid for with their labor. They decided to found in them Ejido Emiliano Zapata. The situation being what it is, what reason is there to quarrel over the heritage of Charis? Many remember him with fondness, others have their doubts or reserve opinion. But the one thing of which all can be certain is that Rojo Altamirano bears the burden of the Charis heritage.

Although Rojo was the first to betray Charis, he still dares to bear homage to the general. He frequently speaks of him and even brought the governor to that affair in Revolution Park. But just as the *colonos* of Alvaro Obregón and the *ejidatarios* of Emiliano Zapata are "the pillar of the Coalition," so Rojo's history is soon incorporated into social discourse. The more that Rojo Altamirano bases his electoral campaign on the continuity of the trajectory of Heliodoro Charis, the more his disloyalty to Charis will be revealed. At the beginning of July 1983 it was insistently commented on and denounced in COCEI meetings that Rojo had altered the general's will, falsifying his signature so that the *colonos'* lands, those later sold to Federico Rasgado, would remain in his wife's hands.

For a couple of months, the *priístas* had sought to forge a hero who might unite the community, a figure in whom the people might recognize themselves and that might serve as a conduit to channel them toward the new leaders of the official party. Although Charis might not have been a great devotional saint worshiped by the Juchiteco masses, the *coceístas* did not abandon him. In the first place this was due to the roots that Charis has among some peasant groups, but above all it was because COCEI could not afford to cede an image that could also be converted into a weapon in enemy hands. Without drawing the general's life into the discussion, everything that might be of value in it not only was uprooted by Rojo Altamirano but returned as a boomerang against him.

"JUST IN CASE IT OCCURS TO THEM TO COME BACK"[11]

A comparison of the political dependency Alvaro Obregón with the municipal seat of Juchitán leads one to recognize that some traits deriving from Zapotec culture manifest a greater force and clarity in the first. Evidence suggests that the differences might be explained through reference to the "folk-urban continuum"; in one case there is rural life and in the other a city. But the "folk-urban continuum" does not provide answers to some new questions. For example:

Up to what point did a struggle for land and a confrontation between the same Zapotecs, earlier in the political dependency than in the municipal seat, mobilize identity and put into play the collective memory with different rhythms and modalities? Are not the peasants of Alvaro Obregón, who claim that they are the pillars of COCEI, also a pillar that enriches the culture of all Juchitecos?

The approach that emphasizes different projects to redeem the past runs into similar problems. A first interpretation—a bit ingenuous—suggests that the *coceístas* propose a return to the past, while the *priístas* are undertaking regional modernization. But the myth of "primitive communities" that take refuge in their ancient traditions is exploded in this case with one question: To what past do they seek to return? Because it is not to the immediately past period, the epoch of peace and harmony that arrived with land dispossession and political oppression. They do not seek a heritage similar to that pursued by Teodoro Altamirano. Is it necessary to return, then, to the past of the community's primordial land titles? To the period of Che Gorio Melendre? To that of Che Gómez? If the Juchitecos are going to the past in search of an essence, of a continuity, they come back to the present above all with the strength of their rebelliousness. And in this sense, yes, an effort is made to return to the past: beyond the conformity that characterized the years preceding the renewal of combat.

From the perspective of their uninhibited essence, which must be mobilized daily, the Juchitecos interrogate and decipher their history, a history conscious of its aspirations and one that is alienated neither from its life nor its destiny. Contrasting with the dynamism that "primitive peoples" display in this area is the immutable character of official history, that of the nation on the march toward modernity, which places upon the people's collective memories all the weight of its institutionalization and its distance from their hopes.

NOTES

1. From "Quienes somos? Cuál es nuestro nombre?" ("Tu laanu, tu lanu"), by Víctor de la Cruz (1983b:81). Translated by Nathaniel Tarn for this volume.

2. From "Han muerto mis compañeros" ["My Companions Have Died"] by Macario Matus, in de la Cruz (1983b:77), translated for this volume by Nathaniel Tarn.

3. John Tutino (1980) discusses the proposals of those who attribute the rebellions of indigenous peasants to a direct response to exterior assault (capitalists or colonialists). Tutino opts, on the contrary, to look for the key to uprisings in the weakness of the enemies. Víctor de la Cruz refutes Tutino and insists in searching for the causes of the movement in the Juchiteco community's defense of its natural re-

sources. This defense required them to oppose Juárez because, as governor of the state of Oaxaca, he allowed the dispossession of the land and salt flats and protected their private appropriation by foreign landowners. From this last perspective, it would be important to add that the oppressed peoples had plenty of reason to protest, at diverse moments of their history. But the articulation of a social force, the construction of a unit sufficient to undertake the rebellion, would have to be looked for justly in the forms in which exterior attack upsets community life. The expansion of capitalist interests in Juchitán from the end of the eighteenth century has coexisted, at various times, with the global reproduction of the members of the community. But discontent has exploded in sustained actions when Juchitecos are denied the fundamental conditions that assure their survival: access to natural resources—the land, fish, and the salt mines.

4. Editors' note: The Idle Lands Law was declared by President José López Portillo in 1977 and published in the government's official journal only on January 2, 1981. As part of the Ley de Fomento Agropecuario (Agricultural and Livestock Promotion Law), the Idle Lands Law gave the federal government the right to seize uncultivated lands in the national interest and contract them out temporarily to individual solicitants.

5. Editors' note: See Binford (1983:215–80) for a detailed discussion of the parastatal José López Portillo sugar mill debacle.

6. Zapotec proverb in de la Cruz (1983b:37).

7. The director of *Neza Cubi* was Macario Matus; the editor, Víctor de la Cruz; the publisher, in Mexico City, Imprenta Ruiz. It appeared between 1967 and 1970.

8. " 'Returning to the roots' is historically possible only when it implicates, apart from a real commitment to the struggle for independence, a total and definitive identification with the aspirations of the popular masses, who not only oppose the culture of the foreigner but also oppose, globally, its dominion. In a contrary case, 'returning to the roots' is only a solution aimed at securing temporary advantages and, therefore, a form, conscious or unconscious, of petit bourgeois political opportunism" (Cabral 1981:169).

9. From "La vida" ["Life"], Zapotec song written by Juan Jiménez, in de la Cruz (1983b:91).

10. From "5 de septiembre" (of 1867), poem by Eustaquio Jiménez Girón, in de la Cruz (1983b:61).

11. From "La campana" ["The Bell"], by Andrés Henestrosa, cited by Víctor de la Cruz (1983b:129) and reproduced in this volume.

Memories
of
Anastasia Martínez

In the time of Obregón, when they fought in Ocotlán, the gunfire was vicious. Many were injured. When this occurred I was eleven years old. The battle took place near Hometusco. At this time Charis was a colonel. This is when I learned what a military stack was: The rifles were placed crosswise. This meant that Charis's men should remain at ease, while the forces of Felipe López attacked. That is why Felipe López complained, saying that this was not

Many local Zapotec heroes and heroines do not appear in official history books, but their exploits are nonetheless celebrated in Juchiteco oral tradition, of which these "memories" are but a single example. Here we provide a brief introduction to some of the persons and events referred to by Anastasia Martínez.

The battle of Ocotlán, Jalisco, won by General Heliodoro Charis and his band of Juchitecos, was a turning point in future president Obregón's defeat of the de la Huerta rebels and his (Obregón's) consolidation of power during the Mexican Revolution. Many Juchitecos participated in this and other major battles of the period (such as the one at Tacubaya). In Juchitán, Charis also became a leader of the liberal Partido Verde (Green Party), which fought the conservative Partido Rojo (Red Party) during the late nineteenth and early twentieth century for control of the Isthmus.

Che Gómez, the main leader of the Green Party, staged a separatist rebellion in Juchitán in 1911 before he was killed and his movement crushed by the Mexican military.

Feliz (Chato) Díaz, brother of the Mexican dictator, Porfírio Díaz, governed the state of Oaxaca in the late 1860s and early 1870s until he was killed by a group of Juchitecos who took revenge on him for his mistreatment of their town and the mutilation of their patron saint, San Vicente Ferrer.

Albino Jiménez (Binu Gada) led the Juchiteco forces that defeated a French Interventionist army near Juchitán on September 5, 1866, during the Maximilian era.—Eds.

right, since his people had been worn out. Later, López asked Charis for permission to go to Mexico City, and Charis took the train to Juchitán.

Another battle took place in Tacubaya (in San Jerónimo). Many of our people died there also. Toña Gabino's son died. The enemy made a small fortress on a hill and from there fired on San Antonio, destroying its church. All of this happened because we had lost that battle there.

I did not see the battle because I stayed in the Ciudadela. In this place, the Reds of Juchitán jailed Felipe López, but he got out and organized his people. He rose up in arms when they killed Licenciado Che Gómez. My mother buried Lic. Che Gómez here, together with seven or eight men who died in Matías Romero [Oaxaca]. When they recovered the bodies, they were unrecognizable. They had stolen the big ring that Gómez used to wear and only left the scarf he wore around his neck. My mother saw all this!

When Pablo Pineda arrived here the movement was large. He went to the house of Doña Marga Binu Gada, my grandmother, and she said to him, "Come in and look for my daughter," but my mother was hidden in a large trunk because they wanted to apprehend her. They said that she had been in rebellion and had recovered the bodies of the dead in Matías Romero. When Pablo Pineda's men left, my mother went out the window and fled.

When we went on Charis's campaign, other women went also. My mother and I went together with the soldiers. From Hometusco we went to Puebla. I remember that, at this time, Carranza arrived at Mexico City to spend the September fiestas. In Puebla they made a nice fiesta for him.

We were there for six months; this was in 1912. I was ten years old then and went with my mother to the battles. My mother went to feed the *paisanos* that were in the troop. They also took her to cure the sick.

At night she went out to see what was happening on the front. In the morning she returned and fed the soldiers. We made the meals while she was gone. My mother, from her childhood, was a daring woman. She was very brave. Her name was Margarita Jiménez. Her father was Albino Jiménez (Binu Gada), who fought against the French. He died on Tehuantepec Hill.

My mother died of an illness sometime after the battles. She became very angry the day some of our neighbors were captured and jailed while they played cards. The authorities, through rumors, found out that political meetings were held in the house. The mayor was Navarrete. When the neighbors were jailed, they did not even have their huaraches on. You see, the majority of them were fireworks makers, and this job does not require huaraches. My grandmother told them not to wear huaraches [i.e., to dress informally so that the authorities would not know that meetings were going on]. When they arrived at City Hall, there was a gang of people crowding around. My mother told the captured men, "Go like men, you have not stolen anything or killed anyone!" Meanwhile she yelled curses and vulgarities against the authorities.

My mother saw all this and then returned home. Shortly thereafter the cops came to take her away by force. My mother told them, "I am not going with you, go on and I will soon follow. I have not robbed or killed anyone." The cops insisted but they were not successful. As she promised, my mother went to City Hall and cursed the stool pigeons and gossipers who had accused our relatives of conspiracy. "It doesn't matter," she said, "we already know who the accusers were. Just wait and you will find out what our people do to you."

I went with her. When we reached City Hall, the mayor asked why she had defended those men. She said, "Well, Víctor Gómez is the son of one of my sisters. And I," my mother told the mayor, "am the daughter of Colonel Albino Jiménez, and not a son of a bitch like you. Listen well because I am not going to repeat myself. I am not like a clock that repeats itself."

"Okay," said the mayor. "I am going to send you to Chimalapa right now."

"Very good," my mother answered, "that is just what I want, I need to stretch out my legs a bit."

"If that's the case," said the mayor, "I am going to send you to Oaxaca."

And she said, "I like that too, I will thank you in the name of my mother, because with that I can take the opportunity to go see the doctor, because here I have found no one who can cure me."

And faced with this, the mayor had nothing else to say but, "I will leave you here in this jail." And he locked up my mother. She was there for six days and was well taken care of. Her food had to be tested by Tranqui Guiati, the jail cop, and only then would she eat.

Margarita Jiménez was strong-willed. One day she was coming back from Tehuantepec and saw that a Frenchman had fallen dead with his weapon in his hand. The Frenchman was already swollen. Upon seeing him my mother said, "Look, no less, at this son of a whore who fell with my father's weapon and all." And she immediately took the weapon from the Frenchman and gave him a kick at the same time.

When the Che Gómez Revolution broke out she hung a little drum around her waist and went around banging on it to alert people for battle. She was accompanied by the bugler. It was the time of Licenciado Gómez.

The day Carranza's troops arrived in Juchitán they were put in charge of controlling the men and made everyone carry white flags. Some men left for other towns. When Carranza's forces arrived they were congratulated for their efforts to calm and pacify the Juchitecos. Well, they were ordered to wreck Juchitán if anyone opposed them. But thanks to this, calm prevailed, and not a shot was fired.

The men who opposed Carranza's forces were taken prisoner and taken to Ixtepec. There, many of our people were court-martialed, and many were shot two-by-two by the Ixtepec river.

Pedro Trinidad and Pedro López Félix were able to escape. Later they went to Veracruz. Our townspeople were denounced by the Reds. This was during the Carranza era. After that, Magín Blas rose up as a leader and became a rebel.

I saw how they killed Chevíe Salinas in Ixtepec. He died together with a guy named Chiñas, both of them shot two-by-two near the river. There, also, the Labariega brothers died. One of these brothers, before being shot, asked for a cigarette and put on his hat. That is how he asked to die. I went to see when they were submitted to court martial. I was very young.

My grandpa, Binu Gada, became a revolutionary in the following manner. One day he was making oxcarts, his trade, when a group of men arrived commenting that they should take Saint Vincent out for a procession so that the saint would make a miracle and have it rain. We needed the water then for the fields, and this was our belief. The men had gone to take Saint Vincent out but they returned unsuccessful because Chato Díaz (Félix Díaz) did not want them to. And my grandpa said, "How is this possible? We are the ones who should rule in this town!" And thanks to him for orienting the men, they were able to take out Saint Vincent.

After this the troops came to apprehend him for being the cause of the procession. The military man, leader of the soldiers, asked him, "Did you take the saint out into the street?" "Yes, I did," answered my grandpa, "and you can take care of and keep watch over the town [instead of butting into our affairs]." The military leader was Chato Díaz. He had come to apprehend my grandpa. Before the other soldiers arrived, my grandpa gave Chato a hard blow that knocked him over, chair and all. He hit another soldier who was seated there, took his weapons, and left for the hills. When the troops arrived at the house in search of my grandpa, he had escaped. When the troops tried to cross the river, it seemed like a miracle had occurred because the river had risen without rain having fallen.

Then Chato Díaz said, "This man is a witch," because the troops could not follow him due to the swollen river. That is why Chato took Saint Vincent and hid him by the route to Tehuantepec.

My grandpa could not come into town. And he got together a few people until he had a group. They arrived to defend the town and attack its enemies. Evaristo Matus, Tachu Xada, and two other men were with him and went to attack Chato Díaz. They learned then that the French who had destroyed Mexico City were coming and Mexico City was lost.

My grandpa had always gotten along with the Tehuanos, but despite this, the

Tehuanos sided with the French. The order was given for the men to leave Juchitán because the French forces were large.

My grandmother, Na Gada, along with other women, went to live in Estancia Xunaxi [Ranch of the Virgin]. When the French entered Juchitán, they climbed to the top of the church and saw that they were under siege on all sides. The French were scared by the situation. Munaratu's mother and another woman, possibly Tona Tati, egged on our people to attack the French. They defeated them over there by the lagoon.

These women were the ones who rang the church bells and cried out that the Juchitecos should attack the French, who were in retreat. There they killed them. They also defeated the Tehuanos who united with the French. This took place in the morning and not in the afternoon as it says in a poem by Pancho Nácar.

Tierra Fértil (Fertile Land). Watercolor painting by Miguel Angel Toledo of Juchitán, Oaxaca. 1989.

Irrigation, Land Tenure, and Class Struggle in Juchitán, Oaxaca

Leigh Binford

This paper investigates the role that definitions of land tenure played in the transfer of landed property and political conflicts in the area of Juchitán, Oaxaca. I shall attempt to show that in Juchitán, different national political administrations sanctioned mutually contradictory and ambiguous definitions of land tenure and that these definitions have promoted the concentration of landed property while simultaneously opening avenues within the agrarian reform laws for mounting legal challenges to both past and present transfers. After briefly examining land tenure and distribution in periods before the irrigation project, I discuss the history leading up to the present confusing situation. The paper concludes with a brief discussion of competing interpretations of land tenure in Juchitán and situates those interpretations in the context of competing political discourses.

LAND BEFORE IRRIGATION

Laura Nader (1969:333) described the Isthmus of Tehuantepec as "a low rolling plain covered with nondescript brush of brown and gray." The image is one of want, suffering, and scarcity. It is an image that once confronted Isthmus residents during the November to April dry season, when the leaves on the bushes and low trees wilted and dropped off, or lingered to be covered by dust storms whipped up by the strong winter winds, Los Nortes.

Beginning in late April or early May, sometimes not until June, the landscape underwent a transformation nurtured by the life-giving rains generated by tropical storms far out in the Pacific Ocean. Brown and gray gradually gave way to the light green of young tender shoots followed soon by the darker green of full-bodied leaves. But rainfall in the Isthmus was never dependable. Since the precolonial period, the region's inhabitants have grown a short, low-yielding, but drought- and wind-resistant variety of white-grained corn called *zapalote chico* that provided their subsistence base and is the subject of innumerable stories, poems, and songs.

These climatic particularities helped to shape the land tenure situation from the early colonial period through the mid-twentieth century. Juchitán's radical intellectuals maintain that Juchitecos have successfully defended the land in the vicinity of the municipality for hundreds of years from incursions by Spanish conquistadores and the Dominican fathers who accompanied them during the colonial period as well as from mestizo investors and bureaucrats in more recent years. What they fail to note is that with the exception of some relatively large cattle haciendas grazing scrawny herds on an extensive basis, Spanish invaders and mestizo, Asian, and Middle Eastern immigrants—and even those Zapotecs who became rich—accumulated most of their wealth through tribute, usury, and commercial monopoly, leaving the Isthmus peasantry to till the soil and bear the risks to production wrought by wind, drought, and the occasional torrential flood (Binford 1983; Tutino 1981; Zeitlin 1978; Hamnett 1971a, 1971b). In Juchitán and surrounding communities the really wealthy people were (and still are) merchants and/or bureaucrats.

Though some latifundization took place, land was available for the taking until the late 1950s. Most of it was taken and given up again and again as dictated by cycles of production and declining fertility. Liberal nineteenth-century governments ordered that Juchitán's communal lands be divided up and parceled out, but the orders were regularly resisted or ignored (Esparza 1987). Plans to expropriate land for colonization projects in the "underpopulated" Isthmus also came to naught, largely due to the paucity of secure water sources. Alejandro Prieto, who was dispatched to the Isthmus in the late 1870s to pinpoint potential colonization sites, portrayed the region as desolate and backward, noting that there were no legitimate agricultural haciendas and few areas capable of sustaining settlement (Prieto 1884).

Thus there is little documentary evidence to contradict Esparza's (1987:69) conclusion that "Juchitán appears to have begun the twentieth century in relative peace with respect to its land."[1] Some land was lost to the Trans-Isthmus Railroad line, completed in 1907 (Warman 1983:2), and more to the Pan American Highway, built after the Second World War, but into the 1950s the clearing and planting of communal land continued apace, subject to little regulation (Dorsett 1975:128). Irrigation, which might have altered this formula, did not become a factor in the vicinity of Juchitán until the early 1960s.

It is noteworthy that the great rebellions that mark Isthmus history were stimulated less by demands for land than by complaints about excessive tribute (as in the case of the Tehuantepec rebellion of 1660) or the State's attempt to monopolize the output of rich marine salt factories, which supplied Juchitecos with the means of obtaining Guatemalan textiles (instrumental in the rebellion of José Gregorio Meléndez between 1847 and 1851) (Tutino 1981 and his article in this volume).

IRRIGATION DISTRICT NO. 19 AND THE CONFLICT OVER LAND TENURE

Arturo Warman (1983:2), who arrived in the Isthmus in 1967 to work with the Ministry of Agriculture and Water Resources (SARH), maintains that the Benito Juárez Dam and Federal Irrigation District No. 19 were developed and executed by the State with little consultation of the region's inhabitants. The project was a national project, designed to promote capital-intensive agriculture of food and fiber for both domestic consumption and export. The Isthmus human and physical geography was the raw material that the engineers and technicians, like potters, would carefully mold according to a design that already existed on paper. Thus, regional cultural systems and material social relations—including land tenure and distribution—were not investigated prior to actual construction.

Before the irrigation system, land was held and utilized in accordance with several different systems. Most small-scale agriculturalists simply cleared, fenced, cultivated, harvested, and abandoned the land as necessary, leaving it to fallow for some years until they or another producer planted it once again. Claims to land were transient, meaningful only as long as the land was actually under cultivation. On the other hand, latifundists with large cattle herds as well as smaller-scale agriculturalists working better-watered land in narrow strips along the Dogs' River sought to establish permanent claims by filing titles with local accountants and paying taxes to the municipal treasury. Lacking recognition by the federal government, these deeds and titles had absolutely no legal standing (López n.d.:1; Warman 1983:2).

Despite the undefined tenure status, claims to the dry brush country proliferated once knowledge of the large-scale infrastructural investments diffused. Juchitecos with foresight, capital, and political connections bought, stole, or forcefully expropriated land from small-scale cultivators. Moreover, speculators flocked to the Isthmus to claim or buy up land only to sell it once again when prices became high enough to provide them with an acceptable profit. Land values inflated, and the poor were priced out of the market (Binford 1983:100, 137–39). Only *after* this process was well under way did the government, having determined that speculation jeopardized the project's financial well-being, seek to regularize the tenure situation. We shall see in what follows that far from setting matters straight, a progression of ambiguous and conflicting decrees and presidential resolutions led to ever greater confusion.

THE RESOLUTIONS OF 1962 AND 1964

Early in 1959, when construction of the Benito Juárez Dam was already well under way and land speculation was epidemic, the Department of Agrarian Affairs and Colonization (DAAC, predecessor to the Ministry of Agriculture) ordered its local delegation to expedite the confirmation of communal lands of Asunción Ixtaltepec, Juchitán de Zaragoza, Jalapa del Marqúes, and San Blas Atempa so that work related to the construction of the dam and irrigation system could be undertaken. On February 15, 1960, the DAAC posted notices exhorting owners of *pequeñas propiedades* (small private properties) located within the perimeter of Juchitán's communal lands to present proof of ownership within ninety days to the communal lands commissioner so that their landholdings could be exempted from the communal title that was anticipated.

In a major blow against land speculators, President López Mateos decreed on November 21, 1962, the expropriation of 47,000 hectares of Isthmus land in the public interest, exempting from the expropriation "the *ejidos,* communal lands, the lands corresponding to areas of habitation, urban zones . . . the *pequeñas propiedades* legitimately acquired before 1955, which are presently in use." He ordered the DAAC to determine which untitled lands rightly belonged to the indigenous communities and to have them titled and incorporated as *ejidos.*[2]

Since speculation was not a serious problem prior to 1955, the stipulation "*pequeñas propiedades* legitimately acquired before 1955" effectively protected the lands of earlier claimants to private property while returning to the community those acquired by profiteers. The ejidalization of the remaining properties, though not requested by Juchitecos, would have curbed future speculation since the agrarian reform laws prohibit sale or rental of *ejido* lands and contain provisions for the seizure and reassignment of land that is idled for two consecutive years (Gobierno de México 1981). The López Mateos decree can be interpreted as an effort to secure the financial solvency of the SARH, as the sale of water to producers was the government's principal means of recouping construction costs and generating funds for maintenance of roads, bridges, and canals.[3]

Juchitán's lands finally received legal recognition in a presidential resolution of June 14, 1964, which departed significantly from the 1962 decree. The 1964 resolution ordered the expropriation and ejidalization of the entire 68,000 hectares within the municipal boundaries of Juchitán and its five so-called annexes: La Ventosa, Santa María Xadani, Unión Hidalgo, Chicapa de Castro, and Espinal.[4] Of these 68,000 hectares, 30,000 were located within irrigation district limits, and 38,000, almost all rain-fed, were situated outside district boundaries. The resolution stated that "there exist no private properties within the communal area that have to be excluded from the present recognition" and that "the total area of 68,000 hectares . . . is incorporated as *ejido*" to be divided among approximately eight thousand eligible peasants who would receive certificates of agrarian rights and their land titles.[5]

With the 1964 resolution, the protections and guarantees to pre-1955 private property contained in the 1962 decree were abrogated; the federal government unilaterally declared that there was no private property within the municipal boundaries of Juchitán and annexes and that the area was to become an enormous *ejido*. The ejidalization in 1964 also would have augmented State control over land use. It represented, as Bailón (1987:11) observed, "a means [for the State] to integrate the peasantry into the institutionalized credit channels, commercial crops, and official control." There is no evidence that Juchitecos or Istmeños from other affected communities were consulted in the investigation leading to either the 1962 decree or the presidential resolution that followed in 1964.

REGIONAL COUNTERATTACK

The 1964 resolution aroused strong opposition in Juchitán and other communities among the larger and more influential landholders in the region, who had the most to lose in the event of its execution. They organized local "committees in defense of small property" in each affected community. Many small landholders were attracted by propaganda that portrayed the resolution as another in a long line of impositions by external forces, which, if executed, would deprive them of the small parcels that they currently farmed (Warman 1983:2–3).[6] A regional board composed of representatives from local delegations planned protest meetings and rallies that attracted crowds of as many as five thousand people.

Besides mass political protest, the resolution was assaulted through legal channels. Affected landholders inundated the DAAC, the Ministry of Agriculture and Stockraising (predecessor to the SARH), the president, the courts, and, finally, President-elect Gustavo Díaz Ordaz with demands, appeals, and solicitations to rescind the 1964 resolution and ratify private property claims. The multitude of specific challenges tended to coalesce around two basic points. First, aggrieved landholders claimed that the resolution violated rights of due process guaranteed in the 1917 Constitution and the Agrarian Reform Law because the affected parties were given no opportunity to respond before the resolution was written into the law. A second, and stronger, challenge pointed to numerous errors, inconsistencies, and contradictions of the resolution's assertion that "within the communal area there exists no private properties that have to be excluded from the recognition": *error* because, according to the litigants, there did in fact exist private properties in Juchitán that were guaranteed protection under the *amparo* laws passed in 1942 during the presidency of Miguel Alemán; *inconsistency* because the 1964 presidential resolution ignored and contravened the guarantees offered to "private property legitimately acquired before 1955" by the presidential decree of November 21, 1962; *contradiction* because representatives of the federal government had engaged in activities involving concrete recognition of private property in Juchitán. Specifically, SARH had established an Office of Indemnization in Juchitán, where it registered small private properties affected by the construction of the irrigation works (canals and roads) and made damage payments to landowners.[7]

THE DÍAZ ORDAZ RESOLUTION OF 1966

In 1964, PRI presidential candidate Gustavo Díaz Ordaz visited the Isthmus during his election campaign. He met with representatives of the Committee in Defense of Small Property and promised if elected to resolve the land tenure dispute to their satisfaction (Alcerregía 1976:12–13). On April 9, 1965, with Díaz Ordaz ensconced in Los Pinos (the presidential residence), an engineer and topographers were commissioned to survey the area and compile a general census of landholders (or, perhaps better stated, "claimants") to determine who would have use rights over the lands titled by the presidential resolution.[8] At that time, the irrigation authority still had no knowledge of who owned or claimed to own how much land and where, despite the fact that the irrigation system had been dispensing water for at least the better part of a year in Sub-Region III, which encompassed 22,000 hectares in the vicinities of Juchitán, Ixtaltepec, and Espinal.

Engineer Cosme Verdura Mier, who was entrusted with the task, entered his report on July 17, 1965. That report and corresponding documentation were turned over to the Agrarian Consultative Body on January 3, 1966.[9] Eventually the Agrarian Consultative Body decided to limit execution of the 1964 resolution to 43,000 hectares (5,000 hectares of irrigated land and 38,000 hectares of rain-fed land) and to exclude from execution 25,000 hectares of irrigated land owned individually by 3,800 persons.[10]

These decisions materialized in the surrender by Díaz Ordaz on March 31, 1966, of 3,900 property titles (3,800 to residents of Juchitán and its "annexes" and 100 to residents of San Blas Atempa, adjacent to Tehuantepec) protecting the rights of up to thirty hectares per landholder. Each title was numbered in accordance with the now-completed topographical survey and the boundaries of the lot specified by reference to surrounding lots.

The government thought that issuance of titles backed by the survey would solve the Juchitán land tenure problem. Yet the 1966 resolution was a retreat from earlier efforts to reverse the land speculation that had plagued the project from its inception and that later played (and continues to play in 1991) an important role in COCEI organizing, propaganda, and demands (Toledo and de la Cruz 1983). First, thirty hectares is a significant amount of irrigated land, more than any small-scale cultivator can work with ox team and machete. Second, large landholders have been able to get around the thirty-hectare limit by dividing large extensions into smaller lots and registering them in the names of friends and family, a strategy that placed them in technical compliance with the law but that immunized them against its intended effects.

With the 1966 Díaz Ordaz resolution, the committees in defense of small property disbanded, since their demands appeared to have been met. Only later, when COCEI challenged the Díaz Ordaz resolution, did the ambiguity of the titles become clear. Even government officials eventually acknowledged that serious errors had been committed both in the wording of the titles and in the expedition of the act. The tenure situation became increasingly confused.

First, the titles referred not to *pequeña propiedad inafectable* (protected private property) but to *terrenos inafectables de origin comunal* (protected lands of communal origin), a nonexistent status in Mexican agrarian law.

Second, they guaranteed recipients *possession* of lands of communal origin but did not confer upon them *ownership* rights. In other words, the Díáz Ordaz titles lacked the legal standing of private property titles. They empowered recipients to use designated plots of land, but not (according to the articles of the Agrarian Code, which govern communal lands) to rent, sell, or in any other way alienate them. These problems went unnoticed for some years, and Juchitecos bought, sold, and rented land, justifying their right to do so by reference to the titles distributed by President Díaz Ordaz (López n.d.:4).

Third, inscription of the titles, required by the law, in the *Diario oficial* (which records official acts and proclamations) and the National Agrarian Register was accompanied by irregularities. In several cases two claimants possessing identical Díaz Ordaz titles to the same lot sought credit from the federal agrarian credit bank (BANCRISA) or the parastate José López Portillo Sugar Mill.

POLITICS AND THE INTERPRETATION
OF THE LAND TITLES

The titles' ambiguities and the irregularities surrounding their issuance and inscription opened the door to contradictory interpretations. The agrarian and merchant bourgeoisies, the small landed peasantry, the COCEI political opposition, and representatives of involved federal and state agencies (the agrarian banks, SARH, the sugar cane refinery, etc.) each interpreted the titles differently. By claiming the only legitimate interpretation of the titles, that is, the "truth," each group sanctioned its role in regional political struggle and condemned and delegitimized opposing groups favoring different interpretations by counterposing its putative "truth" with their putative "falsehood," its legal sanction with their lawlessness.

For instance, a 1976 letter from the subdelegate of organization and economic development indicates how the agrarian bourgeoisie justified its right to sell and purchase land by reference to the Díaz Ordaz titles:

> Some landowners, protected by their titles . . . alienated all or part of their possessions and no one could or can avoid it, less so when the authority expediting the title, accepting that it was treating a lot recognized as private property, left a space on the back of the titles in which to record the transfers.[11]

On the other hand, the COCEI includes many victims of the monopolistic and speculatory movements of the prerevolutionary *caciques* and the *nouveau latifundists* (speculators and others purchasing land since the inception of the irrigation project). The organization has consistently rejected the legitimacy of the land titles issued by Díaz Ordaz and demanded recognition of Juchitán's communal claims. Their position was expressed in a public proclamation issued April 9, 1976:

> Thousands of hectares of land in Juchitán were monopolized because of greed and ambition, when these persons [monopolists and speculators] enriched themselves from the Benito Juárez dam; from 1964 to the present date Irrigation District 19 has been marked by monopolization [of land] clearly violating the

presidential decree which recognizes and titles 68,112.54 hectares as communal lands of Juchitán and its annexes: La Ventosa, Chicapa de Castro, Unión Hidalgo and Xadani.[12]

COCEI employs its interpretation of the land titles to justify the invasion and seizure of fields claimed by some of the wealthiest and most powerful Juchitecos. In April, May, and September 1978, September 1979, and December 1980, for instance, irate landowners accused COCEI of sparking illegal land occupations in Juchitán. Thus the ambiguity of the titles provides fertile ground for the work of local activists who favor redistribution of the region's natural resources in favor of the economically weakest segments of the population.

It is important to note that COCEI's appeal is not restricted to peasants, nor its interest to agrarian problems. Juchitán is a thriving commercial town with a small industrial sector, and many active COCEI participants are workers, petty merchants, and artisans, as well as peasants. Although family and fictive kin ties certainly draw nonpeasants into COCEI (Campbell 1990; Rubin 1987:159), the organization's struggles to improve health and sanitation, education, and access to credit give it a wide appeal, as does its dedication to Zapotec culture, language, and ethnic identity. For instance, COCEI has sought agricultural credit at reasonable terms, fair prices for local producers, and honest municipal administration; it organized to clean up the municipal park and improve sanitation in the central market, developed a garbage pickup service, paved streets, and carried out a literacy program.

Local and regional representatives of the agrarian bureaucracy such as SARH, Agrarian Promotion (a government development agent), the National Sugar Industry Confederation, BANCRISA, and the Ministry of Agrarian Reform tend to be allied by class position with larger landowners and the merchant capitalists whose interpretation of the tenure situation they favor. Both groups are committed to private property and threatened by COCEI. The conflicts that might derive from ethnic differences (mestizo bureaucrat versus Zapotec landowner) are mitigated by voluntary adoption of symbols of national culture by rich Zapotec merchants and landowners (Campbell 1989); and by the fact that some mestizo officials have purchased land in the district while others have been involved in more or less corrupt commercial and administrative practices in collusion with other officials or with members of the local agrarian and merchant bourgeoisies.

Higher-level government authorities, without obvious vested interest in the local situation, sometimes take a different tack. Some officials of the banks and SARH, whose job is to see the land used productively, have opposed an interpretation of the titles as supporting private property. Officials of the Agrarian Reform Ministry, further removed from the situation and often concerned with legalistic criteria—though by no means divorced from political struggles or unaffected by local sentiments—are the judges of last resort (along with the president) of the titles' legal status. Into the early 1980s they consistently maintained that the Díaz Ordaz titles protected use rights only and were *not* titles to private property.

Yet the gap between Mexico City and Juchitán, between the higher-level federal government bureaucracy and its local representatives, and between legal ideology and political reality helped preserve an ambiguous situation in which, contrary to the opinion of the Agrarian Reform Ministry, landowners appealed to the titles as legal sanction for the purchase and sale of land. Moreover, the passive character of the intervention of the Agrarian Reform Ministry, limited to interpretation of the situation only, and the domination of the terrain of action by local officials and politicians has helped maintain the contradiction. Even local officials would encounter great resistance from the wealthy and powerful were they to attempt to enforce a concrete redefinition of the situation (e.g., to halt land transactions and land rental).[13]

It is possible that with major shifts in the regional (and national?) balance of political power, the federal government could be convinced to implement communalization or ejidalization, *which already exists according to some interpretations of the law.* But such a possibility becomes increasingly remote as the hand of local agrarian capital is strengthened through credit and material assistance provided by the agrarian banks and the sugar mill. In 1981 some officials of the sugar mill in Espinal stated quite clearly that control over agricultural output is difficult to achieve when land is fragmented in small terrains of dispersed ownership; for the sake of administrative efficiency they preferred greater concentration. The reprivatization drive begun by Miguel de la Madrid and now pursued with great fervor by the Salinas de Gortari administration promises to reinforce official views of the economic superiority of private property and to decrease official support for alternative tenure arrangements (Reding 1989:713–22).

COCEI did not exist during the early battles over the tenure status of Juchitán's land, but organized formally in 1973 following years of land speculation and concentration that altered the class structure and broke ground for new forms of political organization. As COCEI grew into an important regional political force, a strategic alliance developed between local representatives of the federal government and property owners to oppose COCEI efforts to create a widening sphere of autonomous control.[14] This alliance required the federal government to acquiesce to continued land speculation and concentration in the irrigation district, much of it violating the thirty-hectare limit placed on land ownership within Irrigation District No. 19 by the 1966 presidential resolution.

In March 1981, COCEI representatives entered municipal offices as the officially recognized victors in municipal elections. During the next seventeen months they governed the community despite an economic boycott by the state government, political intimidation, and physical harassment before they were impeached by the Oaxacan Congress in August 1983 on account of their supposed inability to guarantee the public order. COCEI refused to leave and occupied the Juchitán City Hall for four months, until physically expelled by the police and military. New elections of dubious legality brought in a PRI government and a wave of repression that forced movement leaders underground (Chávez 1983; Ramírez and Reyes 1983; Hinojosa 1984; Amnesty International 1986). The leadership surfaced again in 1984, entered into a coalition government with PRI in 1986, and, perhaps benefiting from the election of the "liberal" Heladio Ramírez, were officially recognized as victors in the August 1989 municipal elections. Once again, COCEI ruled Juchitán.

The struggles over land continue, although the State has allowed the land tenure issue to recede into the background. The issue has not disappeared, however, because the ambiguous character of the Díaz Ordaz resolution and titles lend them susceptible to constant challenge on the part of the poor and dispossessed and the COCEI militants who speak forcefully in their defense (Toledo and de la Cruz 1983).

NOTES

1. One exception to this peace was the competition for land between adjacent communities. In 1845 Juchitán was embroiled in boundary conflicts with Espinal, Ixtaltepec, and San Dionisio del Mar (Esparza 1987:58–59). In 1947, a little over a century later, a group of Juchitecos asked the Agrarian Department to provide them with title to their communal lands to resolve long-standing boundary disputes with the neighboring municipalities of Asunción Ixtaltepec, San Dionisio del Mar, and Niltepec. Expedient No. 3383 of the DAAC, June 23, 1964, Archives of the Ministry of Agrarian Reform (hereafter AMAR), Juchitán, vol. 1. An earlier solicitation for the restitution of *ejidos* dates from April 22, 1930. Expedient No. 375, AMAR, Juchitán, vol. 1.

2. Presidential decree, Nov. 21, 1963, AMAR, Juchitán, vol. 1. *Ejidos* are State property, formally owned by the nation and parceled out for use to eligible recipients.

3. As it turned out, the region's peasants appreciated the regularity of water supply but resented having to pay for what had previously been a gift of nature—despite the fact that nature had often given too much or too little for their needs. Vehe-

ment protests resulted when the Directive Committee of Federal District No. 19 raised the water user fee, as it did in 1964 from nine pesos to thirty pesos per irrigation per hectare. Many producers ceased purchasing water except in cases of severe drought, sustaining their crops from the summer rainfall. Letter from Professor Domingo Márquez Cueto, vice-president of the Sociedad Agrícola de Pequeños Propietarios del Distrito de Riego de Tehuantepec to Sr. Alfredo del Mazo, secretary of SARH, Jan. 2, 1964, AMAR, Juchitán, vol. 1.

4. Presidential resolution of July 13, 1964, AMAR, Juchitán, vol. 1. Figures have been rounded off for the sake of comprehension.

5. Presidential resolution of July 13, 1964, AMAR, Juchitán, vol. 1, pp. 2, 50.

6. A great deal of oral and archival work remains to be carried out for this period. Ideologies of private property were firmly embedded in the Isthmus long before the federal government decided to intervene to "regularize" the tenure situation, and my guess is that most small-scale agriculturalists regarded the land as private property, regardless of the actual ways in which they utilized it or what they called it. At the time of the announcement of the López Mateos resolution, there were no *ejidos* in the immediate environs of Juchitán through which a knowledge of *ejido* operations might have been acquired. Ixtaltepec, about five miles north of Juchitán, received communal title to 10,579 hectares on October 9, 1954, and converted to *ejido*—but not until November 30, 1963. *Diario oficial*, Oct. 9, 1954, and Nov. 30, 1963, AMAR, Ixtaltepec, vol. 1.

7. Notes from a protest lodged by eight litigants, n.d., AMAR, Juchitán, vol. 1. They pointed out, too, that when the lands of Asunción Ixtaltepec were titled in 1954, the private properties owned by Espinaleños in the zone denominated "Huamichal" were exempted from the resolution. A summary of objections to the resolution appears in Alcerregía (1976:10–11).

8. Letter from Jorge Milagro Ross, n.d., AMAR, Juchitán, vol. 1.

9. The Agrarian Consultative Body is an organ of the executive power composed of members freely designated and removed by the president (Gobierno de México 1981:547–48). It has the power to make judgments about presidential decrees and to give opinions when there are conflicts over the execution of presidential resolutions (Gobierno de México 1981:550). That this body made the final decision is evidence of the direct involvement of Díaz Ordaz.

10. Letter from Jorge Milagro Ross to Lic. Pastor Murquía González, director general of agrarian rights, Nov. 7, 1974, AMAR, Juchitán, vol. 2. In a letter to President Echeverría several years later, the engineer represented the decision as the most humanistic option permissible under the agrarian reform laws:

Having had conversations with the *comuneros* individually, in informative assemblies, in general assemblies with all the representatives of every one of the annexes, the conclusion was reached that it would not be convenient to change the communal lands to the *ejido* regime, since in this case the individual holding would have been 10 hectares; in consequence, with the 27,000 hectares of irrigated land only 2,700 peasants would have benefited, thus having to relieve 1,300 of their possessions, which they have occupied since time immemorial. (Letter from Verdura Mier to President Echeverría, n.d., AMAR, Juchitán, vol. 2)

He was referring to Article 220 (in the 1981 edition) of the Agrarian Reform Law, which fixed ten hectares as the minimum individual *ejido* grant of irrigated lands (Gobierno de México 1981:87). This article was passed during the Alemán presidency (Reyes Osorio et al. 1974:41). The 1964 resolution was to have been implemented by providing each *ejidatario* with approximately four hectares of irrigated land, which would have violated Article 220. In my view the government was less concerned with the economic fate of the 1,300 peasants who would have been displaced than with the political turmoil and antigovernment sentiment that a forced ejidalization would certainly have engendered.

11. Letter from Franco Gabriel Hernández to Ruben Ramírez Cruz, Dec. 29, 1976, AMAR, Juchitán, vol. 3. It can be argued that the existence of a space labeled "transfers" on the back of the titles proves nothing. Use rights (rather than rights of permanent alientation) of communal and *ejidal* lands are also transferred to legally designated descendants.

12. Also see Toledo and de la Cruz (1983 and this volume) for an interview with Daniel López Nelio, one of COCEI's most prominent and astute agrarian leaders.

13. This is illustrated by an important dispute, which lasted from 1974 to 1976. In 1974 elements of COCEI backed the invasion of 170 hectares of irrigated land in an area known as Los Arbolitos in the vicinity of La Ventosa, a political dependency of Juchitán. The landowners sent urgent telegrams to agrarian authorities demanding support for their titles. A meeting was eventually convened on August 8 by the Banco Nacional Agropecuario and attended by representatives of just about every government agency and political group active in the Isthmus. A resolution was drawn up, signed by all, and sent by telex to the director general of inspection, procedure, and complaints of the DAAC (telex to Manuel Avila Saldado, Aug. 8, 1976, AMAR, Juchitán, vol. 2). Requested was "an investigation of the origin and validity of the titles expedited by the Department of Agrarian Affairs and Colonization . . . as well as an analysis to determine if they protect the rights of private property owners or are titles expedited individually as *comuneros*" and the commissioning of two topographers of the DAAC to determine whether or not there was land monopolization in the region. The director general responded on December 11, 1974, to the request for title clarification. He emphasized that the titles could not be considered to protect private property within a community, *ejido,* or irrigation district because that "is a violation of the Constitution, of the Federal Agrarian Reform Law and the Federal Water Laws" and that the titles "protect *ejido* rights, which must be respected always and when the original users . . . are subject to the dispositions of the Federal Agrarian Reform Law" (letter from Manuel Avila Saldado, Dec. 11, 1974, AMAR, Juchitán, vol. 2).

The work of the topographers provided evidence for both monopolization (more than the legal amount owned) and noncultivation of land, either of which are grounds for deprivation of *ejido* rights. After the results of this survey were made public, an assembly of *"ejidatarios"* in Juchitán voted to suspend the land rights of 226 *"ejidatarios"* who were monopolizing land and voted to deprive more than 6,000 *"ejidatarios"* of agrarian rights "by virtue that they abandoned personal cultivation of their endowments for more than two consecutive years . . . without justified cause." The assembly, controlled by COCEI, also voted rights for 1,313 landless individuals without indicating the destination of the remaining units of land (AMAR, Juchitán, vol. 3).

The Mixed Agrarian Commission took the assembly's request under consideration (document of Feb. 6, 1976, AMAR, Juchitán, vol. 3). However, on March 5, 1976, they ruled against the request, citing insufficient proof. The considerations that led to the ruling focused on the failure of local authorities to adequately carry out a number of technical requirements of the Agrarian Code. As a result, nothing changed. The federal government had defended its definition of land tenure without altering the concrete situation in any significant way, except to earn the enmity of both sides in the conflict.

14. Evidence for this assertion can be found in the letters, comments, and reports of government officials contained in the Agrarian Reform Archives, Juchitán, vols. 1–3.

The Future
of the
Isthmus
and the
Juárez Dam

Arturo Warman

The first time I worked in the Juchitán area was in 1967, if I am not incorrect. I was sent to develop a crop and agricultural development plan for the irrigation district of the Juárez Dam, which had been inaugurated three years before and was not effectively irrigating any new terrain. The dam is a very large engineering work that was designed to irrigate forty thousand hectares. The State had an almost exclusively financial preoccupation. For the construction of the dam it had obtained an important external loan, and it was thought that the money, which the country had to repay in hard currency, was being lost due to the lack of production in the irrigated lands. For me it was a process of discovering catastrophe after catastrophe. What perhaps makes the greatest impression upon me still is that the enormous hydraulic work was planned, decided on, and constructed from the center of the country. The local population was never consulted. The State never permitted it to participate in the decisions nor even informed it regarding what might be the intent and objective of the enormous irrigation work.

Those in charge of planning the engineering of the dam knew nothing about agricultural practices in the Isthmus of Tehauntepec, nor did they have any valid knowledge of the geographical conditions. What they did have was a purely statistical knowledge. The most important factor for any Isthmus agriculturalist, the winds that blow during the dry season, was never taken into account by those who planned the dam. They thought that with the water it would be possible to obtain a second crop in the dry season. That is precisely when these winds reach extraordinary velocities of more than a hundred kilometers an hour, resulting in very serious problems for the planning of agricultural crops. Of course, they thought that the costs of the dam were going to be paid with the cultivation of cotton, completely impossible under those conditions.

One of the most serious problems of this region, as of all indigenous Mexico, is the system of land tenure. The land of the Isthmus of Tehuantepec was once communal land that had been retained in the power and under the control of the descendants of the original Isthmus settlers. When railroad concessions were made in the last century, in order to install the Trans-Isthmus Railroad, a very important part of the lands of the indigenous communities were expropriated. From that point sprang up private properties, especially in the region of the Tehauntepec River plain, an area with many advantages. It is well protected from the winds because for hundreds of years a true windbreak has been maintained. This makes it possible to maintain perennial crops that are very difficult to grow in the remainder of the Isthmus. They were originally introduced by the inhabitants of the plain who use water from the Tehauntepec River.

The community of Juchitán, the largest town in the Isthmus, was not so affected by the expropriations because it had little land in the plain. But the mere presence of private property began to break the unity, and two alternative models of land tenure developed: one private, in which land tenure served fundamentally a commercial aim, that of the reproduction of capital; and the other, the communal form in which land tenure served as a basis for the reproduction of life and the society. The agrarian reform of the twentieth century practically passed the Isthmus by, although on diverse occasions the communities initiated the administrative procedures necessary to obtain recognition of their lands. Not one of these agrarian judgments was carried to its end. The property of those surviving Isthmus communities was never recognized.

Under these conditions of legal confusion, many private and State interests sought to transform the communal land of the Isthmus into private property. The mechanism for accomplishing this was and is illegal. It consisted of paying taxes to the municipalities (which always have an enormous need for their own resources) on fractions of communal land as if they were private property, although there was no documentation that might have proved them to be so. After a number of years have passed, the claimants point to the peaceful possession of that territory and the payment of taxes as evidence that the land is private property. A small group of people had appropriated for themselves an enormous area of land compared to the land used by members of Isthmus indigenous communities. This private property is illegal from its origin, but complicity between the individual interests and public interests of the State (who gathered funds from any source) created a false distance between small private property and the communal lands that was without justification, because the private property was never legally founded. It is also questionable whether it was socially founded, at least in the sense of being necessary.

When construction began on the Benito Juárez Dam at the end of the 1950s, the group that had appropriated the communal lands perceived that with the construction of the dam it had a historic possibility of legitimizing this false private property. The small private property owners began to maneuver so that one of the State's powers, which is to expropriate all the land that was going to be benefited by irrigation works, might be applied in benefiting and securing their land rights. Those were the ones who also controlled a large proportion of the economic and mercantile life, commerce, financial institutions, distribution of national products, and usury. Usury was the normal means by which the *comuneros* obtained money in exchange for planting sesame seed. This enormous economic power was converted into political power by taking advantage of the centralism of the State that constructed the work, and the lack of information and participation on the part of the population. They converted themselves into mediators of information. They began to generate rumors that all of the land benefiting from the water would be expropriated to benefit people who were not from the Isthmus. In this way they succeeded in converting themselves into leaders of a false regional movement. Among themselves, they seized every advantage and captured for their own interests the protest and uneasiness of the Isthmus *comuneros*. The State could not, did not want to confront this situation, and left unresolved the land tenure problem during the entire period of the construction of the irrigation work. Thus it became possible for this group of big landowners-merchants-usurers to capitalize on all the rumors, the legitimate concerns, and all the protests.

They alleged in the name of the entire regional population that the State would have to legitimize the status quo; that is, it would have to recognize their properties as such and leave the remainder of the land in its present condition. The State, lacking information and incapable of requesting the participation of the people, after a very *complete* process, ended up legitimizing this situation, as requested by the landowners. In the Isthmus of Tehauntepec there has developed the only situation where communal lands were converted into *ejidos* by one decree, only to be converted into private property by a second decree, both expedited by Díaz Ordaz.

All of this took place, moreover, in an atmosphere where there were great hopes of wealth. The people thought that the result of the irrigation project was going to be an enormous generation of wealth, that the Isthmus would be transformed totally beginning with this irrigation work. These promises were unrealistic since the dam project was inappropriate given the environmental conditions, the population, and the internal conflict between false private proprietors and communal landowners. The promise of wealth was not going to be fulfilled in the short term for the bourgeois group that promoted the legitimization of its situation, and less for the *comuneros* who fought for their survival as a social group. The cultivation of the *zapalote* corn, which was basic for the *comuneros* because they obtained their own food from it, could not be advantageously replaced by any other crop. Sesame, the commercial crop, not only failed to benefit from irrigation but was damaged by diseases. The State had tried to impose new crops and new economic activities without planning and with little success. Rice was introduced with disastrous results. Cattle grazing on an extensive basis was promoted with the same results. The State found itself with an enormous irrigation district for which it had no agricultural alternative and that caused it to fail in its promise to supply great wealth in the Isthmus of Tehauntepec.

In general terms, that was the situation that I recognized when I wrote the book [*Los campesinos, hijos predilectos del régimen*] in 1972: a great failure for the State and a situation of apparent defeat for the *comuneros* who had been evicted from a very important part of their lands when small private property was legitimized. There was a great pessimism in what I wrote, a pessimism loaded with irony. The communal culture suffered attacks related to the development of the irrigation work, which had strengthened its exploiters and its dominators. What I did not imagine at that time is that the *comuneros* would encounter and open up a new front for struggle, that of the political struggle, which has been so successful. Many of the acts that appeared irreversible in 1980 are now processes in open struggle.

The fact that COCEI has achieved an indisputable electoral triumph in the municipality of Juchitán illustrates the enormous strength and great capacity for struggle of the *comuneros* for maintaining the continuity of their project. I believe that a parenthesis is in order, because when I speak of continuity of their life project, it is many times understood that "continuity" means to turn back or to conserve unacceptable situations. No, when I refer to continuity it is to the continuity of the power to decide one's own destiny, not a continuity obedient to ancient models. For me continuity is the possibility of deciding one's own destiny in such a form that the changes may not be brutal impositions from outside, from the capital, but decisions taken with the participation of the people. Continuity means neither conservatisms nor traditionalisms, but from my point of view, autonomous participation in the selection of whatever destiny one wishes to pursue. It is in this sense that I speak of continuity, and the political front that, I believe, supplies an enormously rich foundation for this struggle for continuity to be able to strengthen autonomous decisions and win space in the decisions that other groups have expropriated from local people. Probably, if an authentic free municipality had existed in the Isthmus zone before the project was conceived, the dam would never have been completed, because the people know about their work, how to improve it, and what obstructs it. The construction of an enormous irrigation work did not have the priority of other more concrete and less expensive actions.

The *comuneros* have served as a pioneering example by organizing themselves into a regional political organization [COCEI], a modern organization sustained by people who respect and love their traditions. It is, perhaps, a type of organization that speaks to us of a political future where there will not only be large national parties but also regional political organizations with very firm bases that are going to acquire control over municipal life and are going to be fully capable of participating in alliances with national political parties. I believe that, in this sense, COCEI heralds what is going to be an important political reality—regional political organizations aligned with national political interests. COCEI has promoted the recuperation of many local elements that, perhaps in other conditions, would never have returned to integrate themselves into local life, or would have become integrated after the stage of the formation of the local oligarchy or bourgeois sector. The participation of COCEI students is also, I think, an advance toward what can be a future political reality. And the organization has proven its ability to unite people, who in the context of capitalist development in Mexico would be destined to abandon the region to defend the Isthmus as a popular rather than a capitalist project.

I do not want to overly idealize the situation. No evolution of this type of organization is free of conflict. At odd moments, I like to think that the great Benito Juárez Dam might end up as a great monument to the political evolution of our country. In the struggle for the recuperation of communal land, water has enormous potential if it is not used for immediate gain but to transform in a gradual and successive manner the entire agricultural panorama of the Isthmus of Tehuantepec. The communities can plan over ten, fifteen years to construct a windbreak, before establishing that the water has to produce this year and produce profits. The community can plan a series of alternatives that the private farmer and the capitalist agriculturalist cannot because the alternatives take so many years to mature. If it can manage this resource, the community can concern itself not only with improving the current conditions of life but also with the improvement of life in the future. For the central struggle is the recuperation of continuity not only as a territory but as a productive organization, not only as a certain amount of land surface but as an organization with the capacity to lead productive activity over the long term to generate collective benefits. I believe that at the moment it is only possible to point out the front of the struggle. Who knows what battles will have to be undertaken in order to win it? Who knows what organizational model will result? I think that in this sense it is not legitimate to try to ascertain the future. The important thing is that the people participate in its construction. Insofar as the future is centrally decided far from the land, far from the winds, and above all, far from the people who have lived there and who live there, the future looks very pessimistic. I believe that the Benito Juárez Dam will at some point be rescued by the hands of the communities, that they might recuperate not only the municipality's political space but also the economic space of the land and of decisions.

The
One
Who
Rode Duarte's
Horse

Gabriel López Chiñas

Garapa, garapa, rapa,
Duarte's horse comes flying
along the Tehuantepec road.
Eight soldiers like a dust-devil
rush following close.

— And what did he do, lady?
hey man, what was his crime?
— He rose against the soldiers
who had made our lives a shame.

Covered with dust he comes,
the soldiers cannot see him,
his horse goes flying through the air
down the Tehuantepec road.

Come out of your houses, my friends,
fellow-villagers, come out on the road,
those who go with Duarte
the people will cherish and praise.

Gabriel López Chiñas

The roads, they come and they go
between the hills, between the rocks,
their horses' hooves
an eruption of fireflies
scoring the feet of the night.

Take back your waters, O sea,
from out of the pupils of my eyes,
the waters were sleeping in them
dried up from so much crying.

— And what gives with you, my lady,
hey man, what gives with you?
— Silence! They killed Duarte
along the Tehuantepec road.

Full seven years went Bodo Chiñas
a'riding on his horse—came back to the village,
came to lay these heavy words
Upon the people of his house.

Dark night, deep darkness,
light up your stars,
so that they weep with my heart
While Duarte catches fire in the sky.

PART TWO

Representations of the Juchitecos by Themselves and Others

A n important contemporary issue in anthropology and literature, as we noted in the main introduction and the introduction to Part One of this book, is the manner in which agents of politically and economically dominant cultures represent subordinate cultures. These "colonial discourses" commonly establish hierarchical scales in which the dominant culture is portrayed at the top as the norm, with all other cultures aligned below as various shades of abnormal on a scale of normality (Pinney 1989). Many of the articles and excerpts in Part Two demonstrate that Juchitecos have frequently been subjected to "normalizing discourses" by foreign and Mexican intellectuals, artists, travelers, and government officials.

The Isthmus of Tehuantepec has been an object of interest and commentary by foreign visitors to the region at least since the Spanish colonial period. Soon after the conquest, a genre of travel accounts emerged describing the "exotic" customs and "idiosyncratic" characteristics of the Zapotec people. For Thomas Gage (1958:117, original 1648), who traversed Mexico in the 1630s, the Isth-

Photo by G. Iturbide.

mus was a mysterious land filled with witches, devils, and Indians in the shape of beasts. In an amusing and colorful account, Brasseur (1981, original 1861) set the tone for much future writing about the Isthmus with his depiction of "unruly," dangerous Juchiteco bandits and the mysterious, matriarchal woman ("the *Didjazá*")[1] who flirted with Porfirio Díaz, shot pool with the soldiers, and cast spells on vulnerable men.

The section that follows provides an example of such writings in Von Tempsky's description of Gregorio Meléndez, that "formidable" rebel leader, and his "primitive" but amiable Juchiteco followers who fought the Oaxaca government in the mid-nineteenth century. The other essay of an outsider presented here is the gubernatorial address of Benito Juárez, who viewed the Juchitecos as anarchic troublemakers and enemies of the State, social order, and public morality. Juárez thought it unfortunate that Juchitán caught fire when government soldiers went to restore order in the region, but he rationalized the destruction as a necessary cost of preserving the peace.

There is another history of commentary on the Isthmus, however. It is the thinking, oral discourses, and writings of the Istmeños themselves (about themselves). Almost half a century ago, Covarrubias (1946:310–37) described the rich, nativistic intellectual culture of the Zapotec poets and musicians. For Zapotec intellectuals, Juchitán is the point of departure, the vantage point for understanding local and foreign life ("foreign" referring to anyone from outside the Isthmus). "Juchitán es el ombligo del mundo" (Juchitán is the world's navel), say the Juchitecos. From a Juchiteco standpoint, Zapotec culture "is the purest and the most beautiful." As Gabriel López Chiñas wrote in his poem "The Zapotec Language,"

> Ah, Zapotec, Zapotec!
> language that gives me life,
> I know you'll die away
> on the hour of the death of the sun.

For Juchitecos, the question, "Who are we, what is our name?" (the title of Víctor de la Cruz's poem in Part Two) has an answer, and that answer is very different from the answer presented by foreign visitors. We are not Zapotec, they say, we are the Za, descended from the clouds or from trees (López Chiñas 1982:103–4). We have survived, say the Juchitecos, because we are tough and because we have been able to resist the incursions of outsiders like Benito Juárez. He may be a hero in every Mexican child's schoolbook, but for Juchitecos he is a villain and an enemy (see "Juchitán Political Moments" by Macario Matus).

COCEI peasant leader Daniel López Nelio, asked by a reporter to describe the Juchitecos, replied, "The Juchitecos, they are a bunch of no-good bums, rabble-rousers, and drunkards . . . and I am their leader." But it is one thing for outsiders to say such things about the Juchitecos and it is another thing entirely for the Juchitecos to say them about themselves. Doing so they subvert the discourse about Juchiteco identity and history created by outsiders and celebrate their own feisty self-image and view of the Isthmus past (Keesing 1989). Although the Juchitecos are very aware of outside discourses about them (and are very amused by them—indeed, the Juárez and Meléndez commentaries were published by the Juchitecos in *Guchachi' Reza*), their self-representations and self-images are their own, undiminished by the stereotypes and prejudices of others. COCEI has its own version of Juchitán's history. It is a rough and violent history, a history of suffering and martyrdom, but it is also a history of local autonomy and self-determination. As Macario Matus portrays it in his contribution to Part Two, Juchitán's history is marked by a lineal continuity of resistance and struggle beginning in the colonial period and culminating with the victory of COCEI.

In Andrés Henestrosa's article on sexual life in Juchitán, originally published in 1930, we encounter a defense of local beliefs and behaviors against the stereotypes perpetrated by tourists and other visitors. Henestrosa is adamant in his rejection of the claim that Zapotec culture is characterized by moral laxity, supposedly manifest in the "double bathhouses" and nude women bathing and washing clothes in local rivers. In his view, sexual relations are closely regulated and female virginity highly valued. But to whose advantage? This question Henestrosa does not address, despite the fact that he describes and apparently sanctions the custom of *rapto,* in which a prospective bride is carried away by the young man, sometimes without her permission. Obdulia Ruiz Campbell, however, uses her perspective on this custom and other aspects of Zapotec women's lives to challenge both Henestrosa's interpretations of Isthmus gender relations and those of Western feminists. Ruiz Campbell's article highlights an important issue often glossed over in anthropological treatments of others, namely, that not only are "dominant" outsiders' representations contested by local groups, but the self-representations of such groups are also the subjects of internal contention.

The articles by Elena Poniatowska and Obdulia Ruiz Campbell address women's status and conditions of life among the Isthmus Zapotec. Poniatowska's representation of Juchitecas as strong and domineering has a lengthy heritage in previous writings about the Zapotecs and has become *the* dominant foreign image of the Isthmus (and is accepted by many Istmeños as well). The few passages treating the Oaxacan Isthmus in Mexican travel guides usually focus on the phenomenal Isthmus Zapotec women, who are said to control the social, economic, and, frequently, the political life of the area. Here the common Western male stereotype of women is reversed: In the Isthmus, strong, burly women are portrayed as controlling their weak, dependent husbands, who must ask their wives for beer money when they wish to go drinking and lean on their broad shoulders for support as they drunkenly weave their way home from fiestas. These images were popularized in Covarrubias's famous *Mexico South: The Isthmus of Tehuantepec* (1946). That such views are common in Mexico is illustrated by Elena Poniatowska's description of the Juchitecas' strong wills, power, and feistiness, as well as by the dignity and strength that radiate from the faces in the striking photographs of Graciela Iturbide (examples of which are included in this volume).[2]

Zapotec women do control Isthmus markets and manage household budgets in many rural and urban households as well; they are large in size and forceful in the presence of strangers, rather than shy and withdrawn, and they have played a critical role in COCEI's political victories, as we shall see in the testimonies recorded by Marta Bañuelos in Part Three. Yet there is a darker side to their lives, one slighted by tourists and overlooked even by sympathetic observers. Obdulia Ruiz Campbell, from San Blas Atempa, discusses her view of the reality of Isthmus Zapotec women and compares it to the stereotype. Ruiz Campbell notes that although foreign observers, feminists as well as others, have characterized Isthmus Zapotec women as Amazons, the harshness of their daily lives belies this portrayal. While noting the many spheres of Isthmus society in which women enjoy prestige and a degree of power, she also describes how the custom of *rapto* is oppressive for women. She gives examples from her own life to illustrate Zapotec women's struggles against culturally rooted gender inequalities. Despite all this, Ruiz Campbell remains proud to be a member of a Zapotec community and concludes that urban non-Zapotec women may be attracted to the Isthmus because they "find" there things they lack in their own societies.

In the final selection of Part Two, by Víctor de la Cruz, we see how far things have come from a discourse by Westerners about the exotica of the primitive to another discourse, in which the Zapotecs write about themselves and the outsiders coming in to study them. As it originally appeared in *Guchachi' Reza,* the de la Cruz selection prefaced a translated article critical of COCEI, originally published in French by two French anthropologists who had worked in Juchitán. De la Cruz questions why the writers never bothered to consult the Popular Government's extensive list of publications and why they failed to re-turn copies of their work to the Isthmus for commentary and critique. He ob-serves that the relationship between researchers and subjects is inherently unequal. Ignored by or vilified in the government-controlled media, popular movements are compelled to cooperate with visiting independent journalists and social scientists in the hopes that through them, the message of struggle will reach a wider audience. Once leaving the community, however, research-ers customarily utilize this information to bolster their careers and seldom so much as return copies of their completed work for evaluation and critique by their informants. De la Cruz asks why COCEI has received more support from writers, graphic artists, and photographers than social scientists. In this article, then, he turns the tables on the "civilized" researchers from the intellectual capitals of the Western world, who are subjected to scrutiny by their former subjects, and whose shortcomings are criticized.

We view this as a harbinger of the future. With the spread of literacy and media of communication (already there are satellite dishes and video cassette stores in the Isthmus, and televisions are almost as common as radios were a few years ago), social scientists will find it increasingly difficult to justify their forays into the Third World by reference to "scientific neutrality" and "truth production" without being subjected to criticism of the sort leveled by de la Cruz. Social scientists will be increasingly engaged in political dialogues when studying and analyzing Third World cultures, societies, and economies, and they will have to be prepared to defend their views before their informants as well as among their academic peers. It has even been argued (Tyler 1987b) that it is precisely this voice of the Other, speaking more forcefully and in broader channels to Western anthropologists, that is the basis of the discipline's current crisis of representation. In an interview with Jonathan Friedman (Friedman 1987:117), noted anthropologist Eric Wolf observed,

> It's getting to be difficult to teach people anthropology. It used to be that we taught our students about the people out there. Now the very same people sit in my classroom. Some tell me of their direct familiarity of the places in the text-book photos, others explain the virtues of various medicines and the physical power of witchcraft. Many are there to establish the importance of their identities. The former distance of investigator to object is no longer possible. The object has become a talking subject with a definite point of view.

NOTES

1. *Didxazá* (rather than *didjazá*, as in Brasseur 1981) is actually the indigenous word for the Zapotec language. Here Brasseur has used it to refer to a Zapotec woman who, many have suggested, may be Juana C. Romero of Tehuantepec.
2. One exception to the matriarchical characterization of Isthmus Zapotec women by tourists, social scientists, and other observers is the work of Chiñas (1983). Chiñas denies the Zapotec matriarchy thesis but does conclude that Isthmus Zapotec society is gender egalitarian, a view challenged by Obdulia Ruiz Campbell in her contribution to this part.

Who
Are We?
What
Is
Our Name?

Víctor de la Cruz

Speech. Saying yes to the night,
saying yes to darkness.
Whom to speak with, what to say
if there is no one in this house
while I feel so lonesome at the cricket's sadness?
If I say yes, if I say no:
to whom yes, to whom no?
Where did that yes and that no come out of
and with whom did I talk in the heart of darkness?
Who got these words down on paper?
Why write on paper at all
instead of on the ground?
Earth is huge,
broad, extensive.
Why don't we write below the sky's surface
everything our minds speak out,
everything born in our hearts?
Why don't we write on the green leaves,
on clouds, on water,

on the palm of the hand?
Why on paper?
Where was paper born
that was born white
and imprisons our own speech,
the word our fathers sculpted among flowers,
they sang at night
when they created their dance,
they used to decorate their houses,
inside their shrines,
in their royal palaces?
Who brought that second language
coming to kill us with our own word,
coming to trample down our people
as if we were maggots
fallen from trees, scattered over the ground?
Who are we? What is our name?

A German Traveler's Observations in Juchitán

G. F. Von Tempsky

We left Tehuantepec on the 29th of March [1854][1] and arrived, the same day of our exit, in the Indian town of Juchitán. Juchitán contains about 10,000 inhabitants, being the most populous community in southern Mexico. Its inhabitants have the reputation of being a very unruly set, turbulent politicians and revolutionists.

In the south, no political movement is made without weighing its opinion in the balance of success, which nearly always turns in favour of the side the Juchitecos are on. They have been in Oaxaca often, as well as in Tehuantepec, enforcing their opinions at the point of the bayonet. They have besieged and taken Tehuantepec twice, and Oaxaca once. In the revolution that put Santa Anna again in the presidential chair, they aided the movement, and a large quantity of muskets and ammunition was distributed amongst them. The newly-established Government remanded the arms after they had benefited by their use, but were disappointed in their expectation. The Juchitecos refused to give them up, and the Government had not the power to take them. This village was, besides, reputed for its hostility against white strangers, or strangers of any kind, and we had been warned not to enter its confines, as the people would, at the least, steal our horses. All this, of course, determined us to go, and see the matter with our own eyes; expecting to find some new phases of character and interesting excitement among this peculiar people.

A Frenchman [Alexandre de Gyves] was said to reside amongst them, doing a very good business, and being tolerated on account of his liberality and otherwise worthy character. This gave us sufficiency of confidence in our undertaking; and for my part, I resolved to go and ask hospitality of the most formidable of their leaders [Gregorio Meléndez]. There is nothing like showing oneself fearless in the intercourse with Indians; shake them vigorously by the hand, look boldly into their eye, and you have got them as servants, who would have been your masters had your footsteps been wavering, your hand timid, and your eye winking in approaching them. They are, in that respect, like the wild beasts of their forest. Turn your eye from the tiger, attempt a retrograde movement, and he flies at your throat; but fasten your eye upon him, he will quail, and not dare to injure you.

We rode unconcernedly through the dense crowd of villagers, who assembled from all sides on our arrival. We asked our way to the house of the famous Indian, and every one indicated to us the whereabouts, with an ominous smile. We arrived at his house; and it is the fashion in Mexico to ask *posada* [shelter] without dismounting. I therefore rode right up to the verandah before his door, where the host was standing. He was a tall, fine-made man, of massive and deeply-marked features, an eagle's eye, dark and flashing from underneath thick eyebrows, and an arched and muscular brow. He was wrapped in his Mexican *serape*, exhaling the smoke of a paper cigar through his nose, and looking with ineffable contempt upon our approach. Not in the least astonished at his looks, I said my rude say of, "Me hace el favor de darnos posada?" ("Will you do me the favour of giving us shelter?"). He directed a long look at me, and then courteously touched his hat, and said, as usual: "Pasa Usted adelante, cavallero" ("Come in, sir"). And thus pleasantly—the more so from the sheer novelty of the thing—were we ushered into a goodly house, with an obliging host.

Our horses were cared for, cleaned, rubbed, washed, fed, and were as safe as if they were in a double-locked stable, with ourselves sitting on their backs all night. We showed, of course, not the least anxiety in regard to either horses or baggage; for that would have spoiled everything. A sumptuous supper, *à la Mexique,* was set before us, and we did justice to it, with our host presiding, a dense crowd of lookers-on darkening the door, and the privileged filling the room itself. In a quarter of an hour's conversation, I knew the bearings of my host's opinions, and recognised the main feature of his character—an inextinguishable hatred of Mexicans in general, and Santa Anna in particular. His feelings on these subjects rested on so just a foundation, that I did not hesitate to pander a little to his prepossession, by drawing, impromptu, a caricature of Santa Anna, which set him a laughing and chuckling with intense enjoyment, which was joined in by a subdued and respectful echoing chorus from the lookers-on, who now crowded faster and faster into the premises. I found a little potful of liquid indigo, and, with an extemporised brush, I executed a sort of caricatured likeness of Santa Anna, in full uniform, upon the white walls of the dining-room. This first picture finished, their curiosity was awakened, and I had to paint the wonders of ships, sailing and steam vessels, railway and mail coaches, European soldiers with Napoleon at their head, until I was tired, and dismissed the spectators till next morning.

My friend and I tried to start that next day, but there was no chance of accomplishing it; our host nearly got seriously angry with us, for thus depreciating his hospitality, and we had to stay. That day the first prelections on geography were held in Juchitán. No European has any conception of a Mexican Indian's idea of the rest of the world. Mexico fills the globe, and, in some remote corners, are some few other countries, whence the white and black men come. I filled all the walls with maps of land and seas, and broke off my lecture only in the evening, when lecturer and audience were thoroughly tired. I must acknowledge that I never have seen such willing and intelligent disciples as these Juchiteco ruffians.

We had to stay a third day, during which I gave them an idea of fencing, which astonished them still more, as they consider themselves very good fencers with their short sabres, called *matchetes* [*sic*]. To finish the enjoyment of the day, we had some wrestling, of which they literally understood nothing, and were consequently bumped mercilessly to the ground, to the intense enjoyment of all the lookers-on.

On the morning of the third day after our arrival, we managed our escape. We left a little present with our host, who gave us a guide for the first day's journey through a labyrinth of roads, not of the safest kind as regards either life or purses. Thus we got away from all the blandishments of Juchitán, where we were hard pressed to stay and settle among them: men promising to cultivate our fields for us, and pretty women assuring us that they would keep our household in good order; our host added, "and then we will go to Mexico and cut Santa Anna's throat, whenever you have taught all of us to fence and fight like soldiers."

NOTE

1. Although Von Tempsky gives 1854 as the date of his visit to Juchitán and his encounter with Gregorio Meléndez, some sources claim that Meléndez died a year earlier, in 1853.

The Juchitecos as Seen by Benito Juárez

Excerpts from a speech, July 2, 1850

I should point out that in order to maintain the state's internal peace I have principally taken care of two things: (1) To respect individual rights and ensure that they are respected, so that citizens will have no justifiable motive for launching a revolution to assure their rights against arbitrary acts of power; and (2) To organize and maintain public forces and prepare the elements of war, so that when peace is threatened or interrupted, the instigators can be repressed and punished as rapidly and efficiently as the security of the Oaxaqueños and the dignity of the Government demand. . . .

With the aforementioned measures, public peace has been secured, in general, in the state. Only the town of Juchitán (last March) has scandalously altered the tranquility enjoyed by the District of Tehuantepec. This was done neither to carry out a political plan, nor to propose any useful reforms, nor to complain about its current government, nor to change administrative personnel, as is falsely affirmed in apocryphal writings published in Mexico City by the enemies of the state administration. It was done to evade obedience to all authority and the healthy burden of the law, and to rob with impunity and engage without obstacles in excesses that morality condemns.

It would take a great deal of time to describe to you the state of immorality and disorder in which the residents of Juchitán have lived since very ancient times. You know well their great excesses. You are not unaware of their depredations under the colonial regime and their attacks against the agents of the

Spanish government. You know that during the centralized government they mocked the armed forces that the central power sent to repress their crimes, defeating and causing damage to it, making fun of its leaders, and scorning the local authorities. You have been witnesses to these scenes of blood and horror. You know all this, which is another reason why I omit a history of the events that have passed before your eyes and that, moreover, did not occur during my administration. I will address recent events below and will remind you of the past so that you will know better the unruly character of these rascals, and will see also that this is not the first time the state has been faced with such scandals from them.

Juchitán Political Moments

Macario Matus

The political situation that Juchitán is experiencing is not gratuitous or extrane-
ous. It is a result of many years of struggle. Juchitán is a branch of the great
tree that is the Zapotec race—newer than that of Tehuantepec—and as such
inherits rebelliousness and detests subjection. That is to say, the Zapotec race
has always been free.

One hundred years before the conquest we had already left the center of
Oaxaca, Teotitlán del Valle, and arrived at Zaachila, or Teozapotlán del Valle.
Thus, when the conquest occurred, we—a branch of the Zapotec wise men,
high priests, and warriors—were already on the banks of the Tehuantepec
River. We came here out of the mysteries of fate and for practical reasons:
There was abundant fishing, hunting, and fruit—in other words, exactly the
opposite of what there is today.

And here we remained, not without first defeating the Huaves, who had in-
habited these bountiful lands since before the time of Christ. The Zapotecs and
Mixtecs, who earlier allied to defend themselves against the Aztecs and Toltecs, repelled the Huaves and confined them to the territories where they live
today. Numerically, we were superior to them. As a matter of fact, no one
knows where the Huaves came from. Some think they came from Peru.

A few years after the Spanish conquest, which wiped out the center of
Oaxaca, religion and missionaries put an end to our idols, our stone gods. They
wanted to do away with our language too, but they could not. Where there had

been a ceremonial center they put a Spanish saint: Santo Domingo or San Vicente Ferrer. They could not overcome the Zapotecs, not because we were stronger but because we were geographically remote.

Of course, the last Zapotec king was converted because the priests (friars Bernardo de Alburquerque, Juan de Mata, Córdova, and others) set a trap for him. They surprised him worshiping his guardian gods. They seized and excommunicated him, and jailed him in filthy cells. Finally he asked for pardon because they offered him the heavens as a reward. There, momentarily, the direct line of the great Zapotec race was lost.

A few years after the conquest (March 21, 1660), the first rebellion against the Spaniards occurred here in Tehuantepec. A woman beheaded a viceroy or *encomendero* who was in collusion with the church to abuse the Zapotecs and extract from them tribute in gold, fabric, and precious stones. And because the Zapotecs could not take gold from where there was none, could not draw blood from where there was none, they protested, assassinating one of the aforementioned personalities. The Spaniards had done the same thing, and with worse cruelty, throughout the Mexican nation.

This affront was punished severely by the viceroys, King Charles IV, and the priests. On this date several men and women were flayed with children watching the spectacle to prevent a repetition of the uprising. In other words, if someone protested any injustice, the punishment was flaying and public torture (just as justice is carried out today also). The seed was planted, the seed of protest against injustice and the iniquities of man and religion.

We have to take giant steps ahead to arrive at more recent times. In 1850, when the "national hero of the Americas" [a common Mexican reference to Benito Juárez] was in his heyday, a man, a Juchiteco rose up against Benito Juárez protesting exploitation of the Juchitán salt flats by outsiders. The hero was named Gregorio Meléndez, or Menléndrez. He opposed Juárez's arbitrary actions and demanded that the salt flats be exploited by the Juchitecos. In reprisal, Juárez—the defender of the fatherland—twice ordered the burning of Juchitán. This is why we cannot love Juárez. Porfirio Díaz, who used the Juchitecos for their bravery and toughness to decide his major battles (such as Carbonera and Dos de Abril), did the same thing to Juchitán. Again we paid dearly. Díaz razed the town because of more discontent and rebelliousness from the Juchitecos. The 1866 battle of Juchitán against the French we will skip over for reasons of space.

On November 4, 1911, José F. Gómez ("Che Gómez"), who fell into the hands of the henchmen of Benito Juárez Maza (yes, the son of the patrician Benito Juárez), was assassinated. Che Gómez protested because an outsider (Pancho León) had been imposed as *jefe político* (what is today the mayor).

That is, Che Gómez was opposed to what was the PRI of that era. He was killed along with three hundred Juchitecos, and one thousand were injured to silence his struggle and outcry. *Porfirismo* was in agony, and its last death knell was given by Governor Juárez Maza.

In 1913, during the Huerta era, a Juchiteco congressmen, Adolfo C. Gurrión, who did not fall in the trap set for congressmen by Huerta's killers, returned to his homeland to search for allies to fight against Huerta's puppets. Of course, he was cruelly tortured and assassinated along with his mother and son—all for protesting for his rights to free expression and action.

Another leap in history. Juchitecos have been murdered and killed throughout the years mentioned. Some martyrs were great and well known, others were unknown, but the struggle was never forgotten. History harvested this pain and suffering in support of the great struggle for freedom in 1981.

The struggle of COCEI, not the PCM [Mexican Communist Party], as everyone thinks and uses to soil the struggles of the Juchitecos of today, has been congruent with the history of physical and intellectual battles of its predecessors. It is the first time that the people's vote has been respected after many years of fraud, mistreatment, and lies. It is the struggle of the people, not of COCEI. Juchitán, of this great Zapotec race, has been a town that was beaten, burned, torn up, injured, and tortured to its very soul. The victory of COCEI is the history of a people. It is a history that we can write and comment on because already it is being seen and even scorned by the enemy.

COCEI as a political organization emerged in 1968 with one of its leaders, Héctor Sánchez [mayor of Juchitán from 1989 to 1992], who still remains in its ranks today. The others are Oscar Matus and Daniel López Nelio [federal deputy from 1988 to 1991], who headed a students' association of the Isthmus of Tehuantepec with its headquarters in Juchitán, Oaxaca. From then on they have been concerned with defending the trampled rights of workers, peasants, and students. This all began with the voracity of a doctor who worked in the health center. He sold medicine that was supposed to be given free to the poor. That is, the first action of COCEI was to eradicate corruption at the health center. Afterwards, COCEI leaders became advisors and lawyers for the poor. They demanded payment of the minimum wage, restitution of land, indemnizations, rights to strike, and payments from different private and official enterprises. COCEI supported the demands of Isthmus students for scholarships, tuition, compensation from bus companies for accidents and deaths, and lower bus fares. They also defended teachers who were fired or unjustifiably replaced. Later, they supported several local organizations and groups from other parts of the country.

COCEI became the conscience of private and government workers. They had power and a following. By helping the poor, they made the poor their allies. And, of course, the state and federal government had COCEI in their sights and thus could repress, kidnap, disappear, and assassinate their leaders, such as Víctor Pineda Henestrosa and Leopoldo de Gyves Pineda, who had roots in the masses. The principal leaders of COCEI were pursued. They were fugitives for crimes they never committed. Years of struggle, hardship, torture, and disappearances passed until the elections of 1980–81. COCEI's actions have been drastic and adventurous but effective.

The Forms of Sexual Life in Juchitán

Andrés Henestrosa

Often one hears foreigners who have visited the Isthmus of Tehuantepec say that there is sexual promiscuity, free union, and a price on female virginity there. The most unusual comment is the affirmation of the existence of "double bathhouses." This assertion is not supported by reality. In the entire Isthmus there is not one public bathhouse. There are many rivers, and there are artesian wells in most houses. Women do bathe nude in the rivers but not because of a lack of modesty. Either a man should not pass by when a woman is bathing, or he can go by but cannot stay to watch. Only the tourists—because they travel through in a hurry—or superficial men like them can make such claims as mentioned above because they are ignorant of the fact that all Isthmus life, or more strictly that of Juchitán, obeys customs rooted in ancient tradition. There is no sexual looseness of any kind, nor can there be in a town that scrupulously follows ancestral custom. I am talking about a form of being and a form of conduct.

Along these lines I hope to explain how the forms of sexual life originated and persist by virtue of their classical past. In reality, these sexual behaviors are neither offensive nor of great consequence. It would not occur to anyone in Juchitán that the honor and decency of a family resides in sexual functions. I speak, naturally, of those people in whom primary forms of thinking remain intact. Others among whom these forms of thinking exist are now influenced by a foreign spirit—"foreign" referring to all that is not from the Isthmus.

There have always been two routes that lead to marriage in Juchitán. One, the way that we could call legal, consists of a marriage that conforms to foreign customs. The other, which begins in *rapto* [abduction], involves a search for virginity, the results of which determine whether or not there will be a marriage.

The first form involves the following: the groom (by way of his parents) has a group of honorable old men ask for the woman's hand in marriage. In Juchitán these old men are most frequently called *xuaana',* and in Tehuantepec *chegola.* They approach the woman's parents, and one of them, always the oldest, gives a rhetorical speech we call *libana,* in which he praises the beauty and virtues of the woman, and the virtues of the man. The speech concludes with the marriage proposal. Then the father calls his daughter to ask her if she wishes to marry. She may give her response right away, in which case the messengers convey the reply to the groom; or she may give it later, in which case the messengers will return for it. If the answer is yes, there is nothing else to do but set a wedding date. A *padrino* is named, in whose house the bride is left a few days before the wedding. The wedding celebration may last for three days, full of the sound of fireworks. During the celebration there occurs one of the most picturesque aspects of indigenous custom: the material proof of virginity— recovered on a sheet—that the *padrino* takes to the house of the bride's parents.

The second form—*rapto*—can arise for several reasons. For example, the groom may ask for the woman's hand in what I have called the legal route but is denied it because, in spite of prior assurances, the woman or her parents reject the request. If it is the case that the parents say no but that the woman is willing, then she voluntarily elopes with the man. With a fait accompli thus presented, the wedding may or may not take place, although the parents always prefer that it does. If, on the other hand, the woman rejects the marriage proposal, the man may take her by force, literally "dragging her away."

The Zapotecs, like all primitive men, have an absolutely fanatical concern with virginity. But it is not so much with material virginity; rather, it is a kind of retrospective jealousy. Hence, most frequently, the man first wants to have proof of his bride's virginity. It could happen that the woman is ready to marry but demands that she be asked. The man may ask to marry her, but sometimes his mistrust causes him to abduct [*raptar*] the woman. In these cases, the woman may feel so offended that she completely opposes the marriage.

When the *rapto* is consummated, marriage may be a necessary consequence if in the process the woman's prior virginity is demonstrated. In this case, the abductor feels repentance for having acted in this way, repentance that is made more acute if the families are friends. He, his parents, or his representatives go immediately to the woman's parents' house. They explain what happened and promise there will be a wedding. The following day the marriage is legalized in front of a judge. If she was not a virgin, the woman is returned to her parents' home the same night. This is why in such cases in the Zapotec language the word "virginity" has become a synonym for dawn. But in both the first and second forms of marriage, if the woman is not a virgin but the man who possessed her first has died, then events follow their course, and the wedding is realized.

Next I address what ignorant foreigners have called "the price of virginity." This consists of a certain amount of money that is given to the woman or her parents (and may be rejected) when the woman is a virgin but she or her parents oppose the marriage, or when she turns out not to be a virgin and the man rejects her. This is not, however, a payment for services provided, but a forfeiture—which presupposes punishment—of a certain amount of money. In Juchitán, poor people have few possibilities of earning money, and the loss of one hundred pesos, for example, is a real punishment for them. If the woman or her family does not want the money or the marriage, there is an alternative penalty: They can demand the jailing of the abductor. Otherwise, the judicial authorities do not intervene, and everything is arranged between the families. The weight of custom is so heavy that judges, even if they are not of our people, apply the criteria of custom instead of legal standards.

I said at the beginning that there is no laxness in our morality. I repeat this now, and illustrate it with one of the most beautiful Zapotec customs. There are some who assert that this custom is older than the conquest, and I agree, but I believe that, at least in the aspect presented today, it also reflects Spanish influence. One way of maintaining the purity of customs, of conserving them, is public satire of all those who flout them, try to deny them, or act as if they are unimportant. This happens throughout the year. But when December comes around, in the nights closest to Christmas, a group of men go out into the streets. Stationed on a corner or in front of the house of one who would violate tradition, the men notify the public in loud voices of the violator's private affairs. They do not say beautiful words about the coming of Christmas or that a lover will take his loved one to see the crèche. Instead, they talk about sexual matters. They finish by saying that the flower [i.e., the woman], which is the most pure, should know these things and so should the townspeople.

I recognize that there may be a degree of moral or sexual perversion in Juchitán as is natural in all cities, but with this narrative I have attempted to demonstrate that not only is there no moral laxity in Juchitán, but that there is a great purity in the customs that the people defend and strive to maintain.

Hammock seller of Juchitán, Oaxaca. Photo by G. Iturbide.

Juchitán, a Town of Women

Elena Poniatowska

Translated by Cynthia Steele

Juchitán is not like any other town. It has the destiny of its Indian wisdom. Everything is different; women like to walk embracing each other, and here they come to the marches, overpowering, with their iron calves. Man is a kitten between their legs, a puppy they have to admonish, "Stay there." They walk touching each other, playfully. They trade roles; they grab men who watch them from behind the fence, pulling at them, fondling them as they curse the government and, sometimes, men themselves. They are the ones who participate in the demonstrations and beat policemen.

> Long live free Juchitán!
> Long live the municipal government!
> Long live the political prisoners!
> Freedom for the political prisoners!
> Freedom for Víctor Yodo!
> Freedom for Polo de Gyves Pineda!
> In 1981 the people are already the government!

You should see them arrive like walking towers, their windows open, their heart like a window, their nocturnal girth visited by the moon. You should see them arrive; they are already the government, they, the people, guardians of men, distributors of food, their children riding astride their hips or lying in the hammocks of their breasts, the wind in their skirts, flowered vessels, the honeycomb of their sex overflowing with men. Here they come shaking their wombs, pulling the *machos* toward them, the *machos* who, in contrast with them, wear light-colored pants, shirts, leather sandals, and palm hats, which they lift high in the air as they shout, "Long live Juchitec women!"

It is the Juchitec woman who owns the market. She is the powerful one; the merchant; the bargainer; the generous, avaricious, greedy one. Only women sell. With their machetes and their palm hats, the men leave home at dawn for work; they are iguana hunters, peasants, fisherman. When they come back, they hand over their harvest to the women, who carry it to the plaza, in gourd bowls decorated with flowers and birds, their proud lofty heads crowned with splendid and abundant fruit, plantains *(plátanos machos), guayabas* bursting with ripeness, papayas, watermelons, pineapples, custard apples *(anonas),* sapotas *(zapotes), chico zapotes,* guavas that distill their unique aroma. In the market, next to the stalls where they sell green glass pottery from Oaxaca, is the black crockery from Juchitán, jerked beef *(tasajo),* dried beef *(cecina)* covered with flies, brown sugar. Fresh banana leaves grow green again, folded in squares as they are wrapped around dough, meat, and hot sauce for the tamales. Gold chains, necklaces made from coins, hoops for piercing ears, all glitter in glass showcases. Here is the hot chocolate stall, there the booth that sells the prehispanic beverage, *bu'pú,* made with fresh cocoa, sugar, and toasted petals of flowers called *gie'suba,* whipped together into a thick, fragrant foam. A refined drink, fit for kings. And over there, palms, brooms, ropes; and over here, huaraches, stirrups, harnesses, chairs, spurs; and right here, locks, hinges, latches that resemble round shrimps curled up into themselves, piled up in baskets, brought by the Huave Indians, together with fresh turtle eggs and dried, sun-roasted fish. Right over there, the Isthmus *totopos,* those giant tortillas that are cooked underground, crunchy and rotund like the perimeter of a skirt over the earth. They are proof that life has no bitterness. *Totopos* laugh. They keep on laughing. They even laugh in the middle of a bite. Ensconced in the shelter of the ground, they seek the shelter of the mouth to partake of its language. . . .

The women of Juchitán are strong-willed, in contrast with other regions, where women shrink back and cry: in Jalisco, in the Bajío, in Mexico City. They have nothing in common with self- sacrificing Mexican mothers drowned in tears. Isthmus women impose themselves with the white ruffles of their skirts, the tinkling of their jewelry, the golden lightning of their smiles. "Get your gold caps, Exaltación, so your teeth will shine." Women, unique and inimitable, like the ocean, who carry within them hidden treasures, red coral trees, dark shells in the very center of their grace. Because of them, traditions are not lost: dresses and customs, holidays and candles—the *vela* of the Plum Tree; of the Lizard; of San Vicente, patron saint of Juchitán; of the San Isidro Labrador, San Juan and San Jacinto. Since the whole year is a holiday, there are no holy days. The morning after, the market opens late because everyone wakes up sleepless and hung over. Women help each other grind chocolate, cook chicken, prepare candy; the vigil is organized collectively in one place, the home of the *mayordomo*. Candles are bathed, ready to be placed in the church the next day. In one house sweet egg bread is kneaded, for the snack; in another *totopos* are clapped flat with the palm of the hands; in a third kitchen, stews begin to simmer. Meanwhile, women chat and joke with each other; what they say always has an erotic connotation. They pat, coax, knead, taste their dishes: "It needs salt." In the streets they ask each other, "So, you're going where they beat eggs" [an allusion to testicles]. And their laughter resounds. Zapotec women have always been openly erotic, and they wear their sensuality on their shirtsleeves. Sex is a little clay toy; they take it in their hands, mold it as they please, shake it, knead it together with the corn of their *totopos*. Everything reminds them of it, the humming of the *zanate de oro* bird, the fluttering of the butterfly, the color of the red snapper. So much so that foreigners—and in Juchitán everybody is a foreigner, except the people from the Isthmus—are either scandalized or fascinated forever, like Eisenstein, who filmed the women from Tehuantepec lying in their hammocks, nude from the waist up, and wrote in his diary, "A portion of the garden of Eden remains before the closed eyes of those who have ever seen the unlimited Mexican vistas. And you are left with the tenacious idea that Eden was not located somewhere between the Tigris and the Euphrates, but, of course, here, somewhere between the Gulf of Mexico and Tehuantepec! This does not preclude the dirt in the pots of food licked by the mangy dogs that swarm around . . . nor the secular backwardness."

Left to right: Maribel, Yolanda, and her daughter on their way to the corn mill in San Blas Atempa, Oaxaca. Zapotec women use milled corn to bake *totopos,* crisp tortillas that are a specialty of the Isthmus of Tehuantepec. Photo by H. Campbell.

Representations
of
Isthmus Women:
A Zapotec Woman's
Point of View

Obdulia Ruiz Campbell

When foreign observers visit the Isthmus of Tehuantepec they are impressed by the sight of women's colorful attire. This includes *enaguas* (long, flowing skirts) and *huipiles* (indigenous blouses), worn daily, and embroidered velvet gowns with floral and geometric patterns complemented by striking gold-coin jewelry of different sizes and denominations, worn in Isthmus fiestas. The proud manner in which Zapotec women wear these gowns gives them a robust and stunningly attractive appearance. Foreigners also observe Isthmus women's market activity; the women confidently buy and sell and astutely bargain the merchandise. The hammock- sellers are so insistent that their customers have no choice but to buy. The characteristic sales pitches of the hammock- and *totopo*-sellers are "hamaca, güero" ("hammock, blondie!") and "lleva totopo, güero" ("take some *totopos,* blondie!").

Likewise, outsiders see how women stand out in the social and religious arenas, whether accompanying their neighbors or friends to the burial of their relatives or attending novenas after the funeral. Women also help with the preparations for the masses offered to the souls of the dead nine days, one month, and one year after the burial. Additionally, women organize and attend the annual celebration of the Day of the Dead in the cemetery. This involves taking marigold flowers *(guie' biguá)* to their dead; weeping on the tombs, accompanied by bands specially contracted for this purpose; and participating in the sale of sweets, beer, and soft drinks at the entrance to the cemetery. There is a popular saying that refers to this occasion: "Los vivos al gozo y los muertos al pozo" ("The living to the party and the dead to the tomb").

In popular fiestas, women devote themselves totally to pleasure: drinking, dancing with other women, and creating their own atmosphere by telling risqué jokes and roaring with laughter, accompanied by loud hand-clapping. At times, male homosexuals *(muxe')* join them to "raise hell," and that is when the jokes get racier. From my point of view, this serves as a kind of psychological relaxation or therapy for Isthmus women because they free themselves from the tensions and pressures of their daily responsibilities.

If the visitor lives in a Zapotec household, she will realize that women work hard to provide for their families. At times they have the responsibility to educate their children while also controlling their husbands when they are able to or allowed to by the men. If this should occur, the woman brags about it and takes every opportunity to demonstrate or say that she rules the household. I want to make perfectly clear, however, that although one frequently hears the phrase "te manda tu señora" ("your wife dominates you"), there are in reality few such cases.

Because of their short stay in the area, outsiders—be they anthropologists, sociologists, or writers—having seen these things, leave with the impression that Zapotec women are Amazons or that they live in a matriarchal society, when the reality is quite different. The foreigners are only interested in what they are looking for, what they sympathize with, or what is most attractive or new to them. They romanticize it, exaggerating particular dimensions of reality, depending on their personal interests. For example, many writers exalt the powerful image of Zapotec women. For feminists this is solid gold! One sociologist even wrote that all Juchitecas are lesbians. I wonder, does the social scientist have an aversion to lesbians, or does she support them? The sociologist did not realize that both the Zapotec men and women, when they want to show affection or friendship towards a person, besides showing it verbally, express it physically without any sexual intent.

When women meet their friends in the street, they smile with joy. One touches the arm or the shoulder of the other and says, "How are you sweetheart?" ("Cómo estás, corazón?") or "Are you going, beautiful?" ("Ya te vas, guapa?"). Without being homosexuals, the young men greet their friends by shaking hands. Some hold their little fingers together while walking and talking. Some older men shake hands and then one of them holds onto the wrist of the other while they chat. Recently, I was in India, and while visiting a small town in Rajasthan, I saw two young men holding onto each others' little fingers as they walked along. This is so natural to me that the only thing I thought was that they also have this custom. I never imagined that one day I would have to explain or defend it.

Although Isthmus women definitely do not dominate their men, there are aspects of society in which they enjoy equality, as in the sponsorship of fiestas. A couple shares the prestige or credit when they agree to serve as fiesta *mayor-domos* (sponsors). This requires that they finance a large three-day fiesta in honor of the town's patron saint. Additionally, both spouses share the pride of covering the wedding expenses of their children and giving dowries to their daughters. The dowry consists of the presentation of a cedar hope chest and gold jewelry. Another example of shared responsibilities is that the husband and wife make an effort to provide their children with an education (with the expectation that the children will care for them when they grow old). Also, when a couple reaches old age they are equally highly respected. Likewise, when a widow or divorced woman takes care of the responsibilities discussed above, she is greatly respected.

Another frequently discussed topic is the supposed sexual liberation of the Zapotec woman. If their observations were profound, the foreigners would understand that Zapotec women's conduct and way of being carries with it an innate grace, that in their informal conversations they always allude to sex in a joking way, seeming to be very sexually sophisticated, when it is only word-play. This behavior is more common in married women than among younger, unmarried women, who are supposed to be less bold in their behavior and vocabulary if they want to reach the altar with their boyfriends.

Rapto (when a man carries off a woman to be his bride) is a shameful and denigratory action for women, and they know it. Several of my friends said they felt embarrassment, fear, and pain during the *rapto,* and that sexual pleasure was secondary. It embarrassed them to know that the families of their boyfriends were waiting and asking if they had had sex, eager to see the "proof of virginity" (a sheet or handkerchief stained with blood). At the same time, they were afraid that the boyfriend would declare that they were not virgins (even though, in fact, they were), due to the boy's ignorance, inexperience, or bad intentions. They felt pain because the man imposed himself without consideration and acted brusquely, demonstrating his animality. My mother and other relatives told me that they were abducted with violent force, that they received blows to their legs so that they would not resist so much and were later pulled by their hands to the houses of their boyfriends where they were deflowered. After my mother told me this story she repeated the well-known saying, "the calm comes after the storm" ("después de la tempestad llega la calma"); that is, despite all this, the women felt a certain satisfaction for having gone through the same ordeal as their mother, grandmother, or great-grandmother before them.

In the cases of my sisters and me, we made special efforts to have boyfriends from outside our town (San Blas) to avoid experiencing *rapto.* You see, the boys from our neighbor city (Tehuantepec) had already given up the custom of *rapto*, substituting for it the "marriage petition" *(la pedida de mano)*, in which the sexual act occurs after the religious wedding as part of the famous *lunes* (Monday). At the end of the Sunday wedding party, the bride and groom retire to relax and calmly have sex in the late hours of the night. They show the "proof of virginity" to their parents, and then on Monday celebrate it with a second more exuberant party. The name *lunes* has come to mean not only "Monday" but also the "proof of virginity" itself, as well as the party associated with its presentation.

In my case, my husband and I left for our honeymoon after the religious wedding and completion of the traditional rites of the wedding party: the toast, *medio xiga* (a ceremony in which the couple's relatives and guests donate money to them in a half-gourd), the jar-breaking dance, the blind-chicken dance, the tail dance, the kiss, the waltz with the bride and groom's parents, and the cutting of the cake.[1] We left behind my perplexed relatives because there would be no *pachanga* (wild party) on Monday. You see, there is no *lunes* without the bride and groom.

The Zapotec woman understands that marriage is forever— "until death do us part," as the saying goes—and she is prepared for this, whether she has seen this at home or been counseled by her mother. She has to have children (or otherwise the marriage fails) and, likewise, be ready to meet the sexual needs of her husband when he requires it, regardless of how tired she is from her many daily tasks.

I will give an example of the Zapotec mother's daily life to illustrate some of the above-mentioned points. The example is from my own family; it is a first-hand experience. My mother was self-sacrificing, a hard worker, and an ingenious administrator of her few centavos to serve three meals a day to her seven children. It is very common in an Isthmus family to see between a half dozen and a dozen children seated at the table. It is to the mother's credit that she has bread on the table each day. My father, as a campesino, only sporadically brought home the harvest. Our daily economic needs were satisfied by the sale of great quantities of tortillas, the product of my mother's work. She also raised pigs. When it was harvest time, my father brought home from the fields corn, sweet potatoes, mangos, coconuts, *nanches, guanábanas,* bananas, guavas, and marigold flowers, which my mother sold in the market.

At an early age I realized that Zapotec women suffer from the temperament of their demanding, scolding, abusive, and drunken husbands. Isthmus men frequently beat their wives and children. Without intending to disturb the memory of my two grandmothers, I recall that they suffered a great deal from mistreatment by their adulterous husbands until the days of their deaths. Additionally, my siblings and I know what it is like to kneel on the ground in the sun holding rocks on our heads and in our hands until collapsing from exhaustion. This punishment was my father's favorite. He also commonly punished us with a rain of *cinturonazos* or *cuerazos* (blows from a rough waxed piece of leather used to tie the bulls to the oxcart) on our backs.

An example in which my mother had "ni voz ni voto" ("neither voice nor vote") was when she protested on finding out that my grandfather and my father planned to marry me to an old friend of theirs who was in his fifties while I was just twenty-one years old. When I realized that neither she nor my other relatives could help me with my protest against the arranged marriage, I had to run away from home, although later I was able to return to visit my family.

In spite of all these difficult experiences, and although I left my hometown more than twenty years ago, lived in Mexico City, traveled to other countries, and married a foreigner, I am proud to belong to and form part of a Zapotec community, which I rejoin when I am in the Isthmus. Perhaps this ethnic pride and sense of community that we Zapotec women have are attractive to the *chilangas* (women from Mexico City) and *gringas* (North American women) precisely because they lack them.

NOTE

1. In the jar-breaking dance *(el baile de los cantaritos),* young (mostly unmarried) women holding ceramic jars on their heads dance in a circle around the bride and groom and then break the jars on the ground in front of them. In the blind-chicken dance *(la gallinita ciega),* young women circle around the blindfolded bride, who eventually catches one of them. The woman who was caught then receives the bridal wreath and is said to be the next to marry. The tail dance *(la cola)* consists of the bride and groom's standing on chairs forming a small bridge with the train of the bride's dress. The young girls form a conga line and dance under the bridge until the groom drops the "tail" (i.e., the train) of the dress onto one of the girls. All of these activities are accompanied by particular songs.

Social Scientists Confronted with Juchitán (Incidents of an Unequal Relationship)

Víctor de la Cruz

Many indigenous people have had the honor of living with social scientists (anthropologists, linguists, sociologists, etc.) while the latter carry out studies on their towns or regions. I especially remember two of them, because I know them personally, who even had the good fortune to earn salaries as informants and afterward to travel to universities in the United States of North America. They are Juan Olivares, a Huave of San Mateo del Mar, Oaxaca, and Pedro Pérez Conde, a Tzeltal of Tenejapa, Chiapas. Many Juchitecos have also been so honored, especially during the agitated days our Ayuntamiento Popular survived. During that time we spent pleasant moments in the company of many national and foreign scholars of social reality while serving as guides, interpreters, translators, or informants. We had many concerns and tasks in those days, among which one was most urgent: the necessity to disseminate information about the events (which weighed so heavily upon us), motivations, and goals of the struggle of Juchitán and the Coalition. We urgently needed to denounce the siege we were under, as widely as possible, before national and international public opinion. We needed to do this in spite of the silent complicity of the mass media and the attacks (orchestrated from the offices of the government) launched by a large part of the press. Our concerns, at that time, revolved around whom to inform—because together with Oaxacan "journalists" asking if the Juchitecos were going to rise up in arms, there appeared Harvard students determined to subject us to long interrogations for their imminent theses—and who benefited from the information provided: ourselves (creating consciousness about the repression of a people) or some national or foreign police agency.

From several days prior to the infamy committed against the people of Juchitán until August 3, 1983 (the day in which the state and federal governments repudiated the Ayuntamiento Popular in a farce performed by the state legislature), the manipulation and stifling of information reached extremes of vileness seldom seen in history. All the national and state dailies concealed the facts. A television channel that was given facilities to film our rally from City Hall used those takes to deform the events; the director of a national newspaper covering the event had vacationed several weeks previously, his expenses paid by the State; and so forth. Under these conditions, the only way left for COCEI and the Ayuntamiento Popular to denounce repression was to pay for advertisements in the national press. Local papers refused to accept them. Reading the paid advertisements, one fact stood out: the number of writers, graphic artists, photographers, and others who showed solidarity with the besieged Ayuntamiento Popular and the persecuted organization greatly surpassed the number of social scientists. I proposed to someone that they work out an elementary statistic to determine how many writers' or painters' signatures appeared in the advertisements for each name of an anthropologist, sociologist, historian, or linguist. An explanation could be that those who promoted solidarity with Juchitán were more active in artistic circles than in academic ones.

After the events outlined above, I was invited by the Institute of Sociological Research of the University of Oaxaca to participate as an observer and commentator in the conference "Perspectives on South and Southeast Mexican Social Movements," directed by Pablo González Casanova (November 28–30, 1983).

My participation consisted of commenting on the paper of a young PRI sociologist from Juchitán, who, from his standpoint of academic neutrality and scientific objectivity based on false data and information obtained exclusively from his party, dedicated himself to attacking the "disappeared" Ayuntamiento Popular and COCEI and to giving advice to the government on how it should treat this organization. Taking advantage of the opportunity, I proposed a discussion of the ethics of a social researcher's use of his/her work. Additionally, I proposed to those who consider themselves impartial or feel committed to the liberation struggles of indigenous peoples the creation of a document analyzing the irregularities committed by the government to impeach the authority established by a town after long years of sacrifices and repression. The issue was avoided as rhetoric prevailed. On this occasion, my relations with the students of social reality were not very pleasant.

I make these public reflections apropos of the work of Marie-France Prévot-Shapira and Hélene Rivière d'Arc, originally published in a French magazine in the language of that country, and which reached our hands by chance. How many cases such as this one occur, in which the indigenous people provide information to researchers without its returning to their hands after it is processed? Does this not perhaps constitute a looting, such as that of the archaeological objects of the indigenous people, or the stealing of our raw materials? If, in exchange for the information that they are provided, the social scientists cannot send a copy of their finished work to the place from which it originated, how can they expect to discuss their positions and related propositions with the local people? Who ultimately benefits from the results of social research? It is not likely the social groups, actors of the phenomena under study, for in the majority of cases they do not learn about the existence of such studies. In the best of circumstances, we might think that this research benefits "science" in general and the personal ascent of the researcher in particular. But science also has its beneficiaries, be they national or foreign, who can process and systematize the information to further their plans for domination and colonization. Why, then, is it necessary in some cases to provide information? Because the need for solidarity requires dissemination of the people's struggles. Under such conditions, some people have to assume the responsibility and run the inherent risks.

In the case of the work of the aforementioned authors, we publish it,[1] although we are in disagreement with it, because it exemplifies the unequal relationship between the informant ethnic groups and the researchers who receive the information. But the essay also has its own limitations and errors. Having had the opportunity to talk with COCEI leaders and authorities of the Ayuntamiento Popular, they could have obtained from City Hall a geographic perspective on the struggles of ethnic resistance of the Juchitecos in publications created through our editorial project to elucidate and comprehend the history of indigenous resistance to colonialism. Indeed, it is precisely this lack of historical perspective in analyzing social actors in a period of hardly more than ten years that leaves the work floating in emptiness, with affirmations about the supposed similarity between the origins of the COCEI struggle and Trotskyism or focoism. Reviewing the attached bibliography, one can see that it includes no titles published by the Ayuntamiento Popular from which the researchers could have obtained information about the historical antecedents of the current struggle. From the two works cited in the bibliography, they could not have historically documented the essay. One of the sources they may not even know. I am referring to *Mexico South: The Isthmus of Tehuantepec,* by Miguel Covarrubias. They attribute it to a publisher named Cassel, without specifying the place of publication, when it is well known that this book was published by Alfred A. Knopf of New York. The other work is the noted essay by John Tutino on the Tehuantepec rebellion of 1660.

With these clarifications for our readers, especially for our *compañeros* in struggle, we hope for a critical reading, pages ahead, of the work entitled "Zapotecs, PRI, and COCEI: Confrontations Surrounding State Intervention in the Isthmus of Tehuantepec." We also hope that the relationship between social scientists and the communities or regions they study will be more just and the assertions more serious and beneficial for the people studied.

NOTE

1. The article de la Cruz refers to, "Los Zapotecos, el PRI, y la COCEI: enfrenta-mientos alrededor del Estado en el Istmo de Tehuantepec," by Marie-France Prévot-Shapira and Hélene Rivière d'Arc, appeared in *Guchachi' Reza* 19 (June 1984): 11–26.

PART THREE

COCEI:
Isthmus
Zapotec
Political Radicalism

With the demise of entrenched regimes in the Soviet Union, East Germany, Poland, Rumania, and other Eastern Bloc countries, few monolithic one-party states remain in the contemporary world. Castro's Cuba is often said to be one of the last holdouts of such regimes. Although Mexico is also currently undergoing major political changes, it is seldom mentioned in those discussions, perhaps because historically the Institutional Revolutionary Party (PRI) has permitted opposition parties to exist while limiting their influence through a judicious mix of co-optation and repression, and has legitimated its rule via elections. One can quibble over the degree and extent of PRI hegemony, the nature of changes within the party (and its precursors) over time, and so on, but the longevity and stability of PRI, which has governed Mexico in one form or another since 1929, have rarely been equaled in contemporary world, and especially Latin American, politics.

Now that PRI's long-standing dominance of Mexican public life has begun to erode, particularly as a result of the neo-Cárdenas movement, the study of

COCEI rally in support of presidential candidate Cuauhtémoc Cárdenas and Juchiteco federal deputy candidate Daniel López Nelio. At the microphone is Enedino Jiménez, poet and leader of a local teacher's union. June 1988. Photo by H. Campbell.

"new social movements" opposing PRI and pushing for change is taking on new relevance. Juchitán and COCEI have played an important role in this research. Opposition politicians, intellectuals, and international observers used the COCEI case to evaluate PRI/government electoral reforms of the late 1970s and early 1980s, and COCEI's 1981 election victory attracted much attention when Juchitán became the first and only left-controlled city in Mexico (see Jeffrey Rubin's article in Part Three). The government's ouster of the COCEI administration from office in 1983 was viewed by many scholars as evidence of PRI's reversion to antidemocratic policies and a PRI moratorium on reform (Alvarado 1987; Cornelius et. al. 1989b).

COCEI did not play a major part in the rapid rise of *neocardenismo,* which took political scientists, PRI/government functionaries, foreign observers, and, indeed, the populace as a whole by surprise during the 1988 Mexican presidential elections. COCEI was just one, albeit an important one, of the many regional and local political organizations that banded together with Cárdenas to rock the boat of PRI control. Cárdenas's movement, and the electoral ferment it stimulated, had a profound (some say irreversible) impact on the Mexican political system. The candidate received officially 31 percent of the vote (Cornelius et al. 1989a:19), although unofficial counts indicated substantial fraud (Reding 1988), and left opposition candidates from the Federal District and Michoacán won Senate seats. Yet change at the municipal level, particularly in rural areas, has lagged behind. Reported *cardenista* municipal victories in Michoacán, the movement's stronghold, have been marred by violence and PRI intransigence. Following the 1988 election, dissension and fragmentation within the *cardenista* camp, government harassment, and PRI's rapprochement with segments of the right (e.g., in the Baja California and Chihuahua gubernatorial elections) have slowed the movement's momentum although it remains an important challenge to the PRI status quo.

Within this shifting context, COCEI has persisted as a stronghold of left opposition to PRI control in the countryside. In 1989, buoyed by Cárdenas's support, local PRI divisions, and perhaps national PRI interest in maintaining a democratic image, COCEI once again won municipal elections in Juchitán and obtained the mayoralty and a majority of seats in a coalition municipal council with PRI. COCEI's successful management of city government led to another victory in 1992; barring serious blunders on its part, it will control city government through 1995.

Part Three begins with a poignant poem by Macario Matus lamenting the deaths of his COCEI *compañeros* in Isthmus political struggles. Since COCEI's founding in 1973, more than twenty-five members of the movement have died in violent battles with local *caciques,* their defenders, the police, and the military (see Amnesty International 1986, which documents human rights abuses committed against members of COCEI).

Jeffrey Rubin's article analyzes COCEI's conflictive political history. He focuses particularly on COCEI's role in Mexican national and regional politics and the complex dialectics of confrontation, mobilization, negotiation, and repression characterizing COCEI's interactions with government authorities. Rubin views this history as a process of increased political opening, albeit subject to occasional reverses, beginning with the 1977 electoral reforms. He examines COCEI's changing strategies and those of its PRI adversaries in this fluctuating political environment. Rubin concludes that electoral reform brought increased civil liberties and greater political competition, although it did not institute either electoral democracy or a more equitable economic and political situation. This history, he concludes, suggests two important tendencies within contemporary Mexican politics: that PRI is able to respond to ongoing political challenges and to change its tactics in order to maintain its power in a more contentious and less reliable political environment; and that the successes of COCEI in Juchitán evidence the expanded potential for national-level and grassroots political organizing and change in modern Mexico.

The next three articles of Part Three present COCEI voices describing and analyzing different aspects of the political struggle. In testimonies collected by Marta Bañuelos, COCEI women explain how they came to participate in the movement, the roles they have played, and the hardships they have suffered as well as the victories they have won. These testimonies are reminiscent of Ousamane Sembane's (1970) novel, *God's Bits of Wood,* based on a railroad strike carried out by African workers in colonial French West Africa. In that strike, women organized independently of the men to secure food and water for their families and eventually marched to Dakar and broke the will of the authorities. Many of the COCEI women's testimonies refer to the period following the defeat of the Popular Government when repression peaked and many of the leaders and militants were forced underground. The Juchitecas played a key role, keeping alive the fires of protest during that period. Like the men, many of them have been beaten, jailed, and even murdered for participation in rallies, strikes, and protests. Although their access to formal leadership roles is restricted to particular spheres (e.g., the teachers' movement, market women's organizations, and the cantina owners' association), and there are no women on the COCEI Political Commission or among the top leadership, the testimony suggests that women's contributions to the movement have been critical to its successes and that they have an important stake in its survival (see Campbell's article in Part Four for more on COCEI women).

The following article is the victory speech delivered by Leopoldo de Gyves de la Cruz when he took possession of Juchitán City Hall on March 10, 1981, as mayor of a popular government that was to remain in office until its ouster in August 1983 by the Oaxaca state legislature. De Gyves was unsuccessful in negotiating the 300-million-peso grant (about 12 million dollars at the time) that his administration sought to promote infrastructural and economic development; as he predicted, COCEI was eventually besieged by "new attacks" from the right. Finally, the speech illustrates once again COCEI's anchoring of present struggles in past memories.

Next is a COCEI political pamphlet of interest because it is a concise summary of the official COCEI view of the social, economic, and political contradictions in Juchitán, and of the organization's policy recommendations to counter land concentration, capitalist penetration, and government intervention. Although originally published in 1982 or 1983, the COCEI pamphlet is representative of most contemporary COCEI views and positions. COCEI's analysis links economic, social, and cultural issues, including access to land and the means of production, educational opportunity, ethnic discrimination, and language. The pamphlet moves from general conditions in the Isthmus to the agrarian policies of the presidential administrations of Luis Echeverría and José López Portillo, and concludes that both administrations employed pro-peasant rhetoric to garner popular support for policies that in the end led to further land and wealth concentration. "The State," according to COCEI, "cannot solve agrarian problems. It is the peasants themselves, in alliance with oppressed sectors, who should impose the solutions to their demands." Thus COCEI articulates an ideology designed to appeal to all oppressed and exploited groups: small merchants, artisans, and workers, as well as peasants.

In the last lengthy contribution, Sergio Zermeño addresses what he sees as some of the strengths and weaknesses of the movement, orienting his discussion around a comparison of COCEI with late nineteenth- and early twentieth-century Russian populists. In his survey of the Russian populist movement, Zermeño identifies two distinct orientations, either of which might provide the key for understanding COCEI. The "Enlighteners" were pro-peasant modernizers who thought that the Russian peasant commune might be able to pass directly to socialism without going through the capitalist stage of development. The "Romanticists" critiqued capitalism but looked to the past for their inspiration; they sought to recapitulate precapitalist economy and social relations. Zermeño suggests that the Janus-like COCEI embodies both of these faces of populism, the forward- and the backward-looking. For him the issue for the future is whether COCEI will ally itself with the peasant masses, forsaking interclass alliances, and defend the borders of culturally and linguistically defined localism, or whether it will promote economic development and expand the range of its contacts and influences, suffering thereby the erosion of ethnic and linguistic specificity. The question has no clear and unambiguous answer, since COCEI has never been in a position to freely choose among its possible futures, but developed its policies in a climate characterized by hostility, violent oppression, and economic boycott on the part of the State (although this may be changing). We will return to the issue in the Afterword, assessing Zermeño's question in the light of shifts in both PRI and COCEI strategy since the 1989 elections.

Part Three concludes with two poems. "Naked Speech" by Macario Matus is filled with images of pain and death associated with martyrdom and the overthrow of COCEI's popular government in 1983. By contrast, Alejandro Cruz's "A Birth in the Mountains" is an optimistic poem centered on political struggle in San Miguel Chimalapa, about thirty miles east of Juchitán, but equally relevant to Juchitán and COCEI. Tragically, Cruz, a gifted poet and popular COCEI organizer, was shot and killed in 1987 while leading a group of Zapotec peasants to the Agrarian Reform Ministry offices in Tehuantepec.

The most recent episode of PRI violence against COCEI occurred on December 9, 1989, when local *priístas* killed four *coceístas* and wounded six others who were protesting voting irregularities in Santo Domingo Ingenio, Oaxaca. Indeed, though COCEI governed Juchitán and several other Isthmus municipalities as of winter 1993, vigilante attacks against the movement are an ever-present threat. Yet, despite these risks, COCEI has persevered as a well-organized and articulate challenge to PRI dominance in southern Mexico.

Na China Henestrosa holding a picture of her son, Víctor Pineda Henestrosa, the most famous COCEI martyr. Photo by G. Iturbide.

My
Companions
Have Died

Macario Matus

Mine—whom I never met
but loved with all my soul.
They seeded the fields
but the day the land was taken
that was the end of work.
One time they were sent off to be outraged:
On that day they climbed the sky's crags.
And not only they have gone:
together with our own went one
who could read the word and was great.
Over there, where they murdered them,
we were taught what life is,
what a life of struggle has to be.
They taught us the gist of liberty:
that no one must trample on no one
in this immemorial land.
The day they quit, the sun died,
the light left for another part of the day
and no light remained to our solar kingdom.

COCEI against the State: A Political History of Juchitán

Jeffrey W. Rubin

The city of Juchitán has achieved national prominence as the center of one of Mexico's few large, militant, and independent leftist movements, the Worker-Peasant-Student Coalition of the Isthmus of Tehuantepec (COCEI, or the Coalition). In the 1970s, COCEI fought for better living and working conditions for peasants and workers using primarily direct-action organizing tactics. In the face of considerable right-wing violence, it succeeded in ousting corrupt municipal officials, winning strikes, defending peasant attempts to control local agricultural associations, and developing class consciousness and political organization in the city's poor neighborhoods. In the 1980s COCEI formed an alliance with the Mexican Communist Party that enabled it to participate officially in municipal elections and win office in 1981, making Juchitán the first and only city in Mexico with a leftist government.

For two years, COCEI governed Juchitán with widespread peasant and worker support, along with a mixture of tolerance and obstruction on the part of state and national authorities and considerable hostility from local elites. The COCEI administration acted to improve neglected municipal services, pressured employers to pay the minimum wage, and supported peasants in negotiations with state agencies. In response, the right wing of the local Institutional Revolutionary Party (PRI, or the official party) established its own organization to oppose COCEI, forging new ties with the Ministry of the Interior, and a reorganized local chamber of commerce began to work together with state and national business confederations to oust the leftist government. In 1983, eight months after the inauguration of Mexican president de la Madrid, COCEI was thrown out of office, and the army occupied Juchitán. After that, military forces established several permanent barracks in the city and stationed armed guards on the balconies of City Hall. COCEI remained strong through a period of severe repression, while elections were decided in favor of PRI in 1983 and 1986, despite evidence of fraud, and state and national authorities pressured for reform of the local party. Protests against the procedures and outcome of the 1986 elections, however, led to the establishment of a coalition government, including representatives of both PRI and COCEI, under the leadership of a PRI mayor. This unprecedented outcome was repeated in 1989, this time following recognition of a COCEI electoral victory.

How do we explain the formation of a strong, grassroots left in Juchitán, the national policy changes that first permitted COCEI to take office and then used military force to remove an elected municipal government from power, and the reform project that the regime has attempted to implement in Juchitán? What do these events reveal about the significance of Mexico's political reform, the changing strategies and capacities of the Mexican regime in dealing with opposition, and the structure and potential of the left in the 1980s?

This introduction will be followed by three sections that discuss successive periods of political conflict in Juchitán. The first describes the political conflicts and economic transformations that were central to the development of opposition politics, as well as the principal activities of COCEI in the 1970s. The second section examines elections and municipal government between 1980 and 1983. It reviews the local and national events and decisions that enabled COCEI to take office in 1981, the policies of the COCEI government and the responses of local, state, and national PRI politicians and business people, and the removal of COCEI from office in 1983. The third section of the essay will outline the events of 1984–86, following the removal of COCEI from office.

1848–1980: REBELLION, COEXISTENCE, AND CLASS CONSCIOUSNESS

Political History

In Juchitán, repeated rebellions against the economic and political encroachment of Oaxacan elites in the nineteenth century gave way in the course of Porfirio Díaz's rule and the Revolution to a federalist system of conflicts and alliances involving both partial autonomy and the acceptance of new kinds of political and economic relations with the outside. National-local interaction increased in the course of the planning and running of the Trans-Isthmus Railroad during the last decade of the Porfiriato, and the revolutionary government of Francisco Madero supported a local rebellion against Oaxaca in 1911. The state government, however, was able to defeat this rebellion and prevent a popular local leader and revolutionary general, Heliodoro Charis, from governing until the 1930s.

Charis's rule signified the ascendancy of national political authority in alliance with local bosses. He came to power through a combination of brief, armed rebellion and the mediation of presidential candidate Lázaro Cárdenas during a 1934 campaign visit. From this point on, most state and national politicians supported Charis's control over local politics. Beginning in the 1940s, a loose coalition of reformers gathered increasing local and outside support in a campaign to replace Charis's candidates with leaders from the business and professional sectors of the city, but they never fully succeeded. The inability of this reformist opposition to win power or change the rules of the political game even in the 1960s, when the lack of any effective mechanism for choosing candidates among competing factions was clearest, indicates the tenacity of the system of politics developed after the Revolution. The eventual victory of the reformers in 1971, when they rallied popular support behind the opposition Popular Socialist Party[1] and its charismatic leader, Tarú, occurred outside of the official party and came too late to enable that party to carry out reforms that would recreate a multiclass alliance.[2]

Economic Development Projects

The political turmoil of the 1960s was accompanied by dramatic economic changes in Juchitán. These resulted primarily from national development projects, particularly the construction of the Trans-Isthmus and Pan American highways in the 1950s, the Benito Juárez Dam and accompanying irrigation district in the early 1960s, and oil facilities in nearby Salina Cruz in the late 1970s and 1980s. As these projects brought both temporary and permanent jobs to the region, Juchitán grew rapidly as a regional commercial center.

Before the construction of the dam, yields of local corn, dependent on rainfall, had barely been sufficient for family survival, and many men had migrated to do agricultural work in neighboring states during Juchitán's dry winter season. While the land in Juchitán was legally classified as communal, it functioned like private property in practice and, before the 1960s, was relatively inexpensive and available to those willing to work it. When the introduction of irrigation led to increases in land prices, however, peasant families gradually began to sell some of their holdings, generally to meet expenses in crisis situations, and made up for lost income by increasing their participation in the growing urban economy.[3]

Because jobs were increasingly available in commercial activities, the issue of land tenancy in Juchitán did not involve the economic survival of the region's families, but rather their rights, well-being, and worldview in a rapidly changing economy.[4] COCEI began its organizing by emphasizing the land issue and had well-founded hopes of winning concessions from the Echeverría administration. In the course of the 1970s, however, both COCEI as an organization and its supporters in their daily lives moved from issues of land tenancy to work and political activism based more broadly on commercial and agricultural income. These changes enabled the Coalition to continue to gain support when the land issue did not advance.

The construction of the dam not only changed patterns of land ownership, but also brought peasants into direct contact with state agencies as agricultural planners sought to recoup the costs of constructing the dam and irrigation system and foster the regional economic benefits that the project had promised. While this economic effort has been largely unsuccessful throughout the twenty-five-year history of the district, it transformed agricultural relations in the region, first through the construction of a rice processing plant, which failed, and then a sugar mill. Both efforts were accompanied by pressures on small and medium-sized landowners to abandon corn cultivation for rice and cane, resulting in considerable State control over peasant production, as well as in peasant indebtedness, which in turn provided outside agencies with increased leverage in production decisions (Binford 1983; Warman 1972).

THE FORMATION OF COCEI

In the early 1970s, President Echeverría responded to the deepening crisis of representation and regional succession throughout Mexico by providing new opportunities for peasants and workers to organize politically outside of the existing framework of government-sponsored mass organizations. In 1973, Juchiteco students of middle-class and peasant backgrounds formed COCEI with the tacit support of the president and several government ministries. Through direct-action organizing tactics, the Coalition gained widespread popular support for strikes, marches, occupations of government offices, and skilled negotiations that improved living and working conditions.[5]

Much of COCEI's initial success derived from the absence or weakness of official peasant and worker organizations in Juchitán, a political characteristic of the region rooted in both its economic and political histories. As a result, in mobilizing support, COCEI did not have to break existing bonds tying workers and peasants to PRI through work-based, interest-mediating organizations. When COCEI did encounter such bonds, primarily in specialized local associations regulating land tenure and agricultural production, it rapidly succeeded in gaining majority support within the organization and splitting it into two groups, one affiliated with PRI and one with the Coalition.

While the political activities of the official party continued to involve only a limited group in the early 1970s, largely ignoring both the provision of municipal services and the development of mass organizations, a political transformation occurred among Juchitecos. Building on the ethnic identity of the close-knit Zapotec Indian community (the prevalence of indigenous language, dress, fiestas, and neighborhood residential patterns makes Juchitán more like a small town than like any other Mexican city), the activities of COCEI fostered the development of a thoroughgoing class consciousness among many of the city's poor and lower-middle-class residents.[6] Class consciousness and support for COCEI developed by way of ongoing, daily discussions over the course of years in family courtyards, in the context of fiestas, social obligations, and solidarity in the face of repression. Women and men in Juchitán's neighborhoods began to state clearly, in nonrhetorical language, that they were *los pobres* (the poor people) and that they were exploited in specific ways by local commercial enterprises and government agricultural programs. They said that they were ruled by a local government imposed through fraudulent elections and military force, that they supported COCEI because it fought unequivocally for their well-being, and that they participated in politics—attending meetings and marching in the streets with raised fists, voting, joining communal work projects, contributing financially—in order to carry on this struggle.

While elections represent a form of continuity between the 1970s and 1980s, most of COCEI's successes in the 1970s involved mass mobilizing activities aimed at pressuring the government and government agencies for concessions on agricultural and urban workplace issues. In agriculture, COCEI successfully fought a tax increase and helped small-landholding peasants win control of the local land council (Comisariado de Bienes Comunales) and livestock association (Asociación Ganadera), which had been run by wealthier landowners. It pressured the Agrarian Reform Ministry to award one thousand hectares of land claimed as private property by a wealthy landowner to peasants in the small town of Alvaro Obregón, and a COCEI member was appointed to the local office of the ministry. The Coalition pursued these land issues and fought for the enforcement of the original *ejido* decree through legal and extralegal means, including mass meetings and marches, negotiations with representatives of the Agrarian Reform Ministry, and the takeover of ministry offices in Oaxaca and Mexico City.

At the same time, COCEI supported organizing activities and strikes at the Juchitán rice plant, the regional chain of neighborhood corn mills, a building materials company, the district agricultural research station, and the Salina Cruz refinery, securing wage increases, benefits, and the rehiring of fired workers in most of these cases. COCEI organized previously unorganized workers and supported unionized workers in efforts to overthrow corrupt leadership. It addressed municipal service issues as well, forcing the departure of the head of Juchitán's social security hospital, who had been illegally charging students for essential health certificates, securing indemnizations for a bus accident, and protesting hikes in bus rates.

Along with these successes, COCEI suffered violent attacks carried out by the right wing of the local PRI and hired thugs, resulting in the deaths of more than twenty supporters between 1974 and 1977. Throughout this period, COCEI leaders were harassed and arrested, *campesinos* were killed for supporting COCEI, meetings were disrupted, and COCEI offices and the homes of leaders were attacked with stones and bullets.[7]

1980–1983: THE LEFT GOVERNS AND THE RIGHT REORGANIZES

After the 1977 political reform put democratization on the national agenda and legalized leftist parties, COCEI, after considerable debate, formed an alliance with the Communist Party, gaining an official place on the municipal ballot in 1980.[8] This alliance provided a national forum from which to denounce electoral fraud following the 1980 elections. In the face of national publicity as well as direct action mobilizations that included the occupation of two foreign embassies in Mexico City, the Mexican government acknowledged that there had been fraud and annulled the elections. In special elections held three months later, COCEI candidate Leopoldo de Gyves was declared the winner with 51 percent of the vote, and Juchitán became the first and only city in Mexico governed by the left.

This democratic opening was perhaps the most significant event in COCEI's fourteen-year history. Despite subsequent repression, COCEI's two years in office provided a real opportunity for an *ayuntamiento popular,* a people's government, and secured for the movement a claim to municipal sovereignty and the enduring support of large numbers of Juchitecos. A coincidence of regional and national events made possible the annulment of the 1980 elections and subsequent COCEI victory. On the national level, the López Portillo administration placed considerable emphasis on newly invigorated electoral competition. Between 1980 and 1983, policy decisions under both President López

Portillo and President de la Madrid permitted opposition victories of the left
and right in a number of relatively large cities in Oaxaca as well as in other
states, particularly in the North. Locally, COCEI was strong and able to mobilize considerable mass support in protest activities, while PRI was divided,
its historical conflict between machine politicians and reformist challengers
continuing to fragment the party, despite the consolidation of a new political
cacique, Mario Bustillo, in the 1970s. PRI was also widely seen as excessively
corrupt; accusations of corruption and inefficiency against the outgoing mayor
and calls for his removal from office had come from across the political spectrum.[9] As in 1971, when the majority of voters supported the Popular Socialist
Party, there was sentiment in Juchitán, across classes, that it was time to throw
the official party out of office and that COCEI deserved a chance to govern.

Events at the state level also played a central role in the 1981 opening. Both
political and business leaders were in a state of disorganization. Oaxaca's two
major business groups were engaged in a struggle for control of the State Federation of Chambers of Commerce and could not act as a unified force against
COCEI. At the same time, a new governor, Pedro Vásquez Colmenares, had
just taken office, arriving from Mexico City without a developed base in
Oaxaca politics. Lacking the backing of the business elite, Vásquez Colmenares needed to establish his own political support, and he sought to represent
the national political opening at the state level. A repressive approach to Juchitán, likely to provoke violence, was both risky and undesirable at the beginning
of his term (Bailón 1985).

The opening provided by the *reforma política,* however, was limited and
uneven. Despite his assertion of COCEI's right to govern in Juchitán, Vásquez
Colmenares cut off much of the municipal budget as soon as de Gyves took
office, and state and federal agencies opposed loans and credits to the Ayuntamiento Popular. In response, COCEI organized a march from Juchitán to
Oaxaca, convincing the governor to agree to negotiations before the marchers
reached the capital city. However, the municipal budget increased only gradually, and well-publicized tactics of this sort were needed repeatedly to secure
the basic necessities of municipal administration. Business people in Juchitán
attempted a commercial strike, but only a handful of enterprises participated,
and the strike failed.[10] Local PRI leaders initially found no effective way to
respond to state and national support for the COCEI victory. Both the middle
class and the elite in Juchitán concluded that national authorities had chosen
Juchitán for the site of a political experiment and that they were being sacri-
ficed to the regime's desire to manufacture democratic credentials.

Once in office, the COCEI government worked to end the neglect that Juchitán had suffered under a succession of corrupt PRI administrations. Working

together with city residents, municipal officials repaired unpaved streets, constructed and staffed local health clinics, established a public library on the central plaza, and rebuilt the crumbling City Hall. They took on two of the largest local employers, a beer distributor and a Coca-Cola bottling plant, and, after bitter strikes, secured higher wages and better benefits for workers. In addition, they pressured employers throughout the city to begin to pay the minimum wage and provide workers with the benefits to which they were legally entitled.

In 1982, COCEI participated in elections for federal deputy, and its candidate gained a seat in the national legislature as a member of the proportional representation list of the Unified Socialist Party.[11] While COCEI did not have sufficient support in the electoral district, which included twenty-two municipalities, to win a majority seat, this achievement nonetheless served important symbolic and practical purposes. For COCEI supporters in Juchitán, having a representative in the legislature indicated that their movement was strong and successful and contributed to their sense of multifaceted COCEI success during this period. In terms of political power and negotiation, the COCEI deputy provided an additional, direct means for COCEI to publicize its situation in Mexico City, a tactic of continuing importance in limiting the State's use of repression. Participation in legislative elections in alliance with the Unified Socialist Party also marked a new stage in the Coalition's alliance with the national party. In 1979, COCEI had rejected participation in national politics, and its relationship with the Communist Party in the early years of the Ayuntamiento Popular was characterized by antagonism, with COCEI repeatedly asserting the primacy of its own activity in advancing leftist politics. COCEI's participation in the national legislature indicated an increased willingness to acknowledge the usefulness of a national party in furthering grassroots politics.

The COCEI government negotiated with state and national authorities to secure credit for peasant farmers, and it sponsored the invasion of a large tract of government-owned land, where several hundred families built houses. Furthermore, COCEI emphasized the regional nature of its activities, putting forth the demands of peasants throughout the Isthmus, organizing workers and supporting strikes in an independent Isthmus union, and announcing its intention to participate in the 1983 municipal elections in municipalities throughout the region. In all these efforts, COCEI bypassed the traditional power structure of the local PRI and negotiated directly with state and national authorities.

These advances, especially efforts opposing ownership of land beyond legal limits and demanding payment of the minimum wage, struck at the privileges of the city's agricultural and commercial elites. In the face of elite opposition, the Coalition favored militant rhetoric and action, including veiled threats of violence to property that were occasionally carried out, further alienating opponents. COCEI's exercise of municipal patronage particularly angered the middle class and led to accusations of arbitrary and illegal practices. Furthermore, when the state government cut off the municipal budget, COCEI responded by pressuring local businesses to make contributions to the municipal treasury. These payments became a major point of controversy. COCEI not only fought the economic and political privileges of PRI and its supporters, but also laid claim to the public spaces of the city, encouraging supporters to make use of public areas where they had not previously gathered, such as the plaza in front of City Hall.[12]

Viewed from a long-term perspective, COCEI represented a considerable threat to the status quo, not only in Juchitán, but on regional and state levels as well. The Coalition's activities in Juchitán and throughout the southern part of the Isthmus challenged the existing development model by claiming a greater share of wages, land, and services for peasants and workers. COCEI viewed business people and landowners as opponents and set out to weaken their political power—or, more accurately, their traditional freedom from political control—and their hold on land and labor. These efforts provoked considerable turmoil in Juchitán and met with some success, and COCEI's plans to field candidates and make economic demands on an Isthmus-wide basis became increasingly credible.

In addition to displacing PRI politicians and challenging business interests, COCEI's efforts to effect change disrupted the rhythms of daily life in business and at home on a constant basis, substituting mobilization and conflict for the relative tranquility of daily life in the past. The Ayuntamiento Popular was not only a form of municipal administration, it also fostered a new atmosphere of participation and activity. Political meetings, public gatherings, street theater, and a COCEI radio station changed the panorama of municipal life. Furthermore, COCEI expressed its solidarity with leftist struggles in Central America in speeches and public events and timed its literacy campaign to coincide with the Nicaraguan effort.

In response, local PRI politicians and business people formed new groups that could fight the Coalition on the local level and pressure state and national authorities. The right wing of the official party organized the Committee for the Defense of the Rights of the People of Juchitán; unfettered by official constraints, this group waged a virulent anticommunist campaign, invoking the image of Central American-style conflict in the Isthmus, and made free use of violence and intimidation. In the first half of 1983, members of this group disrupted COCEI meetings and shot at the organization's leaders. While this did not diminish the militance of COCEI supporters, it fostered an atmosphere of extreme tension and provided an effective means of convincing outside authorities of the need for intervention.

Business leaders in Juchitán elected a new, young executive committee to head the previously weak chamber of commerce, and they turned this organization into a focal point for unified opposition to COCEI demands and contact with state and national business confederations. Finally, middle-class opponents, including some who had initially sympathized with COCEI, claimed that the Coalition consisted of illiterate rabble rousers, the city was no longer safe, and government should be placed in the hands of the "educated."

By 1983, then, PRI politicians and business people in Juchitán had formed new organizations that could act more effectively in opposing COCEI than could those that existed in 1980. The pressures exerted by these groups coincided with state and national changes as well. The more conservative Oaxacan business leaders had won control of the state federation, and they joined with the Juchitán Chamber of Commerce to organize a statewide business strike in May 1983. During the same period, Miguel de la Madrid assumed the presidency and replaced López Portillo's minister of the interior, who along with his predecessor had presided over the political reform and been relatively willing to negotiate with COCEI, with his own more hard-line choice, who was more open to the grievances of the right.

In the summer of 1983, an incident of violence, probably provoked by PRI, gave the state government a pretext for throwing COCEI out of office and appointing a PRI administrative council to run the city. The Coalition refused to leave City Hall and called out a massive demonstration, while federal troops arrived to patrol the streets and set up several permanent barracks in the city. After new elections were decided in favor of a young, professional PRI candidate, who officially won 54 percent of the vote, the army attacked City Hall, removed COCEI supporters, and instituted a period of severe repression, during which arrests and beatings of COCEI supporters were frequent. Four COCEI leaders, jailed without charges or trial, were named prisoners of conscience by Amnesty International.[13] The army set up a barracks inside City Hall and stood guard on the building's balconies until 1987, a military role unprecedented in recent Mexican politics.

The shift in Juchitán from political opening in 1980 to the repression of political competition in 1983 can be explained most simply in terms of local elite response to the radical politics of a democratically elected leftist opposition. COCEI challenged the economic and political monopolies of established elites, who then organized to oust the opposition. This explanation is compatible with that of a broad national shift from recognition of opposition electoral victories during the first years of the political reform to the denial of such victories after 1983. However, these analyses do not account for the success of COCEI in gaining office in 1980, its ability to survive and participate actively in politics after being removed from office, or the shape of the regime's reform project. Additional factors must be examined to understand these political relationships and outcomes, including COCEI's strategic choices, the changing role of the regime, the centrality of elections in political conflict and negotiation, the strength and autonomy of COCEI, and the new arrangements that followed the removal of COCEI from office.

First, COCEI made repeated strategic choices between confrontation and negotiation. These choices occurred in the fluid political situation of a new opposition government that had come to power in part because of the willingness of many people to vote for a radical political movement. Much of the political debate in the period during and after the COCEI government focused on charges of COCEI arbitrariness and unwillingness to apply the law impartially. These involved acts of appropriation, enforcement of the law, and distribution of patronage targeted at particular individuals. Although no one could claim that PRI had been less arbitrary than this in the past, and most would agree that its abuses had been significantly worse, the charges of arbitrariness and procedural illegality were leveled with great vehemence against the left and formed a central part of the popular discussion about the COCEI government among most of the middle and upper classes, as well as among poor *priístas*.

In addition, COCEI's approach to workplace and agricultural issues was based on mass mobilization tactics and was seen to involve threats of violence and occasional use of violence. Many middle-class sympathizers fault the COCEI government for its unwillingness to negotiate with local business people and offer them basic guarantees of a secure environment in exchange for reforms. They suggest that COCEI should have demonstrated a clear ability to run the city in a way that satisfied the private sector as well as COCEI's own mobilized supporters, and that if the organization had done this, it would have been able to stay in power longer, consolidate middle-class support, and carry out more reforms.

COCEI's grassroots supporters, however, were pleased by COCEI's successes and approach. They feel strongly that the Coalition acted consistently in the collective interest of poor workers and peasants and cite examples of the ways in which the organization was helpful to individuals. They speak of COCEI's integrity and effectiveness without criticizing the organization's militance with respect to local elites. COCEI supporters do not prefer procedural democracy, which occurs in some situations, to other forms of participation and decision-making characteristic of the organization. They express ongoing satisfaction with existing forms of popular participation and with the involvement and attentiveness of the organization's leaders, who make well-informed decisions based on interaction with supporters.

The involvement of the regime shaped the process of leftist challenge and elite response described above at every stage. COCEI could legally participate in elections and officially win because of regime decisions to change the electoral rules nationally and to permit particular outcomes in Juchitán. Furthermore, the ability of local economic and political organizations to effectively oppose COCEI—through strikes, violence, or influence on government policies—depended not only on their own organizations and political skills, but also on the changing willingness of the governor of Oaxaca and the minister of the interior to support such activities. The regime played a significant role in keeping repression to a minimum, contributing to the Coalition's own ability to continue to function as a strong and autonomous political force in the region. Finally, the regime acted to reshape both the local PRI and the pattern of government investment in Juchitán during the 1984–86 period of PRI government, and during subsequent municipal administrations as well.

Elections had an independent if ambiguous effect on the abilities of COCEI, the local PRI, and the regime to advance their interests in Juchitán, offering benefits and obstacles to each. Elections legitimized COCEI's goals of local sovereignty as well as its claim that majority support should bring with it the right to govern, the regime's own rhetoric about electoral democracy thus providing the opposition with a powerful rallying point. Furthermore, the procedures and norms surrounding elections, although they included many types of fraud, also limited the ability of the regime to achieve desired outcomes without serious complications. The interaction between regime and opposition redefined the rules and the ways they were enforced during each contest, and this process permitted not only opposition legitimacy but opposition victories as well.

The strength of COCEI was another important factor in the process of leftist challenge and elite response. As described in the previous section, this strength originated in the success of a grass roots movement in organizing poor people, fostering class consciousness, pursuing a mass mobilization strategy, and securing economic and political benefits. COCEI's strength enabled it not only to act powerfully against local economic and political elites and their organizations, but to interact directly with the regime, survive electoral defeats, outlast repression, and continue to act as advocates for poor people's interests through mass mobilizations, negotiation with government agencies, and participation in municipal elections.

1984–1986: STATE REPRESSION AND
A NEW REFORM PROJECT

After months of severe repression at the end of 1983 and the beginning of 1984, the regime initiated a variety of activities that would characterize its strategy in Juchitán. These included a public military presence, state investment in municipal services and infrastructure, respect for most civil liberties most of the time, elections without opposition victories, and reform of the local PRI. This strategy was gradually modified in subsequent years, as the regime permitted COCEI to participate in municipal government in 1986, removed the army from Juchitán in 1987, and recognized COCEI's victory in municipal elections in 1989. The actions of the regime in Juchitán neither destroyed nor substantially weakened the opposition, which continued to negotiate with the authorities and agencies of the state from a position of strength throughout the decade. Furthermore, the regime's long-term goals of transforming the region's economic and political structures face the severe constraints of national economic crisis and the strength of both the local PRI and COCEI.

After the army occupied Juchitán in the summer of 1983, it established three permanent barracks in the city, two of them located at the dividing lines between the center of the city and the poor neighborhoods where COCEI enjoys its greatest support, and one inside City Hall. In the course of 1984, constant patrolling of the city by armed vans gradually diminished, but the military and the state police continued to maintain a clear public presence. During this time, which coincided with the national economic crisis, the Mexican government invested unprecedented millions of pesos in Juchitán, building a bridge, beginning the construction of a sixty-bed hospital and a new market, remodeling City Hall and other buildings around the town plaza, cleaning irrigation canals, and extending the small network of paved streets. The new municipal government emphasized its professional character, as well as its ties to Mexican national culture, in public events; at the same time, in response to COCEI's success in using ethnicity to mobilize political support, PRI speeches were conducted in Zapotec more frequently than in the past.

After several months of repression, members of the Coalition were gradually—and unevenly—permitted to exercise their constitutional rights to free speech and assembly. These rights were limited by a tacit understanding that the plaza in front of City Hall was off limits, by police harassment and assault of COCEI activists, and by the continuing imprisonment of four Coalition leaders. However, compared to the repeated killings of the 1970s, the repression of the 1980s was restrained. The military crackdown of 1983 and 1984 acted to intimidate rather than destroy COCEI and neither killed nor seriously injured its leaders or supporters. Paramilitary right-wing violence occurred less frequently and with less intensity than it had in the 1970s. While half of COCEI's most important leaders were imprisoned, the other half resumed their normal organizing activities within months, and those in prison were released within a year and a half.

In 1985, COCEI mounted an active campaign for federal deputy, mobilizing supporters in meetings and marches throughout Juchitán and surrounding towns over a period of three months. COCEI also defended workers in a labor dispute, fought an increase in irrigation rates, and negotiated with housing authorities in Oaxaca to regularize land ownership and services in the COCEI housing development. While it was clear that COCEI would not win a majority in the Juchitán electoral district in the 1985 elections (it enjoyed majority support in a number of cities and towns, but less in others), the campaign for federal deputy served to demonstrate COCEI's survival and continuing strength, thus serving a particularly important purpose in a postrepression period. Furthermore, because the Coalition was assured a place on the proportional representation list of the Unified Socialist Party (PSUM), the campaign resulted in a victory and maintenance of an important channel for national publicity.

Participation in national legislative elections for the second time also marked the strengthening of COCEI's relationship with the Unified Socialist Party. After initial years of antagonism between the allies, the Coalition's respect for the party and the working relationship between the groups continued to develop, although tensions persisted. In 1983, COCEI made use of Unified Socialist Party support in fighting the regime's moves to oust the Ayuntamiento Popular, and its leaders acknowledged the national party's reliability. During the 1984 repression, however, there were disagreements about the strength of the party's commitment to defending COCEI. In 1985 and 1986 COCEI joined with two other national leftist parties, in addition to the Unified Socialist Party, in a statewide Democratic Coalition.

COCEI entered the 1986 municipal elections with its strength undiminished and ran a short, orderly campaign. Javier Charis, an accountant who taught at the regional Technological Institute, was older and more established professionally than COCEI's previous two candidates, and his campaign emphasized a moderate rather than militant approach, made overtures to the middle class, and promised accords rather than confrontation with business. At the same time, the local PRI experienced intensified conflict between its business and professional supporters, on the one hand, and those associated with the local political boss, on the other. This local conflict occurred in the context of important changes in state-level politics, and the interaction between state and local PRI leaders demonstrated both the regime's commitment to internal PRI reform in Juchitán and the strength of local resistance to those efforts.

In May 1986, Mexico City authorities surprised Oaxacans by designating as the official candidate for governor the most progressive of the precandidates, a long-time supporter of peasant claims within the CNC (National Peasant Confederation). The designation of Heladio Ramírez represented a clear effort on the part of the national authorities to recognize some of the claims of leftist groups in Oaxaca. Ramírez in turn chose a young member of the reformist wing of PRI in Juchitán, Jesús Pineda, as mayoral candidate there, demonstrating the regime's commitment to reform of the local party.[14] Political leaders in Juchitán, however, responded by physically threatening the newly appointed candidate, pressuring him to resign, and replacing him with a schoolteacher they could easily manipulate. The business and professional group in Juchitán, which had allied with Ramírez, then formed its own organization, refusing to support the official candidate and campaigning actively for abstention and for annulment of the elections. Looking ahead, they sought to demonstrate strength before the 1986 elections to gain support from the governor for political changes in Juchitán in the future.

As in the first 1980 elections and in 1983, PRI was declared the winner with 56 percent of the vote,[15] despite evidence of fraud in the preparation of the list of registered voters and the issuing of ID cards necessary for voting. In response, COCEI repeatedly blocked the Pan American Highway, stopping traffic between the states of Oaxaca, Chiapas, and Veracruz, as well as between much of southern Mexico and Guatemala, in an effort to pressure the Mexican government to annul the elections. Members of COCEI also carried out hunger strikes in the halls of the national legislature and in the state capital and staged demonstrations in front of Juchitán's City Hall. These actions, which led to long negotiations with state and national authorities, resulted in the annulment of elections in several towns surrounding Juchitán, providing the first official acknowledgment of regional strength for COCEI.

In Juchitán, COCEI's pressures for annulment coincided with similar tactics on the part of business people and the new governor, though each group had different goals for subsequent political arrangements. After both PRI and COCEI refused to participate in a coalition government headed by the newly elected PRI mayor, Ramírez named Felipe Martínez, a Oaxaca-based Juchiteco sociologist who had written a book about the conflict in Juchitán, as municipal administrator.[16] After lengthy negotiations, PRI and COCEI agreed to join in municipal government, with half the offices in the city government going to each group.

Events in Juchitán suggest that policymakers in Mexico City hope to resolve the political conflict in Juchitán through what they call economic and political "modernization." Through massive investment, they would put an end to the pervasive lack of basic services such as paved streets, drainage, and public lighting; improve public facilities such as hospitals and markets; and provide the infrastructure for commercial and urban development, such as a branch off the Pan American Highway that would pass through the center of the city. Politically, national and state leaders would press for the definitive ascendance of well-educated business people and professionals to positions of political authority in Juchitán. These new leaders, well aware of the economic costs of corruption, extreme poverty, and explosive class conflict, would work to clean up both municipal finances and the streets of Juchitán, extend public services, educate the "ignorant poor," and calm political tensions, thereby fostering a good investment climate and regaining support for the official party. Finally, while this plan is being carried out, the presence of the army would prevent the opposition from physically seizing power, an act that it could probably carry out with majority support. The army would avoid confrontation, and both civil and military authorities would act to permit the exercise of most civil rights so as to avoid provoking and thereby strengthening the opposition, as occurred in the past. The presence of the army would thus pave the way for a legal and orderly future.

This plan is not likely to work for both economic and political reasons. First, the continuing economic crisis brought the ambitious projects begun in 1984 to a halt within a year. Neither the hospital nor the market had been completed by the fall of 1986, rerouting of the highway had not begun, and drainage had been extended only several blocks. Second, the projects actually implemented favored improvements in public image, such as reconstruction of the public buildings around the central plaza, which addressed middle-class concerns, rather than efforts to extend education, health care, potable water, or drainage services to Juchitán's populous poor neighborhoods. As a result, people attributed what changes they saw to the success of COCEI in scaring the government into action, noting at the same time that they themselves, and poor people generally, benefited little. Third, public investment and even the possibility of temporary jobs did not easily buy off COCEI supporters. The movement's organizing success of the 1970s and early 1980s, based as it was on ethnicity, class consciousness, and municipal self-government, fostered the development of steadfast loyalty. Fourth, COCEI will act to take advantage of the regime's economic and political projects in the Isthmus, using the tensions and transformations of economic development as well as political conflict within PRI to strengthen itself as an organization and secure gains for its worker and peasant supporters.

Finally, the local PRI had resisted political reform for forty years, despite state and national pressures. Although this may have endangered what reformers have seen as the long-term interest of the party, the local political system, tied always to state and national networks, served effectively to enrich a political class, provide a handful of leaders with considerable authority and prestige, and maintain public order. After the formation of COCEI in the 1970s, when reform was perhaps most necessary, it was least likely, because the old-style political leaders were those most capable of taking charge and opposing the new movement, however ineffectively. National leaders supported the establishment of a new political *cacique,* willing to countenance and even promote right-wing violence, and this boss and his supporters played a central role in removing COCEI from office in 1983. Despite the initiation of a new round of reform efforts on the part of national authorities in the subsequent period, these politicians continued to participate actively in managing both repression and municipal administration.

The difficulties encountered by Heladio Ramírez in exercising the customary rights of an incoming governor to designate mayors demonstrates the tenacity of the *cacique* system, however modified it has been since the 1930–60 period. At the same time, Ramírez's appointment as gubernatorial candidate, his overtures to leftist groups statewide, and his naming of a municipal administrator in Juchitán may indicate a reform commitment of unprecedented strength in recent Oaxacan history, and Ramírez may exert continuous pressure for political change in Juchitán. However, the combination of economic crisis, COCEI strength, and entrenched political bosses, together with the continuing high level of political consciousness and class conflict in Juchitán, suggests that the reform process will yield unintended consequences and virtually ensures that it will be uneven. One predictable consequence will be the continued activity of COCEI as a permanent opposition with majority or near-majority support in Juchitán.[17]

NOTES

I would like to thank the Doherty Foundation, the Inter-American Foundation, and the Social Science Research Council for their financial support for this research. All views expressed are my own. Much of the discussion of local history as well as the views of different groups in Juchitán are based on field research I carried out in Juchitán in 1985 and 1986. This article was written in 1987 and does not include discussion of the effects of coalition government between 1986 and 1989, or of the 1989 COCEI victory. A longer version of this article appeared in Alvarado (1987).

   1. The Popular Socialist Party, in contrast to the Communist Party and its descen-

dant, the Unified Socialist Party, is not a leftist party and was recognized as an "official" opposition party long before the political reform legalized the Communist Party in 1978.

2. For a brief history of opposition activities within PRI, see Marco Antonio Gutiérrez (1982).

3. Changes in land tenure patterns did not happen without conflict. For details on the López Mateos administration's plan to turn the region into an *ejido,* a move that might have protected peasant landholdings, see Binford (1985:179–85). Binford describes the successful, elite-led, anti-*ejido* movement in the Isthmus. As a result of this effort, virtually all the irrigated land in the Juchitán district remained in private hands, to be freely bought and consolidated in subsequent years. Data on the shift from agricultural to commercial, industrial, and service work between 1960 and 1980 appears in Jhabvala (1982).

4. A number of authors, as well as the leadership of COCEI, argue that these economic changes were indeed a threat to the survival of the region's poor, and they would disagree with the interpretation presented here. A good example of this view is presented in López Monjardin (1983). I agree that economic changes indeed caused enormous economic and social disruptions and that these were central to the development of class-based politics. I argue, however, that the means of economic survival were available in the urban economy and that people took advantage of these opportunities. The struggle, in this view, was not over physical survival, but rather what kinds of lives people would lead and on what terms.

5. For a variety of basic histories of COCEI, see Bailón (1985), R. J. Gutiérrez (1981), López Monjardin (1983b), Martinez López (1985), Matloff (1982), Ornelas Esquinca (1983), Prévot-Shapira and Rivière d'Arc (1984), and Taller de Investigación Sociológica (1984).

6. Zapotec identity in Juchitán withstood the destructive pressures of Mexican national culture in the nineteenth and twentieth centuries partly because economic advancement in the city was not equated with the casting off of indigenous language and other traditions, as it has been in other parts of Mexico. In Juchitán, middle-class and lower-middle-class families often live in communal courtyards in poor neighborhoods, participate in family and neighborhood traditions, and consider themselves to be part of "the poor people." Furthermore, the bourgeoisie in Juchitán, in contrast to economically similar groups in other parts of Mexico, has not rejected its indigenous identity and generally insists that its children speak Zapotec and participate in customary rituals, even as they learn to function in the educational and business environments of wealthy Mexicans.

7. In addition to sources listed in note 5, see Amnesty International (1986:47–63).

8. For examples of the debate about electoral participation, see Saul López, "La COCEI ante las elecciones," *Satélite* (Juchitán), Apr. 8, 11, 22 and May 6, 20, 1979; and Alberto López Morales, "Votar o abstenerse," *Satélite,* Apr. 29 and May 6, 13, 1979.

9. The best discussion of the conflicts within PRI appears in Martínez López

(1985). For reporting on municipal corruption, see the issues of the local newspaper *El Satélite* (Juchitán) throughout 1978 and 1979.

10. Thorough coverage of these events can be found in the Oaxaca newspaper, *Hora Cero,* 1981–82.

11. The Unified Socialist Party of Mexico (PSUM) resulted from the union of the Communist Party and other leftist parties.

12. My thanks to Adriana López Monjardin for her observations about the political and social use of public space.

13. See Amnesty International (1986:47–63). Three of the four were released after twenty months in jail.

14. Without acknowledging the underlying causes of poverty or challenging prevailing patterns of economic development, those whom I call reformists within PRI support administrative efficiency and an end to corruption, much like the reformers who fought to oust machine politicians in U.S. cities.

15. Official results gave PRI slightly more than 50 percent in 1980, 48 percent in the subsequent 1981 contest, and 54 percent in 1983. These relatively constant electoral figures were accompanied by an 84-percent increase in the number of voters between 1981 and 1986, a result of the increased importance of elections during this period and the efforts of both PRI and COCEI to mobilize voters.

16. In his 1985 book, Martínez López argued that the strength of COCEI arose more from PRI weakness and errors than from enduring mass support, thus suggesting that reform of PRI would enable the party to regain support in the city.

17. COCEI's 1989 electoral victory and President Salinas's 1990 visit to Juchitán, including a meeting with Mayor Héctor Sánchez, demonstrate COCEI's enduring strength and the ongoing nature of political negotiation between COCEI and the regime. Salinas's visit brought promises of major development projects in the region, along with acceptance of the Coalition's demand for participation in the planning process.

Coceístas in front of Juchitán City Hall awaiting a political meeting in support of Mexican Socialist Party presidential candidate Heberto Castillo. March 1988. Photo by H. Campbell.

Testimonies
of
COCEI
Women

Collected by Marta Bañuelos

TOGETHER IN STRUGGLE

"Ten years ago, when COCEI began, my husband joined the struggle. As his *compañera,* I was at his side. Thus, I am also on the side of COCEI, the people, workers, peasants, and students of town. From the moment he joined, I would follow him, and he never said, 'Don't go.' On the contrary, he said, 'We must fight together for the good of our children.' Then I had an idea, and I still maintain it: I am fighting for the people. My children also participated in the rallies, neighborhood meetings, and assemblies because they are in agreement with me and the ideas of their father." —Hermila Guerra (market vendor, widow of Rodrigo Carrasco, a former COCEI city councilman, and mother of five)

I ADMIRE THE ENTERPRISE OF THE WOMEN

"One thing I have admired in the people of Juchitán is the women's drive to engage their *compañeros,* children, and brothers in the struggle for the rights of their people. And I have seen, throughout this time, that the women of the Isthmus, Juchitán, and especially COCEI have participated decisively in hunger strikes, office seizures, and other types of protest. We know that our *compañeros* cannot take part because of the current climate of repression in Oaxaca, principally Juchitán. Therefore, women have stood alone; they have conducted protest vigils by themselves." —Vicenta Pineda (teacher, member of the COCEI teachers' organization, divorced with one child)

INSTEAD OF HOLDING MEN BACK WE SUPPORT THEM

"I began to participate in COCEI after they kidnapped Professor Víctor Pineda Henestrosa [1978]. That is when women began to mobilize, because men could not leave their work to investigate where they were holding him. We met several times to see what we could do, and then we did it. Yes, it is important for women to participate in the movement along with men, because instead of holding them back and telling them not to go, quite the opposite, we support them and go with them. We participate in the rallies and marches, and do what work we can, such as distributing literature and attending meetings. Recently, as a result of PRI/government repression, it is at times more dangerous for men to protest. Hence the women organize themselves and go to the district attorney's office." —Lucila Villalobos (housewife, four children)

OUR COMPAÑEROS WERE IN DANGER

"My husband began to participate politically after he retired from the army. Earlier he was one of the founders of the Frente Unico Democrático. I, as his wife, and the wives of other leaders formed the Women's Committee in one neighborhood. Now we have fourteen neighborhood committees where everyone, man and woman, participates. When the government took over City Hall, they jailed many *compañeros,* and we women were the ones who went to protest. We were aware of the danger to our *compañeros.* I can tell you, as a mother and wife, that I am proud of my son and husband, but I am also proud of the townspeople who struggle for a better life." —Luisa de la Cruz (wife of Leopoldo de Gyves Pineda, COCEI elder statesmen, and mother of Leopoldo de Gyves de la Cruz, former mayor of Juchitán)

WOMEN ARE MERCHANTS
AND THEIR OPINIONS ALSO MATTER

"Women participate in labor problems, but still not as much as they should. However, their participation in the COCEI political struggle is very important. Women work in commerce, which is based on interchange. The husband gives her the harvest and she sells it and returns home with the money or whatever is needed. Women take care of commerce and, therefore, have a right to their opinions. Women's opinions are decisive. On the other hand, in the teacher's movement, many *compañeros* prevent their women from taking part. I am divorced and that is why I participate more. Women are made to study education because it takes less time. In the teacher's colleges there are always many women." —Vicenta Pineda

WOMEN ANALYZE AND MAKE DECISIONS

"Before, the women only attended assemblies. Now they are the ones who analyze and make decisions." —Modesta Antonio Girón (teacher, representative for female members of her teacher's union)

I AM FROM A POOR FAMILY, I HAVE THEIR SUPPORT

"I do not like to be a parasite on my family like some of the rich kids [*burguesitos*] of Juchitán. But it is necessary for my parents to support me so that I can work full-time for the organization. There is no other way. My mother is very sentimental and has suffered a lot. Her gray hair reflects her sixty years of age. The first time I went to jail she cried and asked me to stay out of politics. That is why I told my father not to have her come see me behind bars. My father is different: He says he will make them pay for what they do to me. I am from a poor family, the poorest in the country, but I have their moral support." —Vicky (COCEI activist, taxi driver)

I ALSO SUFFERED THE REPRISALS

"I am the wife of Professor Víctor Pineda Henestrosa, who was kidnapped on July 11, 1978, by the army. I had been participating in COCEI, like any other militant, since the movement began. As a result of the kidnapping, I became more fully involved. I participated in rallies and strikes that the organization held in order to free him and the other imprisoned *compañeros*. One of the neighborhood committees (of Ward Seven) meets here in my house. My neighbors from the seventh ward meet weekly on Thursdays to present all of their problems of a social nature, problems between neighbors, and between spouses. Compañero Lorenzo, who is the neighborhood representative, and other *compañeros,* resolve all of the problems. That is how the committee of Ward Seven functions. For example, in the electoral struggle we prepared food, distributed pamphlets, and held rallies together with our *compañeros*. We have also been speakers at rallies or other COCEI events.

"My husband began to participate in COCEI from the beginning, advising peasants. He was adviser to the Commissioner of Communal Lands in 1977, but in 1975 the peasants themselves named him agrarian representative and he also became head of Promotoría Agraria [Agrarian Promotion] for the Ministry of Agrarian Reform branch in Juchitán. He worked there for two years because the peasants wanted him to. Later, he was only an adviser, and precisely because of his assistance to the peasants they kidnapped him.

"I participated in COCEI's government as a council member. I also suffered all the reprisals against the Ayuntamiento Popular. July 31, 1983, to January 1, 1984, were the most terrible moments for *coceístas*. Miraculously, I was not there the day the military took over City Hall. I left at midnight because my children wanted me to be with them. At times it was difficult to take care of the house and work in city government because I also continued to teach, and it was sometimes very tiring.

"I always got my work done. In my free time I can do whatever I want, but I always go to class and do my job during work hours. In this respect, I have been very careful because we depend on my job. I have never given them a motive for criticizing me or saying that I did not go to work. When it was necessary to march in the streets on Saturday or Sunday, some kids greeted me and called me 'teacher.' After that, the *compañeros* told me, 'You can see that nobody knows you.' " —Candida Santiago (teacher, mother of two children, and spouse of the only "disappeared" member of COCEI)

CONSERVING TRADITION

"Juchitán is one of the few towns that conserve their traditions. The Ayuntamiento Popular held several contests related to Zapotec culture. We are Zapotec in our way of dressing, our speech, and our origins. Here in the seventh ward, we all speak Zapotec. Many are monolingual. The older people speak only Zapotec, but the children speak it too. My children also took part in COCEI. When Radio Ayuntamiento Popular operated, my two children were announcers. They sang and read poetry and folklore in the children's program. My son also recited or sang in the civic programs of the Ayuntamiento Popular." —Candida Santiago

I NEVER TURNED BACK

"On January 1, 1984, they detained and tortured me. I was disappeared for three days. My mother, children, relatives, and *compañeros* did not know where I was held. But I stood firm against the bandits. They did not scare me for a minute because I knew that the struggle of COCEI was just. Four days later they turned me over to the municipal jail. There they kept me for ten more days, but I never turned back. On the contrary, I returned with more desire and courage to keep fighting. The days when I was disappeared I knew where they had me, but they threatened and tortured me." —Hermila Guerra

IN SPITE OF HER PREGNANCY, SHE PARTICIPATED

"There have been *compañeras* who have died in the struggle. We have the case of Lorenza Santiago, who was shot down in protest against vote fraud by then mayor-elect Mario Bustillos Villalobos, who, in fact, is currently president of the local PRI. Compañera Santiago was shot down. I should mention that despite their children and their pregnancies, women participate. Compañera Lorenza was pregnant, and one of the bullets that hit her destroyed the skull of the fetus. Instead of scaring women, these things have made them more politically aware. Although such things could happen to them also, they remain in the struggle." —Vicenta Pineda

IN A ROOM WITH SIXTY *CABRONES*

"The first time they caught me [May 30, 1984], they held me along with *compañeras* Paty Peña and Antonina Pineda, who is in charge of the neighborhood committees. The first day we were incommunicado, and they would not let us have food. Then they took us to the main jail. We left City Hall with our hands in cuffs behind our backs. Once again, they took me back to City Hall, pulling me by the handcuffs. At eight o'clock at night they took me to a room with sixty *cabrones* that was one and one-half by two meters. I had not eaten all day. The prisoners invited me to eat when they were brought food, but I was not even hungry. It was very hot. We got out on June 3. They charged us with damage to private property—forty-three houses—and to federal property for having painted political slogans in the plaza. The damages were for who knows how many thousands, I don't know. The point is that after a new investigation we made bail. Now we have to sign our names every three days in the district attorney's office [Ministerio Público].

"The second time, I was caught alone. Before that time, the repression was much worse, especially at the beginning of 1984. By February and March we held rallies in the seventh ward. To avoid problems we did not go downtown— because we are not violent, we are valiant, which is different, and we are valiant by tradition. On November 18, we held a large march to the center of town, which hurt the State very much because we had returned downtown once again to demand freedom for our prisoners. On the nineteenth, I left my house at ten o'clock in the morning to go to the committee office and later see Jesús. At one o'clock in the afternoon they detained me. When I saw them I ran to a soft drink stand but they dragged me out with a pistol to my head. I had heard rumors that Rojo [powerful local *cacique* and until recently a PRI supporter] wanted to grab me. But this time they had no charges to bring against me. They took me to City Hall. As I went up the stairs I saw many people from the state government and the army. Rojo gave them direct orders: 'Take her to you know where.' They waited until the municipal workers left City Hall. At 9:30 P.M. they blindfolded me and tied my arms behind my back. I had my hair in my face, and I told them that it itched. When one of them scratched me, I spit on his hand. Then they grabbed my hair and shaved me with an old razor blade. At about 11 P.M. I was very sleepy, but I could not sit down because the floor of the jail—which is actually a secret room—was all wet, my huaraches were wet, and I was cold. At about 12:30 A.M., one of the four that detained me came to tell me that they were going to let me go free. They were such bastards that (after the fact) they could not even believe they had shaved me.

"When I got out I found out there had been a rally outside. COCEI negotiated directly with the State for my release. They told the government, 'If you don't let her go, you will have to detain others also, but the important thing is that she not be alone, that she have a *compañera* with her.' The twelve hours I was held they never let me have food or see my family.

"I will be at the next rally [March 17, 1985], which is the beginning of the campaign of the PSUM-COCEI candidate for deputy, because if I do not go, PRI will say that by shaving, raping, and torturing our *compañeras* they can scare us. But no, I will be there.

"My blood is not hot, but it boils every time I see a PRI member. Yes, I am scared, but with a pistol to the head, who would not be? They should not violate the law like that. But there are limits to this, and for me to stop participating is impossible [*está cabrón*]. They can fuck their mothers, but I will not leave the struggle. I lost my hair and many more things, but I did not lose my life." —Vicky

Inaugural Speech as Mayor of Juchitán

Leopoldo de Gyves de la Cruz

March 10, 1981

My fellow Juchitecos, all of my *compañeros:*

At this moment, no one can deny a great truth: Today the Juchitán people govern themselves. The road to this great victory has been long. It began in 1911 with Che Gómez in the lead and continued in 1931 with Valentín Carrasco and Roque Robles. There were seventy years of constant struggle to gain respect for the popular will. The long road traveled by the Juchitecos has been fertilized with the blood of Juchitán's most worthy sons; with the blood of José F. Gómez, Roque Robles, Valentín Carrasco, Lorenza Santiago Esteva in 1974, José Yola on January 1, 1978; with the imprisonment of Polo de Gyves Pineda in 1978; and with the recent jailing of six *compañeros* in Mexico City for the seizure of the Guatemalan and Indian embassies.

Fertilized with the sacrifices of many Juchitecos, that road today bears fruit with our conquest of municipal power. We have now written the most brilliant pages of our history. With the occupation of City Hall on November 20, 1980, and the takeover of the embassies on February 18, 1981, we taught the Mexican people that in order to win, registration and voting are not enough. It is also necessary to maintain ironclad unity, to struggle combatively, and to have the full support of the people. We have set a great example. We have demonstrated that our enemies, the exploiters, are not invincible. We have shown that with unity, struggle, and national support it is possible to take away their power. Today, my countrymen, Juchitán governs itself.

Beginning today, we will plan great projects, and we will confront new problems. If we strengthen the unity of Juchitecos, remain permanently mobilized, and can continue to count on the support of the Mexican people, we will overcome all obstacles. We have struggled for a new type of government, and for the elimination of the puppet regimes composed of *priístas* and run by the state government. Now we want to establish a relationship of mutual respect and equality between the people's government and the state government. From this forum, we appeal to the people of Juchitán to remain united and vigilant and to make sure the state government fulfills its promise to grant to Juchitán a three-year budget exceeding 300 million pesos, which will serve as the basis for furthering the great projects we have proposed and for carrying out the popular measures Juchitán needs in order to escape once and for all from backwardness and abandon.

Today, more than ever, it is clear that our electoral victory would not have been possible without the Juchitecos' trust and great faith. This victory is the greatest homage to the martyrs of the people of Juchitán.

Our enemies, the *caciques,* exploiters, and land barons, have initiated a campaign to prevent this town from having a new government. In their first offensive, our enemies were defeated. Juchitán now has its new government, but new attacks will come. Smear campaigns have already begun against the Coalition: "Subversives take over City Hall, armed men and delinquents from terrorist organizations occupy City Hall." Newspapers like *Noticias* and the magazine *Tesis* are trying to ruin the reputation of this new government, but no slander campaign can be effective in our town. All campaigns of lies will shatter in the face of the Juchitecos' confidence in their organization, the Worker-Peasant-Student Coalition of the Isthmus of Tehuantepec (COCEI).

Alternatives
for Struggle:
The Context
of the
COCEI
Alternative

COCEI

First we will address the economic, social, and political situation of the region. There we find a clear polarization. On one side are the monopolists, possessors of the means of production and political control. On the other side are the proletarianized peasants, some of whom are owners of about five hectares, but who sell their labor power to meet their families' expenses. Others form part of the sector that owns nothing and is obliged to offer its services during the agricultural cycle and work as artisans the rest of the time. Monopolized agricultural land constitutes the key factor for capital accumulation. Similar economic units have been created in the fishing industry.

Industrialization is still on a small scale; thus there are few workers, most of whom are from peasant and artisan families. In spite of this, workers have played an important role in the COCEI struggle.

Artisanry and commerce constitute other sources of income for Isthmus families. The artisan's products are also monopolized. On the other side are merchants with capital who maintain a sector of the population in misery with monthly salaries ranging from 300 to 500 pesos. This sector is made up primarily of women.

The inhabitants of the Oaxacan Isthmus of Tehuantepec conserve their autochthonous culture and, as part of this, their language, Zapotec. From birth, children are educated according to the traditions and customs of the region. For that reason, the vast majority are monolingual, that is, they speak only Zapotec.

"No Money, No Food; Stop Attacks on the People's Government! COCEI Women in Struggle." Photo by E. López.

The children of peasants, fishermen, artisans, musicians, etc. enter the first phase of education lacking any knowledge of Spanish. Primary education is given in Spanish, which is difficult for them. On the other hand, there is another kind of child, who comes from the families of the dominant classes. These children have the advantages of preschool education and knowledge of Spanish, and because of this are granted many privileges and facilities. Consequently, children of the popular classes are treated as if they were handicapped. Education, then, benefits the children of the dominant classes.

This educational contrast is due to the fact that the workers' children do not have access to preschool, where the other children learn Spanish and how to work with class materials. We should also point out the lack of bilingual teachers. These deficiencies carry on into future studies.

Another factor that intervenes in the educational environment is the economic condition of the parents. On one hand, the children of the rich have the means to obtain books, private tutors, or assistance from their parents, who have enough education to be able to help them. These children have enough time to dedicate to their studies and are well nourished and healthy. On the other hand, the children of the poor, in the majority of cases, have to work from a young age as shoeshine boys, paper boys, or gum sellers to sustain their families. They therefore neglect their studies. Their parents are illiterate and cannot help them. They are victims of malnutrition and diseases resulting from unhealthy conditions. All of this contributes to, and is directly reflected in, the deficiencies in their education. When these children go on to secondary school they take with them the same economic and social problems. Now they must confront teachers who, because of family ties or economic interests, or because they identify fully with the sons of the exploiters, represent the *caciques*. Scholarships, the highest grades, and other facilities are destined for the privileged ones. The humble students are attacked, humiliated, and mistreated in the classrooms.

High school and post-high school education have one goal: to create technicians to serve the privileged classes. Hence the students study to become industrial, agricultural, and fishing technicians. Because of the low level of industrialization in the Isthmus, peasants' children have a difficult time finding work. The few available jobs are set aside for the *caciques'* children. As a result, there are many unemployed technicians who, because of the lack of funding to continue their education, are forced to work as peons and unskilled laborers, thus wasting their studies.

Because of poverty or because the colleges reject them as a result of their academic deficiencies, there are fewer poor students at the university level. Of those who do make it to college, the majority have to work to support themselves. Economic problems, together with a lack of study time, lead to a high dropout rate.

The situation outlined herein is not an isolated case; it forms part of the social reality of the country. Throughout the country, misery, injustice, and oppression permeate both the countryside and the city. The peasants are marginalized with minimal incomes and no education or medical care. They live with the illusion that one day the State will give them a piece of land. They have been soliciting land for ten or twenty years, and the documentation for land redistribution cases has turned yellow from sitting in the files so long. The life of workers in the city is much the same.

When the rural and urban workers organize to demand their rights they are brutally repressed. Protest is countered by jailing or even assassination. The State also employs its organs of social control to implant modern models of Mexican dependent capitalism. A clear example of this is the Echeverría regime. Without pretending to make a profound analysis of what the Echeverría regime represented, we will point out some central elements of his government. This will be the second reference point for locating the COCEI alternative.

The Mexican political system has dressed up the national model of capitalist development in new clothes. Echeverría used populist politics to gain a social base. From this foundation he proposed the modernization of capitalism and fortification of the State so that it could efficiently carry out its role as the guardian of capital. Modernization involved increasing production. In both the countryside and the city it entailed modernization of the instruments of production. To achieve this, it was necessary for Echeverría to look abroad in search of capital and technology.

To advance his project he needed to strengthen the State, which was then in crisis because of the brutal repression of the previous regime. Echeverría mounted a campaign, demagogically proclaiming that, at that moment, there was a greater margin for democracy. His famous "democratic opening" signified a supposed dialogue with different sectors of society and an announced, but not respected, freedom of the press.

This project had a strong impact on the countryside. The sold-out organizations denounced the existence of *latifundios*, raised demands for collective *ejidos*, etc. This can be explained. Collectivization implemented by the State is the basis for modernization of capitalism in agriculture. The new Federal Agrarian Reform Law gives legal recognition to *ejidos* so that they can obtain credit. This permits modernization of the means of production, initiation of capital accumulation in the countryside, and the creation of an *ejido* elite. It promotes the renting and monopolization of land.

Peasants have been struggling for many years to reclaim the country's *latifundios*. Echeverría used *agrarista* [proagrarian] jargon and promised to turn over the solicited lands. Nevertheless, only a minimal portion of the *latifundios* were affected, many of which have not been turned over to the peasants because they are protected by restraining orders.

The modernization project came into conflict with the most reactionary elements of the national and international bourgeoisie, who could not comprehend that Echeverría was neither an *agrarista*, nor a unionist, nor (even less) a communist, as some called him. Instead, he was the faithful guardian of the long-term interests of the bourgeoisie.

With the advent of López Portillo, the situation changed for the reasons mentioned, particularly in the countryside. López Portillo declared that there was no land left to distribute and proclaimed the alliance for production. He attempted to reconcile his government with that fraction of the bourgeoisie that had clashed with Echeverría. This defines López Portillo's agrarian politics and permits us to predict repression against organizations independent from the State that struggle to improve workers' living conditions.

This brand of politics has begun in the Isthmus of Tehuantepec. We are aware that the State, given its class character and the interests it represents and defends, is incapable of solving the economic, social, and political problems of the region or the country. These problems can be resolved to the benefit of the popular classes when those classes are exclusively responsible for resolving them. In the meantime, the people of the Isthmus and COCEI prepare to assume their responsibilities in this historic moment. We can advance by extracting partial solutions to our problems from the State. This defines the character of our alternatives for struggle and the method for implementing them: wide popular mobilization.

The current López Portillo regime does not intend to resolve the region's agrarian problems. Instead, it guarantees the interests of the monopolists and *caciques,* as in the case of the Juchitán *ejido.* Faced with the impossibility of protecting the Isthmus rural bourgeoisie with the Federal Agrarian Reform Law, the government is applying the Idle Lands Law. This is clearly anti-constitutional, because this law is applicable only to private land and not to the Juchitán *ejido,* which consists of communal lands converted to *ejido* status.

The State was forced by its loss of power and real control over the peasant masses to abandon demagoguery and use the military to impose solutions that favor the bourgeoisie. The army began to intervene more frequently in the life of the villages, not only to control the popular movements but also to impose on the workers and peasants the conditions favored by the bourgeoisie and the State. Thus they displaced legally constituted authorities. Little by little, Mexico is turning into a country governed by the military and the repressive forces it represents.

We can summarize this exposition in the following way:

The predominant forms of land tenure in the Isthmus are communal and *ejido.*

The State and the *caciques* are trying to impose (with maneuvers and military pressure) private property on us, because the form of land tenure creates the organizational forms the peasants will use in their struggle.

Land monopolization is promoted by the credit banks and the Agrarian Reform Ministry.

Monopolization has generated and increased the number of agricultural workers.

North American imperialism intends to penetrate the Isthmus as an alternative to the Panama Canal.

The Isthmus peasants are joined in a struggle for the recovery of their lands and for better living conditions in alliance with workers, students, and the people, and this alliance has been decisive in the progress not only of the peasant struggle, but of the popular movement in general.

The Worker-Peasant-Student Coalition of the Isthmus of Tehuantepec (COCEI) is the organized expression of the masses in struggle.

The peasants struggle for democratization of the *ejidos.*

The peasants have overcome the economistic stage and now engage in political struggle.

The State cannot solve agrarian problems. It is the peasants themselves, in alliance with oppressed sectors, who should impose the solutions to their demands.

In view of this situation, COCEI proposes the following:

Ouster of monopolists from the land.

Collective exploitation of land for the benefit of the communities and under the direction of its authentic representatives.

Return of the land to the Istmeños.

Satisfaction of peasant demands for credit, timely irrigation at low cost, and better prices for their crops.

Organization of agricultural workers independent from the sold-out *(charra)* unions.

Struggle for better living and working conditions for rural and urban workers.

Struggle for an education that responds to the interests and needs of the region's indigenous people and that addresses their specific characteristics.

Removal of the army from our communities.

An end to the use of the army as a form of government control.

An end to repression and freedom for peasant political prisoners.

Promotion of regional peasant movements in alliance with the workers, popular sectors, and students.

Linkage of these movements to learn about each other's problems and engage in support actions. Formation of a national revolutionary peasant organization.

COCEI:
Narodniks
of
Southern Mexico?

Sergio Zermeño

The activities of the Narodniks, wrote Andrzej Walicki,

> began at the end of the 1860s in a movement known as *khozhdenie u narod* (Going to the People). The intellectuals, dressed in the style of the peasants, traveled over the Russian countryside spreading their ideas of reform. The persecutions they were subjected to led them to create, in 1876, the secret organization, *Zemlya i Volya* (Land and Liberty), and turn from nonviolent propagandizing to terrorism and conspiracy. (Walicki 1970:81)

The Russian populist movement, as it was generically known, had a strong ideological and cultural content derived from the very character of its instigators. Nevertheless, it was opposed to the "abstract intellectualism" of certain more purely Marxist revolutionaries who tried to educate the peasants by imposing on them the ideals of Western socialism, instead of learning what their true needs were and supporting the interests and ideals of the peasants themselves (Walicki 1970:83). Around 1870, one of its currents reached the extreme—paradoxical because of the very character of the movement's promoters—of declaring that the "intelligentsia" should leave room for the opinions of the people.

But populism consisted, fundamentally, in the preeminence of the "principles of the people" in opposition to capitalism. Lenin precisely stated that populism was "a protest formulated against capitalism from the point of view of the small direct producers who, ruined by capitalist development, saw in it only regression, but at the same time demanded the abolition of ancient feudal forms of exploitation" (Lenin, quoted in Walicki 1970:85). For the populists, capitalism was equivalent to expropriation, proletarianization, and the absolute misery of the masses. It provoked the growing divorce between "national wealth" and the "well-being of the people."

However, the populist movement was not merely a reactionary phenomenon in the sense of always thinking that the past was better (although one must accept that this was an erroneous but very widespread reading of Lenin's theses). In reality, although the populists opposed the bourgeois development of Russia, they harbored the hope that the present form of the commune would make possible a direct transition to socialism. This was the golden principal of *narodnichestvo* (Russian populism). Moreover, in many parts of the world, as Walicki notes, "the idea of a non-capitalist development of backward countries has become a reality" (1970:86). This profoundly undermined the classical thinking about evolutionism (i.e., that there were necessary stages of development) from which had been launched the harshest critiques of the populists, and against which the populists struggled from early on, and rightly so, in the history of Marxism. In fact, populist authors like Mikhailovsky relied on several observations that Marx himself had outlined in *Capital* and detailed later:

> Communism is the rebirth of the highest form of archaic property relations represented by the Russian peasant commune, and, consequently, in Russia it would be possible—assuming that the external conditions were favorable—to pass directly from the rural communes to modern communist production on a large scale. (Karl Marx, cited in Walicki 1970)

Despite forming part of a single movement, the populists divided fundamentally into two groups, a fact that has great relevance for the case that concerns us here. On one side was the group labeled the Enlighteners, whose characteristics Lenin enumerated as follows: "1) Violent hostility to serfdom and all its economic, social, and legal products; 2) Ardent advocacy of education, self-government, and all-round Europeanization of Russia generally, and 3) Defense of the interests of the masses, chiefly of the peasants" (Lenin, quoted in Walicki 1970). The conceptions of the Enlighteners did not reflect the point of view of the small producer. Some of the Enlighteners, such as Chernyshevskii, were decidedly pro-Western. At the same time, they defended the peasant commune with great energy and thought that Russia could modernize by passing directly to socialism without the suffering that capitalism has brought to the masses.

On the other side was a group that Lenin called the economic romanticists. Romanticism "means a criticism of capitalism from the point of view of a backward-looking petty-bourgeois utopia, an idealization of a pre-capitalist type of economy and social relations" (Walicki 1970:93). By considering capitalism as a form of deterioration, the populists affirmed the belief that the traditional Russian economic system, the *artel*,[1] and other similar forms of property were exceptional in character. In this sense, populist economic romanticism meant localism or, at most, regionalism. But it overlooked legal connections with national political institutions and lost sight of or rejected universal or global conceptions of either economic progress or cultural values (and of the ties between local and national economies).

"Progress," wrote Mikhailovsky, "consists in the gradual advance toward the integrated individual, the most complete and diversified division of labor possible among the organs of the human being, and the least possible division of labor among men" (Mikhailovsky, quoted in Walicki 1970:102). "This formula," added Walicki, "expresses the very essence of the backward-looking populist utopia that idealized the primitive peasant economy, placing great value on its autarky and independence with respect to the capitalist market" (Walicki 1970:112).

In any case, populism, in its overall tendencies, proves not to be an absolutely condemnable social, political, and ideological manifestation: "In theoretical matters, populism resembles a Janus who looks with one face toward the past and another toward the future," affirmed Lenin. Andrzej Walicki added, "In approaching populist socialism from the perspective of our times, it is difficult to deny that not only the 'backward-looking' but also the 'forward-looking' face of Janus can be discovered in it" (Walicki 1970:95).

Presently, judging by these considerations about populism, the possibilities for development implicit in the peasant commune seem realizable if autarkic economic romanticism is overcome and if democratic, antifeudal radicalism (read also antilatifundism) is converted into agrarian anticapitalist socialism. Is this possible under modern communal productive forms, though on a smaller scale than Marx imagined?

INTEGRATION INTO THE NATIONAL POLITY AND ECONOMY OR ESCAPE INTO LOCALISM, IDEOLOGICAL PURISM, AND VIOLENCE?

The history and present of COCEI are not situated outside the coordinates marked by this discussion. On one hand, we can clearly discover a scenario in which, supported by a popular, peasant, and indigenous base, a leadership appears that seizes on an ethnic, linguistic, educational, and cultural heritage and

Sergio Zermeño

ends up secluding itself defensively in regionalism, or even more, in *lo juchi-teco* and localism. Several "informants," from Mexico City, expressed little hope that COCEI might become a regional movement or, at least, an organization that would pull together the municipalities that make up the Isthmus of Tehuantepec (at least the Oaxacan Isthmus, let alone the Veracruzan Isthmus). On the other hand, a contrasting choreography is imaginable in which the leadership does not identify exclusively with the popular masses but seeks its bases also among the middle class and even among the dynamic merchants and manufacturers. Economic development would predominate instead of the recreation of the cultural heritage (there would be, in fact, a decline of the latter). Additionally, communication with the political system and the national economy would tend to be fluid.

Naturally, Juchitán has never had a political or economic elite with these characteristics. PRI, always identified with corruption, *caciquismo,* and monopolism, was historically disqualified from fulfilling such a function. In 1981, when PRI wanted to dress up in the clothing of modernity, change, and efficiency, it was too late, and PRI was unable to avoid an electoral catastrophe.

But this does not mean that COCEI is condemned to remain within the first model. We have already seen how a populist current was capable of making the inevitable connection with modern economic and technological development while appealing in an intelligent manner to the property forms and cultural roots to which it was heir. It is true that Soviet power was not very respectful of these positions—modernization took place based on a disintegrating trauma—but there are other examples, such as Cuba, or even within capitalism, Japan, in which articulation [between cultural heritage and economic development] has been much more successful. An elemental question in the case of COCEI is whether or not there is within the movement a current that tends to link cultural heritage with development.

For the time being the central problem in Juchitán is of a political character and has to do with the dexterity or sclerosis of the State and Mexican political system for coping with the changes that, on occasion, it itself proposes in order to be in accord with the national reality. Between 1976 and 1983 the political reform advanced, for better or worse, in the parliamentary realm and even in the electoral area. Juchitán, however, marked the limits of reform. Juchitán demonstrated that the regime's tolerance becomes rapidly exhausted when social movements attain continuity and a leadership (formal or genuine) emerges that forms an alliance with a political party and gains a voice in Congress. This was demonstrated also at different moments in the case of workers at the national university, the nuclear energy industry workers, the popular movement at the Autonomous University of Guerrero, the independent teachers' movement, etc. When apart from all of this the social movement and its leadership show clear signs of autonomy with respect to the electoral and parliamentary rules, and even with respect to political parties (regardless of how leftist they may be), the fancy wrapping around the political reform explodes, and the angry monster in our semioriental authoritarian political womb awakens.

This is what happened in Juchitán. Once COCEI took over the municipal presidency, the federal and state governments began to act like desperate fathers, lamenting their previous permissiveness. Thus, COCEI was very rapidly called on the carpet: "Here I distribute the land . . . look for another source of legitimacy, if you can, although I doubt you can, because as a punishment for your populist whims I am going to reduce your municipal budget to the minimum."

Thereafter, was COCEI enclosed by the State, or did it tend to seclude itself in a fundamentally cultural localism that appeals to its roots, which "goes to the people" and searches out their rage, and which relies more and more on tradition and the small peasant producer? In other words, was COCEI given the opportunity to link past with future, culture with economic development?

SUICIDES AND ASSASSINATIONS: THE LOGIC OF SOCIAL STRUGGLES IN MEXICO

COCEI was not given the opportunity to transform its rich heritage in a positive manner, without ruptures, and to connect nationalism with localism, economics with ideology. COCEI was not given a chance to do politics, politics being understood here as the difficult construction of agreements, as the delicate art of avoiding warfare. On the contrary, COCEI was pushed into doing its politics as the inflexible exercise of principles, of disagreement, separation, rupture, and ideological purism that leads to violence. It seems, then, that the matrix of social and political action in our country acted once again in Juchitán. Despite its declarations of political reform, the assassin, in this case the authoritarian State, corralled its victim until it became suicidal.

Because of this double imposition of suicide and assassination, Mexican social movements cannot be read as manifesting a tendency characterized by a certain continuity and permanence in time, nor can they be viewed as more or less stable forms of organization and ideological content. Rather, they give the impression of being small explosions in igneous magma, such that each little explosion relieves certain pressures but does not cease being a very short moment that destroys itself, extremely localized and without an accumulative connection to other phenomena of its kind.

The radiography of social and political action in Mexico would be similar, then, to a dotted photographic plate—something like a coarse-grained photograph in which it is difficult to find signs of a spectral line, of tendencies with continuity in time, as happens with social movements in other societies (Zermeño 1984).

In the case of Juchitán, in effect, the assassin acted with relentless logic, shunning normal political methods, stripping his victim of all economic means, and engaging in provocation. For this purpose, he installed on the scene in 1983 the most powerful mass media: cameras, microphones, the authorized commentators of official and private television, and many other national and foreign journalists.

Before analyzing the outcome of this event, let us digress to discuss an example in which localism and harassment provoked madness. In that case, backwardness and economic crisis, combined with a lack of professional or political expectations, led a student vanguard to reject economic development, modernization, and the national political system, and to support localism, hyper-ideologizing, purism, and finally violence. I am referring, of course, to the Peruvian guerrilla movement Sendero Luminoso (Shining Path), which adopted the custom of hanging dogs to symbolize its phobia toward the "dog," Deng Tsiao Ping, who caused the Cultural Revolution to fail. They committed these acts in the presence of a peasantry [i.e., the Peruvian peasantry] that often fails to realize that it is Chinese (Vargas Llosa 1983).

According to the *senderistas* (followers of Sendero Luminoso), Maoist China and contemporary Peru have in common the fact of being "semifeudal and semicolonial" societies whose liberation will be accomplished when a prolonged popular war with the peasantry as its backbone makes an assault on the cities. "Besides blowing up electric towers and attacking mining camps to seize explosives, Sendero Luminoso devastated the small agricultural properties of Ayacucho (the large ones had been destroyed by the 1960 Agrarian Reform), killing and wounding its owners" (Vargas Llosa 1983:9). The *senderistas* killed animals, set fire to machinery, and caused millions of dollars of damage. "The true reason for this was the *senderista* desire to cut off all communication between the countryside and the city, that center of bourgeois corruption that the popular army will regenerate one day" (Vargas Llosa 1983:9).

What precipitated the rupture between the poorest Indians and Sendero was "the intention of the revolutionaries to apply a policy of self-sufficient economy and control of production in the 'liberated zones.' " The objective: to cut off supplies to the cities and inculcate among the peasants a system of work in accordance with the ideological model. The communities received orders to grow only what they could consume without producing a surplus and to cease all commerce with the cities. All communities were to provision themselves so that the monetary economy disappeared. Sendero Luminoso imposed this policy with brutal methods. At the beginning of January, it closed the Book Fair with gunshots and dynamited the highway (Vargas Llosa 1983:11). More extreme examples of this phenomenon exist, such as the messianic movement that took place in the Canudos hacienda at the turn of the century (and which Vargas Llosa himself reported in *La guerra del fin del mundo*), or the Khmer Rouge with Pol Pot in Cambodia.

Juchitán is very far from this and is, moreover, one of the most accessible places in the Mexican Republic. COCEI, besides, has clearly rejected violence in any form. But the former example is relevant to the COCEI case because it reminds us what can happen when a movement is prevented from going forward—by an economic crisis and political harassment (or both)—and when ideological fundamentalism and excessive reference to ethnic origins come to the fore.

In September 1983, when I and other researchers made two trips to Juchitán, the COCEI leaders had not abandoned City Hall and did not plan to do so despite the destitution of the town council by the Oaxaca Congress at the request of Governor Pedro Vázquez Colmenares. By then, the point had passed in which their leaders could have been arrested, made to disappear, or assassinated without creating a reaction of incalculable consequences from the COCEI rank and file. Without a doubt, the time had also long since passed in which the COCEI leadership or a part of it could have been "integrated" into national or state-level politics through expenditures or political opening and dialogue. The situation in Juchitán seemed to have reached the low point arrived at by all authentic social movements in Mexico: the moment in which all the intermediate spaces for negotiation between social action and the institutionally established political structures are destroyed or disappear. I had written at the time:

> The social movement and its leadership had been marginalized by the dominant political forces on the national level. The possibilities for a collective suicide, which would be none other than brutal and generalized State repression, seemed to exist in Juchitán, as in so many other Juchitáns around the corner.

And I added:

> The movement's leadership and the movement itself certainly had been pushed into committing errors. But don't tell us that with all of the power of a governor and a national government, like the Mexican one, they have not been able to take advantage of a local movement and of a leadership susceptible to being pushed

into radical positions by merely announcing (however inconsequential it may seem) that the municipal budget had been suspended for fifteen days until the municipal government could demonstrate how it spent its money in the past six months (even though this money had not even been delivered punctually in the agreed upon amount).

Do COCEI and its followers tend to seek refuge in localism, in the Zapotec language, in mythology, in the reconstruction of symbols such as City Hall, in literature, and in painting? Yes. Very well then, it is necessary to prevent them at all costs from transforming past into future: first, by suspending the budget with the pretext of an audit and then by withholding recognition of the town council (after provoking a violent incident between COCEI and PRI); later, by dismantling COCEI with repression; and, finally, by giving PRI all the economic means to construct drainage systems, level and pave streets, build a bridge, bring as many industries to the region as possible, and make it evident that the Alfa-Omega project (which would substitute Trans-Isthmus Railroad transport for shipping through the Panama Canal) to a considerable degree would redound to the direct benefit of the region's inhabitants. How many other things are possible when the national State in a country of eighty million inhabitants focuses its arsenal on a town of sixty thousand souls, the majority of them Indian?

SIGNS OF ISOLATION CORRECTED WITH POLITICAL VISION

There is nothing wrong with utilizing references to Russian populism to suggest a possible tendency; but it is incorrect to confuse reality with its possibilities. It is true that when COCEI took over political control of the municipality, it showed its weak points through its localism, its exacerbated culturalism in detriment to its leadership propensity, and its isolation from national politics. Thus in August 1981 Leopoldo de Gyves himself marked the differences between COCEI and the politics of the PCM, arguing:

> COCEI decided not to participate in the presidential elections, which are a project that have no prospects for the people and create illusions and weak hopes for the people. . . . The PCM is a party that limits itself to electoral actions and does not seek alliances as a party of the masses. . . . Moreover, COCEI differs from other organizations that play at revolution like the PCM and PRT [Partido Revolucionario de los Trabajadores, Revolutionary Workers' Party] who do not work with the masses, organize, or mobilize; it is definitely going to be the people who provide the guidelines. (*Hora Cero*, Aug. 5, 1981)

The state leader of the PCM rapidly answered: "At no time is the PCM responsible for the political movements carried out by the mayor of Juchitán" (*Oaxaca Gráfico,* Sept. 15, 1981).

Relations between the PCM and COCEI improved considerably later, although more at the national than at the state level. The fact is that Leopoldo de Gyves, despite the above quotation, understood perfectly the correlation of national and international forces, at least as of September 1983:

> A socialist government in the Isthmus of Tehuantepec, with the Nicaraguan, Salvadoran, and Guatemalan experiences just a few kilometers to the south, is a possibility that makes the *priísta* military authorities of the state of Oaxaca fear undesirable contagion.
>
> The fear that COCEI could channel the rebellious sentiments existent in the region, impoverished but strategically vital to the country, unleashed repression against the town council and the organization that governs Juchitán.
>
> The State fears that discontent will surpass existing political limits with repression. But we understand that the struggle has to be waged within the constitutional framework by means of the mobilization of the people, political action, and civil resistance. And this is what we are doing. . . . Radicalism and armed actions have no place in this moment. But we will not permit the mediation of our struggle. We know what can happen.
>
> PRI has invested millions of pesos to destroy the organization. The official party favors projects of transnational penetration in the Isthmus. An Alfa-Omega project was established in Salina Cruz to impose a development model based on the seizure of communal lands, exploitation of the region's cheap peasant labor power, and depredation of fishing resources. COCEI is the only force capable of opposing this antipopular project. (Petrich 1983)

Consequently, COCEI's problem consists not only in the confrontation, each time more polarized, of a leadership in danger of accentuating its localism, on one hand, and the capitalist economy and dynamic national state, on the other. It is obvious that "radicalism and armed actions could have no place" in Juchitán, as De Gyves said, but it was also clear that open repression would do nothing but prove the hypothesis that "Juchitán is to the Mexican government what Central America is to the White House." This would be the pretext served on a platter to Washington to destroy the Mexican government's position vis-à-vis Central America. This explains why journalists from *Time, Newsweek,* and many other publications went to Juchitán ready to ask: "Why doesn't Mexico send the Contadora Group to Juchitán?" This clearly presented a delicate problem for the Mexican government and required a gradual strategy, as in the dismantling of a bomb.

JUCHITÁN IN THE GEOPOLITICS OF HUNGER AND WAR

One wonders if an operation of this magnitude [military occupation of City Hall and establishment of a state of siege in Juchitán] will be mounted each time the State-PRI wants to recover a municipality from the hands of the opposition. The fact is that each emergent political situation can be handled with a different degree of intensity. In Juchitán, however, the problem is different, and herein lies the tragedy of COCEI: Juchitán dominates one of the entrances to the Isthmus of Tehuantepec, and the Isthmus constitutes the only military cordon to the North in case of a generalization of the Central American conflict (only 200 kilometers distant without jungles or mountains in between). The Isthmus also forms a strait that separates the Mexican petroleum reserves from the rest of the country and the political capital. It is, finally, the natural canal passage from one ocean to the other and is much safer than the Panama Canal (the Alfa-Omega project consists of two enormous ports connected by modern railways and rapid loading and unloading systems).

COCEI is, then, in Juchitán, and Juchitán is a strategic site not only for the North Americans but for the State and national sovereignty. That is why we said that if things had gotten more serious in Central America, Reagan would have found a pretext in COCEI's people's government to intervene in the region.

For its part, the Mexican government has had to invoke its enormous, but subtle, fraud mechanism because it was necessary to remove the *coceístas* from City Hall in a bloodless operation. Otherwise, Mexican foreign policy, we said, would be "in check." This is, therefore, the situation that prevails in a town where a group of progressive and democratic youth (who have been cruelly harassed but have had the intelligence until now not to resort to violent methods) have to struggle against the titans of East-West geopolitics, the ancestral authoritarianism of the Mexican State, and the area's *caciques* and monopolists.

The question we have to ask ourselves is whether electoral fraud (and the silence of the mass media) is justified under these conditions or if the Mexican government itself and PRI found a perfect justification in the above-mentioned considerations to overthrow (to the detriment of the Political Reform, the supposed promotion of municipalities, and the moral renovation) a town council supported by a leftist party, it is true, but with great legitimacy among the rank and file. This legitimacy is such that if COCEI had not been denied financial and political support from the beginning, it would constitute today the best popular defense of the country's sovereignty in the region (and not by the force of violence but by consensus).

This discussion raises several questions about COCEI's future. Will COCEI be capable of conserving its urban-popular following in the face of a massive investment of federal, state, and municipal governments into Juchitán intended to quell unrest and co-opt COCEI political support?

The answer to this question, undoubtedly, depends on the policies adopted to deal with the agrarian question. However much is invested in improving the city of Juchitán, COCEI will continue to keep the popular sectors on its side so long as the land tenure situation is not modified. Here is the paradox. To attack the agrarian problem it would be necessary to attack both those who have occupied City Hall since 1984 and the social sectors who supported the anti-*coceísta* campaign. Thus, it would be to turn against PRI, like throwing out the baby with the bath water. Thus, it is not that there are insufficient economic resources to expropriate or indemnify the landowners of this key geopolitical region of the country. Rather, the problem is that this would involve attacking the framework of political power that derives from land concentration. In the process, the State would end up realizing COCEI's objectives as a necessary price for finishing it off, while simultaneously damaging the local PRI.

We have returned by another route to the eternal problem: There is no COCEI without references to the land, to the past, and to the people's cultural heritage.

What will be the future of COCEI if the peasants recover their communal lands, and COCEI remains outside the worker's movement, unable to win over the middle classes—if in sum, the future does not belong to them? This brings up another question relevant to this discussion: Will COCEI be capable of breaking a second principle imposed by the logic of social struggles in Mexico? COCEI has been able to inspire a movement that has already lasted for ten years, within a social matrix where collective struggles are rapidly truncated. The question that proceeds is whether or not this social movement and its singular organization will be capable of attacking the second golden rule of action in Mexico, that is to say, whether or not it will be able to abstain from seeking the vertex of the pyramid of political power (which, in a sense, it already occupied when it obtained control of the Juchitán municipal government) and returning to a position in which it practices politics and does politics in and from civil society. Will COCEI be capable of converting itself into a *"basista"* [base] organization? Could it return to its origins, to the neighborhood committees as in 1977–80? Will it succeed in coming and going without trauma, between social power and the political power granted by government apparatuses? Will it be able to consciously overcome its glorious era, the grand moments when repeatedly it was front-page news in the national and even the foreign press?

From March 1984 onwards, news from Juchitán began to arrive: COCEI has regrouped secretly in the neighborhood committees and is attempting to isolate City Hall, today controlled by PRI, reviving and recreating politics in the barrios [neighborhoods] themselves. Fiestas, and various social, political, cultural, and historical expressions, have become the privileged spaces for COCEI popular expressions, now that the street and all of the public places have been privatized by PRI, assisted by the army and the police.

For that reason, perhaps, the great principles of how to do politics should be adjusted to the real possibilities of politics. Maybe a more PSUM-Leninist approach (a strong hierarchical party that strives to take over State power) should be modified to include a COCEI that occupies the hallways and rooms of City Hall (i.e., to include a *"basista"* conception of politics involving movement in the subterranean channels of society and avoidance of confrontation on disadvantageous local, national, and international terrain). This turned out to be an adequate conception for COCEI during moments of exile, persecution, and state of siege.

It is logical, then, that COCEI was born—as a legitimate child of the 1968 political movement—with a Leninist conception (consciousness exterior to the masses, considerable hierarchism, and a strategy of confrontation alternating with clandestinity, as in the case of Punto Crítico and many other groups with the same heritage) which later became "Leninism-Parliamentarianism." As its relations with the masses have deepened and the political system has become more flexible, COCEI now seems to be evolving toward a socialism of the base. Perhaps, then, proposals that understand democracy as the creation of more restricted identities not so focused on the State, and all of the projects not far removed from Poland's Solidarity or that of the *paulista* metallurgical workers (please forgive the lack of alternative examples), acquire great relevance at this time.

But I will repeat myself. If COCEI also succeeds in doing this, it will have overcome—for its own good and for the good of the political opposition in Mexico—two great obstacles of social struggle: discontinuity and over-politicization (in the sense that everything is turned towards and tends towards the State). Hopefully it can also overcome the great danger of the COCEI struggle: the self-contemplation of its glorious past.

NOTE

1. *Artels* are collective forms similar to the *kolkhozs,* but in which the members are permitted to possess certain goods.

Naked
Speech

Macario Matus

Sharp as the word may be,
venomous as the paper,
nothing works against so much blood.
Hushed voice and broken pen
lie in the dust
of these white coffins.

Night has hidden
its light in the fields.
No wind can raise these flowers
the sun has withered today
nor dagger straighten out the laws
of the November cowards.

Where is the baton to arbitrate
between sky and execution wall?
Where the sea to contain
this river's salt tears?
Where the rigor of those arms
crossing under machine gun fire?

Macario Matus

Where the light could brighten
so many black huipiles?

I know where my heart was left
in the hour of the big knives.
It's always the same . . .
a star is born with the dawn
and speech follows after the truncheon.

A Birth
in the
Mountains

Alejandro Cruz

Liberty is giving birth
in the rebel mountains of San Miguel Chimalapa

It is a difficult breach
and I am one more witness to that moment

Men heave grief up to their shoulders
women bear courage in their hands

I want to howl at this bronze moment
this day of armored metals
when liberty is giving birth

A whole people has wept today
announcing itself alive
among the hurting mountains

A people breaking free
a people rebellious and dry

In San Miguel Chimalapa
clean, flushed with the new.

Fandango Istmeño (Isthmus Fandango). Gouache painting by Israel Vicente of Juchitán, Oaxaca. 1989.

P A R T F O U R

Guendabiaani':
The Politics
of
Culture
in
Juchitán

*G**uendabiaani'* is a Zapotec word for intelligence, wisdom, or in a more general sense, culture. Thus, Lidxi (house) Guendabiaani' is the Juchitán cultural center (the Casa de la Cultura), focus of a contemporary Isthmus Zapotec cultural renaissance. Is this movement a resurrection of ancient Zapotec high culture, a return to the glory days of the *binnigula'sa'* (the great Zapotec ancestors), Monte Albán, or Cosijoeza (Zapotec king when the Spaniards arrived)? Or could we understand it better as a form of symbolic ethnicity, invented tradition, or imagined community in the (post)modern world? If it is the case, as Kahn (1989:20) argues, that genuine culture and "objective cultural demarcation" are impossible today, what do we make of Isthmus Zapotec revivalism? What does it mean to be Zapotec in the late twentieth century? These are some of the issues that are explored in Part Four.

Howard Campbell's article examines Juchitán's political and cultural movement and its roots in Isthmus history and Zapotec ethnicity. Since the early part of the century, Juchitecos have stood out among Mexican indigenous

groups for the sophistication of their literary and intellectual culture (see the
Campbell and de la Cruz articles in Part Four, and Covarrubias 1946). In 1929,
Andrés Henestrosa published *Los hombres que dispersó la danza,* a creative
rendering of and embellishment on Isthmus Zapotec folklore and mythology.
This book was a major success in Mexican literary circles. In the 1930s, he
and his fellow Juchitán poet, Gabriel López Chiñas (author of the poem that
follows), founded a lively *indigenista* (indigenous-oriented) cultural magazine
called *Neza,* similar to the avant-garde literary experiments of Mariategui in
Peru. In the late 1960s and 1970s, a new generation of Juchitecos renewed
Zapotec literary fervor with *Neza Cubi* and, later, *Guchachi' Reza.* With the
founding of COCEI, however, the Zapotec cultural movement was integrated
with political struggle. For Juchiteco intellectuals, it was no longer enough just
to write poems and essays about Isthmus customs and the etymology of Zapotec words; it became crucial to wield the pen and paint brush to promote a
political project aimed at redistributing land and wealth and bringing to power
local representatives of Zapotec peasants and workers.

According to Daniel López Nelio ("Interview of Daniel López Nelio"), the
survival of Zapotec culture has always been inseparable from politics and thus
has entailed acts of resistance and self-affirmation. If López Nelio argues that
culture is always political, then Manuel López Mateos maintains the converse,
that COCEI politics is simply a cultural expression of the Isthmus Zapotec
people. Zapotec culture was never more politicized than during COCEI's
Ayuntamiento Popular, "the people's government" (1981–83). At that time,
Juchitán came under siege from the powerful forces of PRI, the military, and
the government bureaucracy. Campbell discusses how the Zapotec writers responded by writing books about COCEI and past Isthmus rebels, recovering
oral histories of struggle, and publishing political and ethnographic photographs. He also describes the syncretistic Juchitán art scene led by Francisco
Toledo, who promoted COCEI and Isthmus Zapotec culture in internationally

acclaimed paintings and sculptures. Samples of the creative literary and ethnological efforts of Juchiteco intellectuals included in Part Four are the poems and *cuentos* (folklore) collected by de la Cruz and others, the *mentiras* (lies) recorded by Manuel Matus, and the article by de la Cruz. Other poems and reproductions of art works appear throughout this book.

Víctor de la Cruz, perhaps the most gifted of the COCEI intellectuals and the editor of *Guchachi' Reza,* discusses COCEI's ethnic revival in his article "Brothers or Citizens: Two Languages, Two Political Projects in the Isthmus." According to de la Cruz, PRI and COCEI support two fundamentally different cultural projects. On the one hand, PRI emphasizes urbanization, modernization, and Mexican national culture. COCEI, on the other hand, advocates reinforcement of the Zapotec peasantry, support for indigenous customs, and defense of the Zapotec language and way of life.

COCEI's first government did not have powerful weapons or much money, but it did have popular support and the rich cultural resources of the Juchitecos. COCEI's radio station, discussed by López Mateos, broadcast Zapotec-language programs criticizing the government in *corridos* (stories told through rhyming songs or verbal recitations), speeches, and news reports. Zapotec artists painted pro-COCEI wall murals with ethnic themes and colorful political banners, and filled canvases with local imagery, symbols from Zapotec folklore, and episodes from COCEI history. Isthmus writers, such as Víctor de la Cruz, Macario Matus, and Enedino Jiménez, wrote poems concerned with the COCEI struggle, local customs, and Zapotec mythology. They also collected Juchiteco folklore and wrote essays and articles criticizing official history and promoting a Juchitán-based view of the past. The Zapotec language was widely spoken in the COCEI mayor's office, among the police forces, in the COCEI-controlled courts, and especially in COCEI rallies, as López Nelio and Campbell note. Fiestas, neighborhood organizations, *tequios* (community work parties), and kinship networks became vehicles for political struggle.

COCEI demonstrations were transformed into ethnic/political performances invoking indigenous cultural style and symbolism and a millenarian view of local history. In short, Isthmus Zapotec culture became one of the strongest weapons of COCEI in political combat with its local, regional, and national adversaries.

While COÇEI invoked the past, it did not (and could not) create anew ancient Zapotec society. Its politicization of local culture entailed the redefinition of existing customs and the revitalization and refunctionalization of old ones in the context of class and ethnic struggle in Juchitán. Shoshana Sokoloff's "The Proud Midwives of Juchitán" is a textured description of women who selectively combine contemporary Western medical techniques with indigenous practices to create something both unique and effective, illustrating the dynamic, synthetic process of cultural change in Juchitán. The Juchiteca midwives are portrayed not as "ethnic traditionalists" but as highly experienced practitioners concerned about the health of their clients and willing to borrow and innovate if that will improve their effectiveness. In the process the midwives are creating new traditions which will be communicated to a new generation of students. Disagreeing with the Zapotec intellectuals who emphasize the "purity" of their cultural practices, Sokoloff sees contemporary Juchiteco culture as a rich blend of "traditional" and modern elements.

Clifford (1988:18) writes that "culture is contested, temporal, and emergent." Rarely in recent Latin American history has an opposition indigenous/peasant social movement had the material resources and the political space that the Juchitecos have had to generate their own versions of their "emergent" and "contested" culture within national and international cultural forums. For this reason, the COCEI case has been an important example of successful grassroots organizing for the Mexican left and a rich subject for anthropological research.

The
Zapotec
Language

Gabriel López Chiñas

They say that Zapotec is going,
no one will speak it now,
it's dead they say, it's dying,
the Zapotec language.

The Zapotec language
the devil will take it away,
now the sophisticated Zapotecs
speak Spanish only.

Ah, Zapotec, Zapotec!
those who put you down
forget how much their mothers
loved you with a passion!

Ah, Zapotec, Zapotec!
language that gives me life,
I know you'll die away
on the hour of the death of the sun.

COCEI march during the mayoral campaign of Héctor Sánchez, Juchitán mayor from
1989 to 1992. July 1989. Photo by H. Campbell.

Class Struggle, Ethnopolitics, and Cultural Revivalism in Juchitán

Howard Campbell

The literature on ethnicity in Mexico is large and rich, but an Isthmus Zapotec peasant leader would say that it misses the point. A central debate in Mexican ethnicity studies concerns whether ethnic distinctiveness or asymmetrical class structure best characterizes rural communities (Díaz-Polanco 1985; Bartra 1977:449–53; Stavenhagen 1970, 1975, 1980).[1] As he stated in his article in this volume, Daniel López Nelio of COCEI sees things differently:

> The Zapotec race is oppressed by an entire economic system, the same as the working class. Now the struggle is not only over an ethnicity because the Zapotecs are also workers. The struggle is also for peasants and the indigenous cultural question. It all comes together. . . . These are the struggles led by COCEI.
> (Toledo and de la Cruz 1983:25)

López Nelio concisely states what many anthropological polemics obscure (Díaz-Polanco 1982; Royce 1982:3; Friedlander 1975). Rather than opposing ethnicity and class, we need to examine their interplay (Bourgois 1988). This has consequences for anthropological theory and political practice in Latin America, where grassroots movements discuss whether to organize along class or ethnic lines (Santana 1981; see Schryer 1990). By abandoning this artificial division, we can understand how ethnicity is simultaneously a weapon wielded against outsiders and a contested terrain of class interests within indigenous communities.

In such struggles, ethnic identity is not only defended but recreated in political discourse. Indigenous history and culture become the disputed product of political process; that is, they become conscious representations sustaining political ideologies (Salomon 1987). Viewing ethnicity as a contended process helps us see how politics is an arena that shapes and transforms ethnic identity and indigenous culture.

COCEI, a political coalition that combines an intense indigenous identity with an equally strong class consciousness, exemplifies the complex interrelatedness of ethnicity, culture, and class. The success of this leftist movement in Mexico, a country dominated by one party (PRI), focused the attention of numerous journalists, social scientists, and writers on the Oaxacan Isthmus of Tehuantepec. Attracted by the rarity of COCEI's victories in Juchitán municipal elections in 1981, 1989, and 1992, its violent removal from office by the Mexican government in 1983, and the colorful nature of the movement, these observers produced a flurry of articles, books, and theses analyzing COCEI. However, analyses have not come to grips with the complexities of ethnicity, class, and politics in the Coalition. What roles do Isthmus Zapotec culture, ethnicity, and class consciousness play in COCEI? What impact did COCEI's politicization of Isthmus Zapotec identity have on indigenous conceptions of history, art, language, social organization, and gender relations? In what follows I will examine these issues, drawing on my fieldwork (1987–93) in the Isthmus.

The dynamics of heterogeneous movements like COCEI cannot be understood within rigid dichotomous categories. For insight into ethnicity, culture, and class in COCEI, we must look to studies in Latin America that focus on processes of ethnic politicization, the social reproduction of ethnic groups, and oppositional aspects of ethnicity within complex class and ethnic hierarchies (Kearney 1989; Varese 1988; Bourgois 1988). These perspectives bring us into the realm of the ideological uses of ethnicity by indigenous groups to resist external and internal enemies.

Oaxaca's sixteen ethnic groups have a long history of resistance to political and cultural domination (Barabas 1986). In recent years, ethnic group survival has required resistance to new challenges from inside and outside indigenous pueblos. Kearney (1989) notes the reconstitution of Mixtec identity in northern Mexico and the United States as a result of economic and political pressures the Mixtecos face in their labor migration. He sees the reconstituted ethnicity of migrants as active resistance, although in Oaxaca their resistance remains passive. Other contemporary studies focus on how Oaxacan indigenous groups use ethnicity to oppose intrusions into their communities or exploitation of indigenous culture by outsiders. Boege's (1988) book on the Mazatecos emphasizes the role of ethnic redefinition in political and cultural resistance to the Mexican state and private agribusiness. Stephen (1988), using the cases of the Oaxaca Valley Zapotecs and Nahuas of Mexico, the Otavaleños of Ecuador, and the Kunas of Panama, analyzes the appropriation and commoditization of ethnic identity by government and commercial interests. She also examines how tourist-oriented craft production results in grassroots economic development, which fortifies local systems of social reproduction. Such processes create a "dual ethnic identity" that opposes local reconstructions of ethnic identity to State commoditization of indigenous ethnicity.

COCEI's use of Isthmus Zapotec ethnic identity, unlike the Mixtec case, is an active, overt form of resistance occurring in indigenous territory. COCEI politics entail a thorough engagement of Zapotec culture against local, regional, and national rivals. In this case, as in Boege's and Stephen's work, indigenous identity is strengthened by opposition to exploitative forms of capitalist development and government domination. However, with COCEI this opposition does not produce a duality, but a single identity invoked against outsiders while it remains disputed turf with indigenous elites. The popularity, resilience, and explosiveness of COCEI reveal that Isthmus Zapotec society is at once a rich source of pride and inspiration, and a class-divided crucible for radical politics. COCEI ethnopolitics also demonstrates that resistance does not simply mobilize ethnic identity but can lead to new uses and creative expressions of indigenous social organization, language, and art. Finally, COCEI and the Juchitán cultural scene show that indigenous societies are capable of more than resistance and survival; they are also fertile ground for political alternatives and provocative cultural creations.

I begin with a discussion of COCEI's politicization of Isthmus history and Zapotec identity, and how this strengthens the movement internally but constrains its possibilities for expansion. This is followed by a section examining ethnic elements in COCEI's organization and leadership. The third section of the essay focuses on an Isthmus Zapotec cultural revival, which flourished as a result of COCEI political activity and promoted the movement's image to a wide audience. The last section deals with indigenous gender relations and Isthmus Zapotec women's roles in COCEI ideology and practice.

LOCAL HISTORY, ISTHMUS ZAPOTEC ETHNIC IDENTITY, AND COCEI POLITICS

COCEI identifies itself as an organization of the indigenous poor of Juchitán and as the continuation of past Isthmus Zapotec struggles for independence from the Aztecs, Spaniards, and French. Thus, COCEI sees itself as the most recent link in an unbroken chain of rebellions, resistance, and defense of Zapotec culture dating to precolonial times. As Macario Matus, a Zapotec poet, puts it,

> Juchitán is a branch of the great tree that is the Zapotec race . . . and as such inherits rebelliousness and detests subjection . . . That is to say, the Zapotec race has always been free. . . . The struggle of COCEI . . . has been congruent with the history of physical and intellectual battles of its predecessors. . . . The victory of COCEI is the history of a people. (in Aubague 1985:30–59)

Juchiteco intellectuals promote these ideas in a series of books and magazines (discussed below), in which they attack official versions of Mexican history and redefine local history from a pro-COCEI perspective. These views have gained wide currency in Juchitán and elsewhere and are a potent call for ethnic solidarity and militancy. For COCEI, local history and Isthmus Zapotec ethnic identity are key elements of a political discourse. This discourse invokes an assumed continuity of opposition to outsiders as a weapon in struggles with regional and national authorities and with the local elites who represent them.

COCEI political rallies are the main setting for recital of the movement's ideological charter and have become a kind of ethnic/political performance. Coordinated yet spontaneous, they begin at the approximately seventeen neighborhood committee offices where COCEI supporters meet. Designated representatives, parallel to the *mayordomos* of fiestas, distribute flags, red bandannas, confetti, and beverages (López Monjardin 1983a). After the neighborhood's *coceístas* arrive and assemble, the large and boisterous group marches through the dusty Juchitán streets holding COCEI banners and chanting political slogans. These marches are modeled after the wedding, funeral, and religious processions that punctuate everyday Isthmus life. As in processions, men and women are segregated, and women wear their most elegant regional costumes in red COCEI colors, complemented by red flowers and gold jewelry. Young boys wearing masks, the *mbiooxho,* dance in the streets, while the women's committee raises its banner, followed by the smaller banner of the "mosquito squadron," composed of COCEI children.

On special occasions, such as the closing of an election campaign, oxcarts decorated with banana leaves, sugar cane, palm stalks, and flowers carry COCEI supporters in imitation of the *convite de flor* (flower parade) processions that initiate religious festivities. During these rowdy celebrations, *coceístas* chuckle at Zapotec jokes and shout "viva COCEI" or "death to *PRIhuela*."[2] The neighborhood committees and contingents from nearby towns arrive one by one to the central office in the heart of Juchitán. Each arriving group is greeted by applause, firecrackers, and bottle rockets as at the end of weddings or mass. Loudspeaker announcements drone, and bands (an essential part of Isthmus festive events) play local tunes. As the different contingents blend into the *communitas* of the red-shirted COCEI crowd, a speaker warms up the audience with episodes of local history. Women work their way through the crowd pouring red confetti on people's hair, as in fiestas, to indicate attendance. Zapotec folk music blares over loudspeakers.

COCEI leaders emerge with *guie' chaachi* flower wreaths and red bandannas around their necks. They mount the improvised stage to roars of applause. Invariably the first word of their speech will be *paisanuca,* the COCEI equivalent of "my fellow Americans," which instantly identifies them with the crowd.[3] Indeed, a high degree of rapport between leadership and followers is evidenced by the close attention the rank and file pay to these talks and the respectful yet familiar way in which they use their leaders' nicknames. COCEI leaders, equally adept in Spanish and Zapotec, are charismatic figures who color their speeches with elegant hand gestures, pumping fists, and local humor.

The audience responds enthusiastically or chants for the release of Víctor Yodo, a major COCEI martyr. After listening to the leadership, the crowd (Cuauhtémoc Cárdenas was received by approximately fifteen thousand *coceístas* in Juchitán prior to the 1988 presidential elections) marches through the poorer outlying neighborhoods of town—COCEI strongholds—and back to the downtown area. The marchers disrupt all traffic and business activity, to the chagrin of local merchants. Finally, depending on the needs of the moment, the crowd may regroup in front of Juchitán City Hall for more speeches and activities, or convene en masse at a local fiesta.[4]

COCEI's principal opponent, the Juchitán PRI, is also composed predominantly of Zapotec people who are proud of their heritage.[5] Yet because of their privileged economic circumstances, the middle and upper classes who control PRI are generally more assimilated into and identified with national culture than are COCEI members; hence PRI rallies are less militantly "ethnic" than those of COCEI.[6] Furthermore, the Juchitán elite's alliances with Oaxaca Valley and national power brokers make them vulnerable to COCEI charges that they have sold out *la raza* (the race) for private gain. Finally, for the PRI upper classes, Zapotec identity is only one ethnic option (Royce 1975:78) because they function just as smoothly in mestizo national society, whereas for the indigenous peasants who are the backbone of COCEI, Zapotec culture and ethnic identity are the sine qua non of their social existence. For this reason, COCEI's passionate, ideological invocation of indigenous ethnicity (versus PRI's lukewarm appeal to Zapotec identity) both reflects and reinforces class divisions within the Juchiteco community.

Nonetheless, perhaps 15 to 20 percent of Juchitán peasants are supporters of PRI. These *priístas* do not differ from COCEI counterparts in their conceptions of Zapotec culture and ethnicity. Although we would expect these peasants to support COCEI, their PRI membership stems from personal ties, patronage links with PRI bosses, and loyalty to the party for granting them *ejido* (government-distributed collective land) plots or titles to small private properties (Martínez López 1985). Given that the Isthmus is an area marked by intense poverty and that PRI controls the purse strings of the agricultural bureaucracy, it is understandable that some peasants join PRI. However, even PRI officials acknowledge that the Isthmus peasant sector is dominated by COCEI and until recently PRI peasant organizations were underdeveloped (Rubin 1987). In 1988, in an attempt to regain peasant support, the Isthmus PRI began to give more attention to these organizations.

The Juchitán PRI has no ethnic project other than Zapotec language classes, painting city walls with ethnic-oriented messages, and promotion of local artists—strategies copied in diluted form from COCEI. Indeed, indigenous culture has little place in PRI's *política moderna* (modern politics), which favors nationalism, capitalist development, and industrialization (PRI 1988). Consequently, PRI cedes the ideological discourse over Zapotec identity to its opponents, even though the majority of its members can also make a legitimate claim to the history invoked by COCEI. Thus, in Juchitán, we have the curious situation of one Zapotec faction (i.e., COCEI) using "we, the Zapotecs" rhetoric against the other (PRI) in intraethnic class struggle. No longer is Isthmus Zapotec style a political weapon used by a "united front" of Zapotecs against mestizo outsiders as described by Royce (1982:181). Since the advent of COCEI, the politicization of Zapotec style and identity and the struggle for political and economic power divide bitter class enemies within the Zapotec community itself.[7]

However, PRI is not alone in misunderstanding the ethnic question and the "dramaturgy of power" (Cohen 1981) in Juchitán. As part of Heberto Castillo's 1988 campaign for president, the Mexican Socialist Party (PMS) held the Encuentro Nacional de Pueblos Indios[8] and a large rally in Juchitán. Unfortunately, the word *indio* in Mexico is used as an insult, implying stupidity, backwardness, and inferiority. COCEI leader López Nelio asked why people persist in calling indigenous people *indios.* Other COCEI leaders were unmoved by the PMS's call for formation of a separate organization to defend indigenous people's lands and culture because COCEI does precisely that in the Isthmus. Further examples of the national left's lack of sensitivity to Juchitán political culture were several faux pas in PMS speeches to the COCEI crowd at the rally: confusing Víctor Yodo, a COCEI martyr, with Pico de Oro;

and *totopo* (tortilla) with *totomostle* (corn husk), which brought roars of laughter from COCEI militants for days afterward.[9] Finally, Cuauhtémoc Cárdenas's emotionless, academic speech left a COCEI audience cold during a visit to Juchitán near the end of his 1988 presidential campaign.

Still, COCEI political discourse has its limitations. Its micro-specific rhetoric, imbued with ethnic and local idioms, plays a self-limiting role in what could become a multiregional movement. At present, COCEI's primary strength is in Juchitán, where it originated, and the nearby Isthmus towns of Ixtepec, Xadani, Comitancillo, San Blas, and several others—all of which have sizable Zapotec populations. COCEI has made inroads into the Huave, Mixe, Southern Zapotec, Zoque, and Chontal areas of southern Oaxaca. It is also spreading into zones where indigenous culture is weak or nonexistent, such as Tehuantepec, Salina Cruz (site of an oil refinery and port facilities), Jalapa del Marqués, and the booming international tourist zone of Huatulco. COCEI has official representation on several Isthmus town councils in addition to Juchitán, and its spokesmen claim they have grassroots support in more than sixty towns.

Yet all of COCEI's ventures outside the Isthmus Zapotec area have been tenuous. This expansion results from the strength of COCEI-controlled peasant organizations and labor unions and/or the appeal of their Marxian political program in areas of extreme poverty. Mestizo industrial workers of Salina Cruz and Huatulco, for example, are uninterested in Zapotec folk history, but they do respect COCEI's ability to pressure employers for higher wages or indemnities. However, the likelihood of COCEI's establishing stronger or more enduring ties to non-Zapotec communities is limited by the imperviousness of its leadership to non-Juchitecos.

This situation is aggravated by the Isthmus Zapotecs' commercial, political, and cultural dominance of the other Isthmus indigenous groups (the Mixes, Zoques, Huaves, and Chontals).[10] Although COCEI reaches out to these groups, such efforts are restricted by the Isthmus Zapotecs' superordinate position and resultant mistrust of the mostly Zapotec COCEI. Another limitation is the high degree of cultural pluralism in Oaxaca and the frequent intervillage rivalries that divide otherwise natural allies (Dennis 1979). Thus, for example, COCEI of Juchitán has little presence in Tehuantepec, partly because of the more than one-hundred-year-old feud between the two towns.

Therefore, although COCEI is not merely a Juchitán movement, it is not a movement of all Isthmus inhabitants, all Isthmus Zapotecs or all indigenous communities of the Isthmus, let alone the rest of Oaxaca. In this sense, COCEI's politicization of ethnicity is a double-edged sword.

INDIGENOUS LEADERSHIP, ISTHMUS ZAPOTEC SOCIAL ORGANIZATION, AND COCEI

COCEI's experienced leadership and tight-knit organization are primary factors in its perseverance. Heirs to a long line of Isthmus Zapotec leaders, Héctor Sánchez (Juchitán mayor from 1989 to 1992), Leopoldo de Gyves, and Daniel López Nelio guided COCEI through a gauntlet of government repression, paramilitary violence, and media slander to its present strength and respectability.[11] Combining audacity, intelligence, and oratorical talent, the COCEI triumvirate has attracted the loyalty of a majority of the Zapotec peasantry and working class of Juchitán. The high level of identification between COCEI leaders and their following is possible because of the leaders' charisma, organizational talents, and success in dealings with their political opponents. As a consequence of the COCEI leaders' power, they can articulate and implement, to some extent, an alternative model of local society and culture.

In addition to the three principal leaders, described as "natural leaders" by journalists, the movement is sustained by a secondary group of political activists who make up the COCEI Political Commission. With few exceptions, this cadre and the three main leaders meet the basic requirements for access to political power in Juchitán, namely, birth in Juchitán or to Juchiteco parents, fluency in Zapotec, and thorough knowledge of local customs and history (Royce 1975). Although there are no women on the Political Commission, a few females play key leadership roles in the movement: Several women were officials in the first COCEI government, and others are leaders of market vendors, neighborhoods, a militant medical worker's union, and tavern owners.

Another critical element in COCEI's success is its organizational structure, particularly the network of neighborhood committees scattered throughout Juchitán and Ixtepec. These committees, established in 1977, wrested power away from corrupt neighborhood bosses, bypassed the imposed PRI municipal government, and provided a forum for citizens to discuss problems with COCEI leaders. Each committee has its own representative, who functions like the headmen (*xuaana'*) of Tehuantepec barrios. COCEI formed the committees by taking advantage of neighborhood solidarity, which is acute in the larger, poorer sections of town, and the profoundly communal and reciprocal nature of Zapotec culture. At the heart of Juchitán social life is the system of fiestas and the *vela* societies that run them. COCEI members, accustomed to being part of fiesta and other voluntary organizations, are quick to participate in the neighborhood committees (López Monjardin 1983a). In fact, in 1984 and 1985, when intense government repression prevented open COCEI political activity, rather than going underground, the organization survived by throwing fiestas to raise money and maintain solidarity (López Monjardin 1986).

Kinship also plays an important role in COCEI's organization, as it does in most aspects of Isthmus life. This appears among the leadership where brothers and husband-wife and father-son combinations are present, as well as among the rank and file. Thus, if one member of a family is a COCEI member, it is more than likely that the rest will be also. This is a serious matter since extended families (in the largely endogamous Isthmus villages) may contain hundreds of united kinsmen. This is manifested in the animated participation of children, youths, male and female adults, and elderly relatives standing together in COCEI events. Pro-COCEI extended families, because of their size, normally include peasants, laborers, market vendors, clerical workers, and teachers. By appealing to the diverse interests of each of these occupational groups, COCEI is able to secure the support of a broad spectrum of family members (Rubin 1987:159). Kinship is especially important in the poor sections of Isthmus towns. In these neighborhoods, the shared patios *(solares)* of extended family households are the focus of a kin unity that becomes militant when channeled into COCEI political activity (Rubin 1987:136). Consequently, the killing or wounding of a COCEI supporter (twenty-five or more *coceístas* have died in political violence) does not weaken the movement; instead, it is often the blow that causes entire families to join COCEI.[12]

Finally, reciprocity and the *tequio* (voluntary collective labor) are culturally stylized mechanisms COCEI uses to mobilize people for marches to Oaxaca and Mexico City, highway blockades, building takeovers, hunger strikes, and daily tasks.[13] For example, if COCEI helps a peasant to obtain credit or land or a worker a job, in the future this same individual might be called on to paint political slogans on walls during an election campaign. Similarly, COCEI invokes the *tequio* to encourage partisans to donate their labor and/or time for diverse actions, such as rebuilding the Juchitán City Hall. COCEI's astute use of reciprocal exchanges and networks of cooperation rooted in Zapotec culture helped COCEI (via donations of food and money, or time spent passing messages or keeping vigil) sustain a several-month-long occupation of City Hall in protest of the government's ouster of COCEI's elected administration in 1983. For these reasons, COCEI leaders say that their organization developed "naturally"—by carrying on or elaborating on existing Zapotec traditions and social forms.

COCEI AND THE ISTHMUS ZAPOTEC RENAISSANCE

A renaissance of Zapotec culture in Juchitán has intensified the political struggle of COCEI. Artists, writers, and musicians play key roles in promoting

COCEI's cause. Analogous to the top three COCEI leaders, Francisco Toledo, Víctor de la Cruz, and Macario Matus lead this Zapotec cultural movement, which COCEI sees as indivisible from its political program. The movement took root in the early 1900s and grew during the 1930s and 1940s with the writings of Andrés Henestrosa and his generation, and the 1946 publication of Covarrubias's *Mexico South: The Isthmus of Tehuantepec*. It blossomed in the 1970s and 1980s after the founding of the Juchitán Casa de la Cultura (1972).[14]

The Casa is a beautiful nineteenth-century mansion, adorned with local flora, which houses art and photography galleries, an archaeology museum, a library, a print-making shop, a stage, and large rooms for conferences, classes, and creative performances. The institution's mission is the study, promotion, and dissemination of Isthmus Zapotec culture and history. A monumental task in an area of deep-rooted poverty, the Casa's activities are possible in large part because of the financial largess of the famous painter and militant COCEI supporter, Toledo; the constant backing of COCEI; and the support of numerous local intellectuals and artists. These efforts are highly politicized because PRI has attempted to wrest control of this key cultural organization from the largely pro-COCEI artistic and cultural community.[15] On many occasions the Casa has been a pitched battlefield in the fight for political and cultural power in Juchitán: in 1975 with the ouster of a conservative director, who permitted soldiers to use the grounds as a staging area for anti-COCEI repression; in 1983, when the National Fine Arts Institute and Oaxaca state government attempted to depose Matus as director, but failed because of the mobilization of prominent Mexican artists and intellectuals; and again in 1988, when Casa workers went on strike for higher wages and an expanded budget (funds have steadily dried up as PRI tries to squelch this center of COCEI support).

I will discuss COCEI's mobilization of Zapotec culture, and the role culture plays in COCEI's success, from three standpoints: language; art, photography, and literature; and popular culture.

Language

COCEI sees the Zapotec language as a foundation of indigenous culture and a tool of political action. COCEI leaders use the language to explain their struggle and politicize monolingual peasants and workers, and establish bonds with the rank and file in rallies and routine affairs. COCEI members spoke Zapotec extensively in the judicial apparatus, police force, and presidency during their first administration. The movement's use of the language creates a powerful in-group mentality and symbolizes resistance to domination by Spanish-speaking outsiders, the local mestizo elite, and upper-class Zapotecs who are not fluent in the native tongue. This strengthens Zapotec pride among the poor and furthers COCEI's image as the legitimate defenders of the ethnic group.

Also during its initial term of office, COCEI carried out a literacy program emphasizing Zapotec language and culture; established Radio Ayuntamiento Popular, broadcasting numerous hours of programming in the native language; and published indigenous poems, songs, and writings on Zapotec linguistics. Additionally, the Casa de la Cultura gives Zapotec language classes, traditional music and dance lessons, and even mathematics classes in Zapotec. Finally, Matus and others created a pedagogical model for promoting the Zapotec language and way of life through cultural dialogue and sociopolitical consciousness-raising à la Paolo Freire and the *sandinista* literacy campaign (UNAM/Casa de la Cultura 1986). Few other Latin American indigenous groups have had the resources and political freedom that the Juchitecos enjoy in their struggle to independently preserve and promote their language.

Art, Photography, and Literature
The Isthmus artistic movement, which developed concurrent with the founding and expansion of COCEI, produces significant painting, photography, and poetry. Francisco Toledo, one of Mexico's finest contemporary painters, leads the way with his vast repertoire of paintings, drawings, and sculpture. Toledo's works are saturated with Isthmus flora and fauna, imbued with key imagery and symbolism of rural Zapotec life, and nurtured by the imagination and fantasy of Zapotec folklore and mythology. One of his recent artistic successes consists of a forty-nine-piece show demystifying Mexican national hero Benito Juárez and juxtaposing official history regarding Juárez with a Juchitán-based view (Toledo 1986). This perspective, linked to COCEI's version of local history, emphasizes the burning of Juchitán by Juárez's soldiers. The pro-COCEI cadre of young Isthmus artists (e.g., Israel Vicente and Miguel Angel Toledo) who follow Toledo also take up political themes, such as key moments in COCEI history or COCEI symbolism. In addition, many of them utilize their skills to promote COCEI directly in wall murals, colorful street graffiti, COCEI political banners, and pro-COCEI paintings on the houses of the movement's two land-invasion communities. Finally, like Toledo, these artists emphasize Zapotec culture and regional animal and plant life in their works.

Juchitán art is not provincial, however, despite its regional focus. Indeed, the state of Oaxaca is home to a prodigious number of important, nationally and internationally known artists (including Tamayo, Toledo, and Nieto), among whom Juchitán contributes its share. The Juchitán art scene was stimulated by the presence in the Isthmus of some of the giants of Mexican painting (Rivera, Kahlo, Covarrubias, etc.), who, fascinated with the region, popularized Isthmus culture and images of Zapotec women from the 1920s onward and inspired local painters (Covarrubias 1946). The contemporary art movement, though, owes more to the fame of Toledo's magical realism and the turbulent years of COCEI's first government. This period provided abundant raw material in the colorful and violent clashes between COCEI and PRI, in which many artists participated, and brought national attention to Juchitán. Local artists benefited from this recognition and the chance to interact with some of Mexico's top contemporary artists and intellectuals, who made Juchitán a cause célèbre and established close ties with the community. Ironically, Juchitán art work, fertilized by these interactions, has a trendy and radical chic quality that does well in the bourgeois marketplace. Toledo's stylish, modernistic, and international work, often bearing Zapotec titles, spread images of the Isthmus Zapotec to elite art galleries of Tokyo, Paris, and New York. Moreover, he almost singlehandedly circulated the news of COCEI's ethnopolitical movement to the world's cultural capitals.

On the local level, this means new opportunities for Zapotec artists to display and sell their canvases (e.g., to hotel owners in the international tourist zone of Huatulco, Oaxaca). Additionally, Toledo sent numerous boxes of the finest paint supplies and expensive art books to the Casa de la Cultura for use by local artists. Toledo's influence was also responsible for the Casa's impressive collection of modern art, including pieces by Tamayo, Cuevas, and foreign masters. Consequently, the Juchitán art scene, inspired by COCEI, has the resources to explore new definitions and images of Isthmus Zapotec culture.

Juchitán and COCEI were also fertile subject matter for some of Mexico's best photographers, who descended on the town to document government repression, the highly picturesque nature of the movement, and the photogenic aspects of Isthmus Zapotec life. Rafael Doniz (1983), Graciela Iturbide (Iturbide and Poniatowska 1989), and Pedro Meyer produced ethnographic photography chronicling the history of COCEI and modern Isthmus life. The books, posters, and even a documentary film made by these individuals diffused COCEI propaganda to audiences in Mexico and abroad.

As in the case of Juchitán painting, the sophisticated photographic account of Isthmus culture has a history that predates COCEI, although it too flourished as a result of the movement. This history reaches back to the 1930s and 1940s, when Andrés Henestrosa began bringing prominent artists and intellectuals, including Langston Hughes and French photographer Henri Cartier Bresson, to Juchitán (Matus 1987). Tina Modotti, Berenice Kolko, and Lola Alvarez Bravo also came and took photos of the town. Eisenstein even arrived on the scene to shoot part of a film on Mexico (Richardson 1988:170–83). The focus on Juchitán by national and international photographers stimulated an interest in photography among Juchitecos. The first significant local photographer was Sotero Constantino Jiménez (1983), whose portraits of Zapotec families, recently rediscovered and published by Toledo and the COCEI government, provide a nearly sociological picture of early twentieth-century Juchitán. Not to be outdone, the Casa de la Cultura has its own excellent collection of photography and an aspiring group of Juchiteco photographers.

Again we find that Juchitán's connections to the national and international art/cultural scene and left intelligentsia fertilized local cultural life and provided multiple outside influences on Zapotec intellectuals. What distinguishes Juchitán from many other Mesoamerican rural communities is that these interactions with outsiders, rather than eroding indigenous culture, stimulated it and provided the raw material for new ethnic self-definitions on the Isthmus Zapotec's own terms. This is possible because of the degree of political and economic autonomy Zapotec people have maintained in Juchitán historically. COCEI claims to be the defender of this autonomy in the Juchitán of the 1980s and 1990s.

The literary movement in Juchitán is also fueled by the struggles of COCEI, and Isthmus Zapotec writers are key COCEI supporters. The poetry of Matus, de la Cruz, Alejandro Cruz, and Enedino Jiménez focus on the rise of COCEI, Isthmus Zapotec culture, and the martyrdom of *coceístas* (de la Cruz 1983b; Bañuelos et al. 1988). These efforts are not without risk. PRI members murdered Cruz in 1987, right-wing thugs constantly harass Matus, and a PRI mob assaulted Toledo and de la Cruz in 1983.

The Juchitán literary movement entails recuperation of local oral and written traditions, history, and mythology, translation of famous poems and literature into Zapotec, and production of original Zapotec- or Spanish-language works focused on regional themes. From 1981 to 1983, COCEI published numerous books and pamphlets dealing with Isthmus history and local poetry, literature, music, and photography. Subsequently, Toledo established his own publishing firm (Ediciones Toledo) dedicated to Isthmus Zapotec ethnology and history. The Juchitecos' key publication is the extraordinary magazine, *Guchachi' Reza* (sliced iguana), edited by de la Cruz and others. Designed by the best graphic artists in Mexico and illustrated with the artwork of Toledo and other famous painters, it is a singular cultural achievement. Concerned primarily with the history and culture of the Zapotec and COCEI politics, this magazine includes poems in Zapotec and Spanish, art, photography, historical documents, social science analyses, pro-COCEI political statements, myth and folklore, and articles on Zapotec linguistics. Ironically, *Guchachi' Reza,* like the paintings of Toledo and friends, is fashionable and upscale despite its relatively humble origins. For example, the translation of Brecht and Neruda into Zapotec reflects the Juchiteco writers circle's awareness of trends in radical literature (see *Guchachi' Reza* nos. 13 and 24). In fact, *Guchachi' Reza*'s readers are more likely to be Parisian anthropologists or urban Mexicans than Zapotec peasants. Nonetheless, PRI was so convinced of the magazine's subversive potential that they burned it and the rest of the COCEI bookstore in 1983 (de la Cruz 1984).

Another major editorial accomplishment of COCEI is the publication *H. Ayuntamiento Popular* (Doniz 1983), which consists of a chronicle of political events during COCEI's first government by Carlos Monsiváis and ethnographic photography by Rafael Doniz. Doniz's photos capture highlights of the 1981–83 period, characteristic Zapotec social activities, and panoramas of the Isthmus. This book and *Guchachi' Reza* disseminated information about COCEI to intellectual circles in Mexico and elsewhere.

Popular Culture and the Politicization of Everyday Life

COCEI's constant mobilizations and its frequent skirmishes with the local PRI make daily life in Juchitán an ideological battleground.[16] In such a context, even the most mundane activities or personal preferences (conversations, commerce, fiestas, what clothes one wears, where one lives, what food one eats, where one drinks beer) may be charged with political significance. This is heightened by COCEI's defense of the Zapotec language and traditional customs and its association with the peasantry versus the rich. These factors, at times, transform everyday actions into forms of symbolic resistance or opposition: wearing red bandannas or red *huipiles* (indigenous blouses) versus green ones; attendance at one fiesta or bar instead of another (one may be primarily PRI and the other COCEI turf); use of different forms of address (COCEI favors use of the Spanish term *compañero* or the Zapotec *bichi'*, my brother);[17] wearing leather sandals instead of shoes; decoration of one's house with traditional furniture versus modern Western items, and so on (de la Cruz 1984).

COCEI WOMEN

Women's extensive participation in COCEI is critical to its strength in Juchitán not only because of their numbers and active contributions but because of their symbolic significance as defenders of the community—which they have been, repeatedly, throughout Isthmus history (Chiñas 1983)—and embodiments of ethnic pride. Women's colorful attire (brightly embroidered *huipiles* with geometric patterns and flowing skirts) and their important roles in commercial, religious, and social life are two of the most prominent elements of Isthmus Zapotec culture. Women invariably comprise 50 percent or more of the participants in COCEI demonstrations, highway blockades, and sit-ins, and their vivid presence (COCEI women dress in their finest and most elegant apparel for important COCEI rallies), militancy, and emotion add zest to all COCEI events. Militant Zapotec women dressed in red *huipiles* and defiantly waving COCEI flags in political marches are among the principal images the movement disseminates in photographs, posters, and political literature.

Unlike PRI women, whose political participation is often restricted to organizational activities and attendance at meetings, female *coceístas* aggressively engage in marches, shout derogatory slogans, take part in hunger strikes, and put themselves at physical risk in building takeovers and the like. Women are sometimes described as the "shock troops" of COCEI, and they are consistently among those wounded or jailed during repression. Several COCEI women have also been killed during political violence. In these political actions, they continue a long tradition of Zapotec women's involvement in issues concerning the control of the community—a tradition not only recognized but extolled in Isthmus oral tradition. Zapotec women's strong character and willingness to fight for their interests in the public arena are key features of this ethnic group, which bolster COCEI.

Nevertheless, COCEI's party line on women—that women have equal rights in the movement and in Isthmus Zapotec society generally—is misleading. Previous descriptions of a Zapotec matriarchy or gender-egalitarian society to the contrary (Covarrubias 1946; Chiñas 1983), Isthmus women experience many of the gender inequalities that affect women cross-culturally, such as fewer educational and career opportunities than men, the "double day," domestic violence, the sexual double standard, and restricted access to positions of political and juridical power.[18] The COCEI hierarchy is uniformly male, and Zapotec women are absent from the Juchitán artistic/intellectual milieu described above. Women who do play prominent leadership roles are mainly wives or relatives of male leaders or the representatives of typically female domains in the Isthmus (e.g., nursing, market vending, the COCEI women's committee, tavern management, etc.). Thus their decision-making power in the political arena, to a considerable degree, is mediated through men or restricted to primarily female activities.

CONCLUSION

Despite the destruction of the first COCEI government and subsequent repression, the movement survived and retained most of its following. From 1989 to 1992 COCEI once again governed Juchitán, has a federal deputy in the Mexican Congress, and is strengthening its foothold in approximately sixty other communities. This provides the movement with substantial control over local decision-making, access to public services for its members, and government spending directed toward COCEI strongholds. However, the organization's leaders continue to state that their primary goal is not electoral victories; rather, it is the defense of Isthmus peasants, workers, and students. They also continue to view COCEI's struggle as the continuation of past movements of the Isthmus Zapotecs for political independence, control of ancestral lands and resources, and preservation of the native language and culture.

In this essay I examined the roles played by culture, class, and ethnicity in COCEI. I focused on the ways in which COCEI discourse and practice have mobilized Isthmus Zapotec ethnic identity, a selective version of local history, and elements of indigenous culture—and in the process given them new politicized meanings. As in Guatemala, Peru, and several other Latin American countries, the Isthmus of Tehuantepec became fertile soil for a Marxist agrarian movement of indigenous people.[19] Such movements reveal the complex weave of ethnicity and class in rural Latin America, a complexity that defies analytical reduction of ethnicity to class, or vice versa. Furthermore, the CO-CEI case shows that indigenous ethnicity is more than a question of "us" and "them": It also involves deciding who and what "us" and "them" are. In deciding this, competing interests within indigenous society not only vindicate their ethnicity but redefine it in political struggle.

NOTES

1. The contestants in this debate are sometimes lumped into the following intellectual camps: *indigenista* (indigenist) versus Marxist, ethnopopulist versus Marxist, or *culturalista* (culturalist) versus Marxist. Another heated polemic concerned primarily with rural Mexico was the *campesinista* (propeasant) versus *proletarista* (proworker) slugfest. The latter discussion, however, largely ignored (or denied) ethnic aspects of the peasantry.

2. *PRIhuela* is a "Zapotecized" COCEI slur on the name of Mexico's dominant political party (PRI). *Huela* is a Zapotec word meaning old woman; here it has the derogatory connotation of something worn-out or used up.

3. This trademark COCEI word highlights the degree to which Spanish words and indigenous inflection merge in contemporary Isthmus Zapotec language. Here the Spanish word *paisanos* (fellow-countrymen) becomes *paisanuca* as a result of a vowel change from "o" to "u" and the insertion of the Zapotec plural suffix, *ca*, in place of the Spanish "s." In Juchitán the Zapotecs creatively mold elements of linguistic and cultural *mestizaje* into new ethnic self-definitions. Royce (1982:176–77) notes, "The Zapotec experience no feelings of inconsistency when they adopt elements of Mexican national culture. . . . The symbols of what is considered to be Zapotec are constantly being revised as Juchitecos move with the times." Likewise, in Francisco Toledo's art, ideas and images from Zapotec cul-

ture are united with European concepts. Instead of opposing "traditional" versus "modern" or indigenous versus international, Toledo bridges these dichotomies to create a rich artistic synthesis (Markman and Markman 1989:196).

4. There are many variations on this basic description of a COCEI rally. Often the main event is a massive demonstration in front of Juchitán City Hall.

5. Royce (1982:169) states that 80 percent of Juchitán's population is Zapotec. Although Juchitán is now heavily populated, the city combines aspects of urban culture with the ambience of an indigenous peasant village. The bulk of the male population is composed of peasants; proletarianization is increasing rapidly, however.

6. The middle- and upper-class Isthmus Zapotecs tend to be increasingly more identified with Mexican national culture than are the peasantry and lower classes for the following reasons: schooling and travel outside the Isthmus, greater access to consumer goods (e.g., cars, televisions, electronic apparatuses, stylish Western clothing, and popular magazines), a growing tendency among elite families to downgrade having their children learn the indigenous language, and their association with PRI and its ideology of nationalism and modernization.

7. Royce (1982:168–83) argues that the Zapotec's unified identity allowed them to maintain political, economic, and social control of Juchitán against the onslaught of rival ethnic groups historically. She states that, in recent times, upper-class and upper-middle-class Zapotecs have promoted Zapotec identity "in order to preserve their dominance" (1982:183). Poor Zapotecs cling to their identity out of poverty and inability to speak Spanish or function effectively in mestizo society: "Any feature [of Zapotec style] exhibited by the lower class is above all, an economic problem" (Royce 1975:78).

Juchitán life has changed considerably as a result of COCEI's ethnopolitics. Since the 1981 election, COCEI—composed of lower-middle-class and lower-class Juchitecos—has taken the lead in promoting and reconstituting Zapotec culture and has bolstered the self-image of poor Juchitecos. Today, Zapotec identity is wielded effectively by a coalition of the poor who view both the Zapotec upper classes and outsiders as their enemies. Additionally, a closer look at Isthmus history may reveal that intense intraethnic cleavages, straining Zapotec unity, did not suddenly emerge with COCEI. Instead they were present in the Che Gómez period, in the struggles between the Red Party and Green Party during the Revolution, and in resistance to Charis's political dominance.

8. National Meeting of Indian Peoples.

9. Víctor Yodo is the nickname of Víctor Pineda Henestrosa, a founder of COCEI who was "disappeared" by paramilitary forces in 1978. Pico de Oro literally means golden beak or golden peak but is also the name of a brand of Mexican beer. *Totopos* are a primary food of the Isthmus Zapotecs.

In contrast to the clumsy use of local names and terminology by PMS leaders in their Juchitán rally, a COCEI speaker evoked delight from the crowd with his transposition of Zapotec slang onto the name of President Carlos Salinas de Gortari. The *coceísta* called him "Salinas de Gueu'tari." *Gueu'* means literally "coyote" but idiomatically signifies cowardice or homosexuality. This is a typical verbal device used by COCEI in demonstrations.

Although there seems to be a refreshing degree of tolerance of homosexuality in Isthmus Zapotec society, currents of homophobia are also present (as this incident implies), despite the frequently espoused view (e.g., de la Cruz 1983e) that discrimination against gays is absent from Juchitán.

10. Bartolomé and Barabas (1986:85) observe the tendency of the Huaves, Chontals, Zoques, and Mixes to be "Zapotecized" vis-à-vis language, clothing, and diverse cultural practices as a result of the superordinate economic position of the Isthmus Zapotecs.

11. Recent Oaxaca state governor Heladio Ramírez was careful to consult with CO-CEI leaders on important Isthmus affairs and acceded to many of their demands. He described the COCEI leadership as "excellent Mexicans and distinguished social activists" in the national newspaper, *Excélsior* (Oct. 16, 1987).

12. Felipe Martínez López (1985:62), PRI mayor of Juchitán from 1986 to 1989, notes the martyrdom of numerous COCEI members as a rallying point for the movement "in a society where the cult of the dead has primordial importance." Daily life in Isthmus towns is frequently marked by large, colorful funeral processions and religious masses for the deceased. Additionally, almost all Zapotec households have altars where photos of dead relatives are venerated. Isthmus cemeteries, especially those of Juchitán, have large house-like monuments in honor of the dead.

13. The Zapotec word *guendalizaa* also means reciprocal or voluntary collective labor among kinsmen, as in preparations for a wedding or fiesta, or building a house. The Nahuatl term *tequio*, however, has replaced it in everyday usage in Juchitán to a considerable extent.

14. Víctor de la Cruz (1983b) discusses the Isthmus Zapotec cultural revival. This movement is heralded in three periodicals concerned with the Isthmus: *Neza* (1935–39), a product of Henestrosa's generation; *Neza Cubi* (1968–70), promoted by Matus and de la Cruz, who attempted to renew the tradition of *Neza;* and *Guchachi' Reza* (1975–present), edited by de la Cruz and others, which is the organ of the modern (COCEI-inspired) Isthmus cultural movement.

The lengthy bibliography and artistic portfolio produced by the current group of Zapotec artists and intellectuals is too extensive to review here. Chiñas (1983:9) suggests that the contemporary Isthmus Zapotec literary movement is the only one of its kind in Mesoamerica; however, similar movements are also emerging in Michoacán, Chiapas, and elsewhere.

15. Several older, more-established Juchitán writers (e.g., Henestrosa and the deceased Gabriel López Chiñas), however, have sided with PRI.

16. Nugent (1987-88:104) notes that popular ideology "is something which social groups create and modify in the course of their day-to-day practices, and through which they organize and transform those day-to-day practices." Nugent observed

a growing ideological separation between Chihuahua peasant-workers and the State as a result of recent economic, political, and ecological crises. This is clearly the case in Juchitán also, although "ideological disjuncture" between Juchitecos and regional and national authorities has a long history that predates CO-CEI politics (see de la Cruz [1983d] and Nugent's [1987-88:104] further comments).

17. Dorsett (1975:240) states that "the term *bichi'* (brother) . . . extends to all men of the town and further to all Zapotecs."

18. Chiñas (1983:117) describes Isthmus Zapotec gender relations as "emphatically egalitarian." The view that Isthmus Zapotec society is matriarchal has been put forth in numerous tourist guides, traveler's journals, and magazine articles and is a common element of Mexican national folklore about the Isthmus.

19. By this comparison I do not mean to imply that COCEI's organization or aims approximate those of any specific movement in these countries. What I am suggesting is that the indigenous people supporting such movements share a common history of colonial oppression and modern-day political and cultural repression that led them to radical resistance. Under such circumstances, some indigenous groups find that class-based politics provide an attractive model for change that is not necessarily in conflict with native culture and local ethnic identity. This highlights the continuing importance of the class/ethnicity question in rural Latin American political practice and anthropological analysis.

Interview
with
Daniel López Nelio

The struggle of the indigenous Zapotec did not originate in the 1960s or 1970s, but began many years ago. It started as a resistance struggle against Spanish colonization and continued as constant rebellion during the colonial period. This struggle is centered on the defense of education, traditions, and Zapotec identity, as well as the rejection of Western culture.

Capitalist development in Mexico has treated the Isthmus as a strategic site for capital accumulation because of its geographic situation and natural wealth. In the Juárez era there were plans to construct either an interoceanic canal, which would unite the Pacific with the Gulf of Mexico, or a railway (as finally happened). Nevertheless, to the extent that this penetration encountered resistance from the Zapotecs, it was not totally successful. Hence Zapotec culture has been an obstacle to capitalism, which is why the capitalists have wanted to destroy it.

The Benito Juárez Dam provides another example of this. It was planned to promote capital accumulation and not to benefit the Zapotecs. It was built to develop commercial agriculture and destroy a culture that throughout history has obstructed capitalist development. I repeat, it was meant to systematically destroy Zapotec culture. Let us examine how development has affected indigenous ways of life.

The Zapotecs have always had a self-sufficient economy based on the cultivation of a variety of plants such as corn, squash, watermelon, cantaloupe, etc. These crops allowed us to feed ourselves as well as retain a surplus for other purposes. If indeed this form of life survives today, it does so only partially. In the irrigation district, traditional crops are no longer planted but have been displaced by sugar cane, an unproductive crop. In the cultural field, today's weddings are celebrated under *stands* [metal structures] provided by the beer companies instead of under the traditional *enramada*.[1] In this sense Warman was right in his suggestion that the construction of the dam was going to have an obvious consequence, the gradual disappearance of Zapotec culture.[2] It seemed as if Zapotec culture was condemned to this fate.

Nonetheless, resistance emerged apparently out of nowhere; yet what really happened was nothing more than our regaining our tradition of struggle. Although they have taken away our lands, they have not been able to make us lose our spirit of struggle. Now we speak Zapotec mixed with Spanish, but our spirit of resistance has not been lost. COCEI recovers this spirit of struggle. Our control of City Hall gives us the protection we need to reconquer our culture and traditions.

In this sense, I understand Warman [see his essay in this volume], and he is right. That is, throughout history unsuccessful attempts have been made to uproot and destroy this culture, but with the Benito Juárez Dam they are succeeding. If we look at the 25,000 hectares in the irrigated area, the majority of them are sown with sugar cane. Where is the cultivation of corn? What is happening to the Zapotecs? There is no rain, and there is no corn in the nonirrigated area, and in the irrigation zone 80 to 90 percent of the land is planted in cane. Therefore, there is little chance for the subsistence economy to continue.[3]

That is why COCEI recovers our tradition of struggle, in the sense of defending the family economy, continuing to grow corn, and reconquering the lands that were taken from the peasants in the irrigation district. COCEI demands respect for the peasants' possession of land and the reinstatement of the 1964 presidential decree, which is nothing more than the recognition of our right to the land that we have possessed for many years.

Control of City Hall opens up the possibility of reclaiming our culture through the radio station we now have. Today in the municipal court, matters are resolved in Zapotec, which PRI would not accept for many years. That is, PRI forced our people to speak Spanish, whether they could or not, in judicial affairs. Today, this policy has been discarded, and Zapotec is spoken in the courthouse, police station, and mayor's office. The previous policy meant the destruction of Zapotec culture by forcing people to speak Spanish. We are reestablishing our culture by converting the neighborhood committees into true people's tribunals, as the Zapotecs did long ago. We have *Guchachi' Reza,* which seeks to recover the history of the Zapotecs. Even if we did not control

City Hall, we would have done this anyway, but not with the same possibilities. Having City Hall, the Casa de la Cultura, and these other means allows us to defend Zapotec culture more effectively. . . .

We know that our culture will not be respected by the capitalist system, which is even capable of militarizing the region to destroy our culture, language, etc. Now, what is our concern? That our children know how to speak Zapotec and play in Zapotec. This is our concern. Why? For the continuity of our history and so that in one hundred years or three centuries, we can continue eating iguana. . . .

In the last instance, our culture will be defended to the extent that we uproot from the country an entire system that oppresses us. The Zapotec race is oppressed by an entire economic system, the same as the working class. Now the struggle is not only over ethnicity, because the Zapotecs are also workers. The struggle is also for peasants and the indigenous cultural question. It all comes together. . . .

At this moment, the struggle of COCEI is not only the struggle of the Zapotecs but the struggle of the Zoques, Huaves, Chontals, Mixes, and Triquis as well. And we are not speaking abstractly, we are speaking of real actions. In fact, there *is* a struggle of the Chontals, Huaves, Zoques, Mixtecs, and Triquis. These are the struggles led by COCEI. But it is not only a struggle of ethnic groups. I want to emphasize this. It is also the struggle of the peasants and workers. Tomorrow, COCEI will be part of an entire project of struggle for the liberation of the authentic owners of the territory of this country.

NOTES

1. *Enramadas* are roofed, open shelters constructed adjacent to many Isthmus homes to provide a shady spot for eating and socializing. Thick, unfinished tree limbs and trunks are sunk into the ground and attached together with smaller beams. The roof is woven of cut palm leaves. At least one or two hammocks are strung from the vertical posts for afternoon siestas and/or nighttime sleeping. Much larger *enramadas* are often constructed for weddings, fiestas to honor patron saints, and other celebrations, although *stands* have replaced them at many contemporary Isthmus social events.

2. "El futuro del Istmo y la Presa Juárez," Arturo Warman interviewed by Francisco Toledo, *Guchachi' Reza* 15 (June 1983): 2–4. A translated version appears in Part One of this book.

3. Editors' note: López Nelio probably overestimates the extent to which corn has been displaced by sugar cane in the irrigation district, but the fundamental point regarding the decline of corn cultivation is certainly accurate. See Binford (1983:102–34) for further discussion of changing cropping patterns in the 1966–79 period.

La Caminante (The Walker). Oil painting on cloth by Francisco Toledo. 1989.

Rain

Víctor de la Cruz

This rain has been falling a long time now,
many rounds of hundreds of years.
Today it was raining the whole day long.
I was remembering you—and you weren't there—
and remembering your name in our language.
That rain comes from a long way away
like our language and our people.
Our ancestors saw that rain fall
and called it: funeral water flower—
because they saw it spill
when a flower opened high in the sky
inside the darkness roundabout it.
Because our lives open
like a flower and close in the gateway of a tomb.
It's a long time now this water has been after us
and a long time we have followed it
and it will not abandon us
as little as we'll let go of it—
because where it comes from: there we were born
and where it ends there we end

in the earth closing down.
The *binnigula'sa',* our ancestors,
those who were the first to speak our language,
saw it fall over their villages
Juchitán, Tehuantepec;
they saw it fall on furrows and cornfields,
filling their rivers, Tehuantepec, Juchitán;
flooding the Biahuido' laguna
and Guichibele, the road to Xadani;
they saw it come at last to the ocean
where the waters we weep have their ending.

The Sun

Enedino Jiménez

Like a dying man waiting
for his family to bless him
I wait for you Sun
to put your light into me.

I've a real strong desire to see you
one more time again:
I'm like some small kid waiting here,
standing in your footprints, conjuring up
your hands on my shoulders, crimson Sun.

Sun: a sentence grows in my hands.
I found it one day when sowing in the fields.
Sun, I want my people to be like you.
No other reason for hoping you'll be by.

Brothers
or Citizens:
Two Languages,
Two Political Projects
in the
Isthmus

Víctor de la Cruz

Apropos of advocacy for indigenous people I will begin my exposition by invoking Octavio Paz (1984:6), who has become their defender in Germany:

> Another important segment of the [Nicaraguan] opposition lives isolated in inhos-
> pitable regions. This is the indigenous minority that does not speak Spanish. Its
> culture and forms of life are threatened, and the indigenes have suffered despolia-
> tion and violent attacks under the *sandinista* regime.

When people talk of ethnic revivals, some feel these cannot be inserted into
wider political projects, and when political projects are mentioned, others believe that these do not imply revival of indigenous minorities. In the Oaxacan
Isthmus, at least, the two projects that confront each other (one imposed and
the other proposed) have ethnic and linguistic consequences. In the case of the
imposed PRI political project, the ethnic element is implicit. And in the project
explicitly promoted by COCEI, ethnic revival is proposed rather than imposed.
This includes the defense of communal land tenure, recovery and revaluation
of indigenous culture, and priority use of autochthonous languages [instead of
Spanish], such as Zapotec in the case of Juchitán. These programs are part of
a broader project that includes revivalism, political strategies, and class alliances in the struggle for a less inequitable Mexican nation. In this new Mexico,
the indigenous minorities recover the geographic and social space that was

snatched from them by the creole bourgeoisie and their allies, who have enjoyed the use of the wealth of this linguistically and culturally rich country.

These initial invocations and advocacy seemed necessary to me now that the great poet Octavio Paz has done well in "seeing straw in the other man's eye," although he has done poorly in not "seeing the stick in his own eye." Here in Mexico he could have easily tried out his ideas earlier by denouncing the ways that the indigenous minorities are fucked over *[chingado]* and marginalized into inhospitable regions, "regions of refuge," as Aguirre Beltrán calls them. The Indian's best lands are taken from them, as in the current case of the "Cerro de Oro" dam, and their cultures are systematically destroyed.

In this essay, I will assess the degree of domination and resistance among the Zapotecs. I will analyze concrete situations in which the contemporary social actors consist, on one side, of *priístas,* the electoral instruments of the Mexican government, which promotes a project of ethnocide and linguistic domination, and on the other side, of COCEI, which offers a project of resistance and ethnic liberation within a broader class-based program.

THE HISTORY OF AGGRESSION AND RESISTANCE

In a previous work, I synthesized the history of language politics in Mexico from the Spanish invasion to the present (de la Cruz 1980a). The measures applied as part of this unfolding politics of colonization are still used today as methods to force the "Castilianization" of the ethnic minorities. This process reveals coincidences not only in the particular histories of the Zapotecs and, for example, the Mixes, but in the histories of all the indigenous groups today called Oaxacans. This is the general history of colonization among our peoples.

In the first stage of Oaxaca linguistic politics, the friars learned the autochthonous languages to evangelize those whom they called *indios* or *gentiles* (heathens). This resulted in the immediate production of *"artes"* (vocabularies and primers of and in the native languages). In the case of the Zapotecs this task was realized exemplarily by Friar Juan de Córdova with his *Arte del idioma zapoteco* [Córdova 1987a, original 1578] and *Vocabulario en lengua zapoteca* [Córdova 1987b, original 1571].

Because the friars felt they could not move forward adequately in the task of evangelization, even in the most perfect of the native languages, the second stage involved teaching Castilian to the indigenes. This stage in language politics was solidified in the decree of June 17, 1550, which later formed part of the Laws of the Indies.

The third stage consisted in discriminating openly against those indigenous people who did not know Spanish by excluding them from occupying public offices in their towns. This was suggested by the bishop of Oaxaca and formalized in the decree of June 1690. The latter decree established sanctions, such as public reproach or the loss of a *cacicazgo* (chiefdom) and all the prerogatives enjoyed by the indigenous nobility, if thereafter they spoke to the Indians of their *cacicazgo* in their native language. This measure was originally prepared in a draft of a decree by the Council of Indies in 1596 sent to King Felipe II for him to approve and send to the viceroy of Peru, Don Luis de Velasco. It was established by decree on April 16, 1770.

We can document the particular history of Isthmus Zapotec linguistic resistance as beginning at the turn of the twentieth century when a Zapotec of San Blas Atempa, Arcadio G. Molina, published a book in which he employed a written Zapotec according to rules he had established in a previous work (Molina 1894, 1899). He finished this earlier study during the time when he was aiding the North American anthropologist Frederick Starr to collect a series of Tehuantepec songs (lyrics and music) in Zapotec (de la Cruz n.d.).

In the mid-1930s a generation of Zapotec intellectuals appeared in Mexico City, grouped around the New Society of Juchiteco Students. They published the newspaper and later magazine *Neza* [1987, first published in 1935–39], in which they made known a series of works concerned with recovering and revaluing the Zapotec language and culture. Only two of them (Andrés Henestrosa and Gabriel López Chiñas) became standouts in Mexican literary circles, but many participated in this enterprise, continuing the seemingly solitary work initiated by Arcadio G. Molina in San Blas Atempa.

Between this author and the *Neza* generation we find a transitional group composed of military men who were born at the end of the last century and who participated in the events of the armed struggle begun in 1910. They were Genaro López Miro, Enrique Liekens Cerqueda (1882–1978), and Jeremías López Chiñas (1901–41). We know of no writings on language and culture by the first. The little we know about him is that he fed Andrés Henestrosa upon his arrival in Mexico City (de la Cruz 1980b). The latter two, however, economically supported *Neza*. Enrique Liekens wrote poems in Zapotec and published an essay about the Zapotec language called *Los Zapotecos no son Zapotecos sino Zaes* (1952) and left unpublished a study of Isthmus Zapotec grammar. Jeremías López Chiñas, whose life ended prematurely, published a study on Zapotec botany. We do not know if this intermediate generation between Molina and the New Society of Juchiteco Students served as a conscious bridge between the two, that is, if they were aware of the Blaseño's work, and if in addition to supporting the younger group of intellectuals, they transmitted to them their knowledge and that of their parents' generation.

The movement to recover and revalue Isthmus Zapotec language and culture did not emerge only among the immigrants to the big city. Other intellectuals with strong attachments to their town and language emerged contemporaneous with Pancho Nacar and Andrés Henestrosa. The same year that Henestrosa was born, Carlos Iribarren Sierra was born in Tehuantepec and Eustaquio Jiménez Girón in Juchitán. In 1910 Manuel Reyes Cabrera ("Rey Baxa") was born in Juchitán, as was Juan Jiménez ("Juan Stubi") at about the same time. All of these men are known and respected for their works in Zapotec or about the Zapotec language. In 1980, a year before he died, Eustaquio Jiménez Girón published a manuscript that he had been preparing for many years: a type of Zapotec- Spanish vocabulary entitled *Guía gráfica-fonémica para la escritura y lectura del Zapoteco*.

One question raised by this history of the resistance of the Isthmus Zapotec language is whether the conscious reaction against the penetration of Spanish began in San Blas Atempa (on one side of Tehuantepec) or elsewhere. Why did Arcadio G. Molina have near his town only this solitary epigone named Carlos Iribarren Sierra, whereas in Juchitán there was a massive response by a great number of people who dedicated themselves to using Zapotec literarily?

We do not know the history of San Blas Atempa or the biography of Molina well enough to determine what exogenous factors might have caused the conflict between the two languages to break out there, resulting in a reaction against Spanish. In Molina's era San Blas was surely almost 100-percent monolingual in Zapotec, since according to the 1970 census 81.74 percent of the population still spoke the indigenous language.

In response to the other part of the question we can point out that Tehuantepec was a community that received a larger influx of Spaniards in comparison to places like Juchitán from the beginning of colonization (Torres de Laguna 1983:20). Tehuantepec was also the center of colonial influence in the region. Consequently, if Tehuantepec was to generate a response to colonialism it would have to take place at the beginning of the colony, as indeed happened historically. The first Isthmus indigenous rebellions occurred there. On the other hand, the then barrio of San Blas Atempa and the town of Juchitán remained relatively removed from the colonization process, perhaps because they lacked political and economic advantages for the conquerors. Then, during the revolutionary movement of 1910, large contingents of Juchitecos and Zapotecs from other surrounding towns moved all over the country to fight for the different factions that disputed power. Undoubtedly this caused the indigenes to confront the other language [i.e., Spanish] in a more prolonged way, whether it was in the community through contact with foreign soldiers, the *dxu'*, or in the places where they went to do battle.

This, I believe, explains the heightened awareness of the military intellectu-als, who reacted to the confrontation with the foreign language and supported and promoted the foundation of the New Society of Juchiteco Students and the periodical *Neza*. Two of these military men, López Miro and López Chiñas, fought in the ranks of General Charis, while Liekens Cerqueda, fighting on another battle front, was made a colonel and member of General Obregón's staff. The initial reaction of Zapotec soldiers confronted with the Spanish lan-guage can be noted in the first *corridos* they composed to narrate their wartime exploits. Their reaction was hesitant; they tried to use Zapotec, but their com-positions were infested with all kinds of words borrowed from Spanish. This is the case in the following *"corridos"* (only in the narrative and not in the form): "The Surrender of the Federales to the Carrancistas in Salina Cruz, 1915," "The Capture of Salina Cruz in 1923," and the "Corrido of the Colo-rado" (de la Cruz 1983a).

As the cultural and linguistic movement becomes politicized, its objectives broaden. Now it is not enough to recover native language and culture. It is also necessary to recover the communal lands that are being monopolized and privatized. Therefore, it is necessary to fight for control of the Communal Lands Commission and City Hall, which are spaces where justice and injustice are imparted and lands are distributed. In relation to this, our history has taught us, since the time of our leader Che Gorio Melendre, that we Zapotecs cannot win the battle by ourselves. We must seek new alliances as Melendre did in his time and, in this way, widen our project.

My generation had the responsibility of taking this step, and I think this occurred because we participated in or closely observed the 1968 student movement. We returned to our towns to fight for and alongside our people. In 1972 the Casa de la Cultura (Lidxi Guendabiaani') was founded in Juchitán. In 1974 COCEI was founded, followed in 1975 by the magazine *Guchachi' Reza*. The Zapotec language is the substrate of these three institutions, al-though in some of them it appears more a goal and in others a medium of activity, but all three go together hand in hand. Thus the municipal political campaign arrived in 1980. If in Tlahuiltoltepec, Oaxaca (Aubague 1983:234), schools are the focal point of conflict over the language question, in Juchitán the political arena is where the Zapotec language began to battle Spanish and defeat it.

Víctor de la Cruz

BROTHER OR CITIZEN? DO WE REALLY NO LONGER WANT TO SPEAK ZAPOTEC?

> Thus, power is manifested also through the use of languages. In terms of politi-
> cal strategy, linguistic domination complements other tactics. It prolongs the ma-
> terial conditions of domination in the realms of consciousness, identity, and
> social subjectivity. (Aubague 1983:211–12)

Not only did they [PRI/upper classes] rob the Juchitecos of their communal
land from City Hall, but they shouted at them in Spanish so that they would
not understand. That is why it was necessary to do battle right there; thus
COCEI speaks Zapotec and seeks the recovery of the monopolized land. It
does not seek a return to the past, but a more equitable route to the future. PRI
also learned the efficacy of using Zapotec to communicate with the Juchitecos,
the majority of whom speak that language. Thus, for the 1980 elections, PRI
ran a candidate who advocated modernization and was obliged to practice Zapotec, which he had stopped speaking, because COCEI speaks in Zapotec to
its militants, its brothers. Stumblingly, the candidate used the radio daily to
expound on the values of the bourgeoisie in the language spoken by the peasantry. Political propaganda, with a photograph of the candidate seated on the
sofa in the living room of his house surrounded by his family, was placed on
the exterior walls of the houses of Juchitán. How many Juchitecos have a sofa
in their living room? Only a few. Images are also part of the modernization discourse.

PRI recognizes that it lost the elections for the second time. Since March
10, 1981, City Hall has been controlled by a government council from the
ranks of COCEI. Now that they have control of municipal government, the
young administrators feel that the pressure of the Zapotec language is greater.
Up in City Hall they shout, tell jokes, charge taxes, and administer justice in
Zapotec. He who does not speak Zapotec cannot hold public office because
the authentic Juchitecos have taken City Hall by storm, and they impose their
language there. The lesson is learned, and in the next electoral campaign (characterized by PRI infamy and repression) the recovery and defense of the Zapotec language are now explicit. They are present in slogans in Zapotec and
Spanish on all the walls of the towns where COCEI participates.

What was the official party's reaction to this? To teach Zapotec to their candidate, who stumbles every time he tries to speak it. This is not only because
he has no command of the language, but also because of the content of his
discourse, which can be likened to bringing the main streets of Juchitán or as
many streets as possible up to the level of the "Houston of the Southeast,"

Tuxtla Gutiérrez [Chiapas]. And the peasants with their oxcarts? Let them go to hell. Let them go to Cheguigo (on the other side of the river), to Ward Seven [a poor barrio], or if possible to Xadani [a nearby peasant village]—the farther away the better. Who ordered them to be so backward and to go on "stuck" to their customs and their "dialect"?

Discourse is a form of life or speaks a form of life. Rather than reflecting the speaker's real world it reflects his desired world, the conception or global project desired for society as a whole. The then president of the local PRI and now mayor of Juchitán [1984–86] has said: "COCEI perpetrates a situation of danger and risk in Juchitán, and that is why we called on the authorities to adopt extreme measures to guarantee security, tranquility, and order" (*Excélsior,* Aug. 17, 1983). Now we know what PRI means by security and order. Their conception of democracy is South American-style democracy although they seek an urbanized Juchitán along North American lines. Those who cannot pay for urbanization can go die in the countryside.

We know well from experience, and the journalists who have been to Juchitán know also, that PRI's discourse translates into actions. It concretizes in actions against *lo zapoteco* for being subversive or Central American. The first action that they took when they recaptured City Hall with the army was to vent their fury against the COCEI-established people's bookstore, throwing out stacks of the publication *Guchachi' Reza* into the street. Well, at least this served to inform the bootblacks that the Zapotec language can be written; thereafter they spent several days deciphering their hidden past in the pages of the magazine.

These few examples and a superficial analysis of them foreshadow the direction to which the *priísta* discourse leads, that is, modernization equivalent to "Castilianization" (perhaps if it were English it would be better), the Zapotec language synonymous with backwardness, and COCEI equal to Central American subversion. This is how PRI began to fight the notorious majority presence of COCEI in certain areas of Juchitán, such as the seventh ward and the Rodrigo Carrasco colony. On another front the Directorate of Indigenous Education of the Public Education Ministry authorized the elaboration of a whole project to "Castilianize" the Isthmus. Is the contracting of Spanish teachers by the PRI administration of Juchitán the first phase of this project? Or is this merely a coincidence? These are questions that only time or those responsible for this project can answer.

Multiple forms have been used to teach Spanish to Mexican Indians, but it is a sophism to say that knowledge of the Castilian language equalizes the economic and cultural situation of the Indian with that of the creole bourgeoisie [as the director of the aforementioned program has implied]. This new project that the government is implementing will not improve even slightly the economic situation of the poor of the seventh ward and the Rodrigo Carrasco colony. But it can serve as a medium to introduce the ideology of dependent Mexican capitalism, and it can push aside socialist ideology as an option for the Zapotec community.

Although disadvantaged because of its lack of resources and the effects of repression, COCEI also defended its project. Its discourse emphasized the defense of Zapotec culture and the reinforcement of the native language through diffusion of its alphabet. For COCEI, the Juchitecos are not equal citizens under the law as in bourgeois-liberal ideology. Treating the unequal equally is an inequality. For COCEI, the Juchitecos are *bichi'*, brothers, and they greet each other by saying "Ma! zeu' la?, bichi'" ("Are you going, my brother?"); "Caziila' dxu'la? bichi'" ("Are you resting, brother?"). One should not exploit, rob, or kill a brother. Cain is not accepted in Zapotec society either.

Citizens, because they are legally equal, must be treated as equals even though this permits the exploitation of some and the enrichment of others. "If they do not become rich too it is because they are lazy, stupid, or weak." But a brother must be helped to go forward, to grow, to construct his house or educate his children. That is why we hold on tightly to *didxazá* [the Zapotec language], because its experience in the past offers us solutions and points of departure toward the future and toward a type of modernity that is less unjust.

The Bell

Andrés Henestrosa

Many wonderful miracles are attributed to Saint Vincent, patron saint of Juchitán—among others, that he turned himself into a saint.

This occurred in a city on earth where day after day a child and his friends carried out harmless works of mischief. One morning, tired of the same games, the child proposed playing *tingui-bidoo.*[1] Two children put their arms together to form a chair, and once formed, Vincent sat in it. Preceded by prayers the children circled around an imaginary temple. Their arms heavy and tired, the children wanted to let Vincent down, but the imaginary saint was now real. His flesh was rigid, turned into wood. From this day onward he was venerated in my land.

One day Saint Vincent left town and disappeared. He left no sign of his absence, and no one, however wise, knew where he might be found. While Saint Vincent was away from the church (which he had imagined and constructed in an instant), he built a bell. He printed his seal on it and went to a white strip of beach to drop it into the green arms of the sea. And he sent a message warning us, the vigilant eyes, to wait at the edge of the water for the waves to wash it up. This strange news ran through the streets, and everyone knew that the saint lived and had not forgotten his church. The whole town ran to the coast. The distance between Juchitán and the ocean was not great, but because of the beach's narrowness the Juchitecos took a while to arrive. Because they had to walk in single file it grew very late before all of them reached the coast.

They waited and waited. The sun heated the air and the sand burned their feet. Getting tired, they looked for tracks, and they found a long trail. The line of footprints went beyond where they were allowed to go without the permission of their elders, so they returned quickly to the city. The old bell emptied its ring into the air, and unknowingly, because their anxiety was great and they could not tolerate more difficulties, the people congregated around the church as if all of the streets passed by its door.

They knew that those who scarred the sand with their footprints were the same ones who had recovered the bell destined for Juchitán. No one doubted that it was the Huaves of San Mateo del Mar. A delegation of goddesses was chosen to go recover the bell. Without following trails, the chosen goddesses walked in the air like shadows without making noise, while the afternoon erased the distance. They arrived in San Mateo very late. The *cortamortajas* bird cut the silence with the scissors of its song. The dogs were asleep, and the church doors were doubly barred. They went up the tower and untied the bell with their fingertips to take it with them. One of the goddesses carried the clapper. They walked with holy fear, as if a vertebral column kept them in line, in order not to break rhythm. As a result the trip was noiseless. Since then the Juchitecas have retained that way of moving (which is like walking in rhyme) in their feet; it appears, even today, when they dress up for a fiesta and dance.

Returning past the wall of brush that interrupts the train tracks for a second, past the murmuring corn fields and near Danibacuza, a goddess let go of the clapper. The clapper hit the bell, and its voice rang all the way back to San Mateo and woke its inhabitants.

Two Huave gods, as light as feathers, climbed up the tower and found the tower silent. With a thousand shouts they brought together their men. The committee that was named there hurried after the Zapotec virgins and soon caught up to them. The Huave voices and the noise of Huave footsteps in the quiet of the dawn announced their proximity from afar. The path got lost with each step, found itself and went straight for a long stretch, and lost itself again. In one of the countless turns, some of the goddesses hid in the brush, and, recalling their ancient origins, others turned themselves into trees. When the path once again found them the bell was by itself. The goddess who had made it speak did not have time to hide herself, so, conserving her shape, she turned herself into stone beside the bell. A Huave god identified her as one of the escaped Zapotec goddesses, and the curse that rolled out of his mouth like a stone petrified her forever.

The Huaves returned to San Mateo with the bronze bell on their shoulders.

The Bell

Once again they could see a bell hanging in their church tower; the bell is reminiscent of the petticoats worn by the women of Juchitán, a sign of its Zapotec origin.

Several nights later, the ocean recognized its guilt. It overflowed its banks and ran all the way to the church to snatch away the bell, but the church had deep foundation posts, and the water was not strong enough to uproot them. Since the first day they got the bell back, each time night passes from shack to shack, tying a flame to the wick of the wax candles, the bell cries out, and the Huaves gather. An individual, the one who carries the wooden staff of author-ity, names a commission of men to take care of the bell, to whom he repeats: "Be careful in case the Juchitecos return."

NOTE

1. *Tingui-bidoo* [swing the saint] is an Isthmus Zapotec game in which two children form a chair or throne by crisscrossing their hands, and another child sits in the chair in imitation of the saints kept in local churches.

Trapped
Lightning

Recorded by Macario Matus

"One day," recounts Sr. Sabino, "I went with my oxcart to collect firewood in the countryside. I went with no worries at all. I arrived at my corn field and began to split logs and collect what I had cut the day before.

"I was cutting wood when all of a sudden I heard a cry, a moan from far away. The lament came from a mesquite tree that was shaped like a forked pole. I approached the area with the desire to help the complaining individual. I saw that pole, and it was the voice of lightning. It said to me: 'Hey, Sabino, look at the trouble I'm in. I have been here for several hours. I don't know how this tree and its fork trapped me. I can't go out into the world and continue doing my duty on earth. You know, making the earth and sky thunder, announcing rain and storms.'

"Well," said Sr. Sabino, "if you are asking me, I will help you." And he took away a stone that was on top of the lightning. He did it quickly, and all he heard was an enormous whistle that went up to the sky.

"This is why," recounts Sr. Sabino, "thanks to me lightning exists in the world. Otherwise, it would still be trapped underneath that mesquite tree. And wherever lightning sees me, it always greets me with lights and thunder. Lightning has never returned to my corn field."

The Tales
of
Moonje'

Manuel M. Matus

Isaac Monje López, popularly known as Moonje', was a liar, but a very charming one. We propose to remember him and ensure that his name is not forgotten and that the charm remains in his stories. He was a tall man (about 1.8 meters) of the Zapotec race, and as far as is known he grew up and lived in Juchitán in the house of a rich sister in the fifth ward. It seems that his real place of origin was Ixtaltepec because his sister was named Concepción, and they called her Chión Guiati' to indicate that she was from that town.[1]

Moonje' was a revolutionary and died at the end of that period when he was about fifty-five years old. His sister gave him an honorable burial. Moonje' was famous, charismatic, and an amusing teller of tales and adventures, all of them exaggerated—folk tales ultimately—full of an imaginary truth. This was his principal attribute, although he was also known for his mighty appetite and his ability to walk for miles without stopping until he reached his destination. He had uncommon strength, but it is said that his soul was harmless.

In Zapotec the literary genre that Moonje' is known for is called *guendarusiguii,* which is the act of tricking someone, the art of knowing how to deceive.

The servants on the nearby ranches were shocked and angered by his gluttony. In one sitting he would eat a batch of *memelas* [corn fritters], a medium-sized pot of stew, and a whole *zabalote* fish soaked in watery corn dough, and drink a bucket of *pozol* [drink made from corn dough]. He was always a bachelor, although he claimed to have lived with a woman. He was judicious and intelligent, but illiterate despite everything. He was hasty and rough in his work, a "real animal" as they say. He wore *piedegallo*[2] huaraches and preferred to walk rather than take the train to save money. He walked twenty-four hours straight with his sack of *totopos* over his shoulder to arrive at the ranches for temporary work. It is known that he worked with the Toledos, "his cousins," as he said, on the San Benito ranch at the edge of Buenavista Hill, twelve kilometers east of Ixhuatán, and also with Mr. Ne Matu on the Carrizalillo ranch near the same town. After 1923 he never returned to these places, and it was learned that he had died from a dangerous fever.

He was a mescal drinker. When he got drunk, he became melancholy and would close both eyes when he laughed. He wore a green shirt in honor of his political party. As a revolutionary, Moonje' belonged to Che Gómez's Green Party under the command of Felipe López, of whom he boasted he was a nephew (although this was not true even though they had the same last name). General López was from Niltepec. When Che Gómez died, the general took his place, and Moonje' went with him to fight.

Moonje' left us many stories, which the older people tell with almost the same grace as he did himself. They knew Moonje' personally, and he told them the tales. As time passed, our personage became the prototype of the Zapotec genre *guendarusiguii*. All of his stories have the characteristic that they are transmitted orally in Zapotec and in Spanish. The following are two of his stories.

MOONJE' AND HIS OXEN

One day the owners of a piece of land sent for Moonje' and told him to remove his oxen because they were doing damage. He went to look for his animals, and when he arrived at the land he saw that his cattle were up in a coconut tree drinking coconut milk. (Version told by ninety-three-year-old Francisco Santiago, who sells perfume and cutlery from a sidewalk near the Juchitán public market. He and Moonje' fought together for the Green Party during the Revolution.)

MOONJE' IN THE REVOLUTION

While fighting in the Revolution, Moonje' had positioned himself in front of a hill controlled by the enemy. From his trench he saw the enemy stationed on the hill. Both of them saw each other at the same time and aimed their weapons. The enemy fired first. Seeing the bullet in the air, Moonje' fired immediately. The two bullets collided en route. Moonje's bullet was stronger and made the other bullet go right back to where the enemy was and kill him.

NOTES

1. Guiati' is the Zapotec name for people from the town of Ixtaltepec.
2. Literally "rooster foot," a type of leather sandal with only one thong separating the big toe from the other toes.

When Radio
Became
the Voice
of the
People

Manuel López Mateos

Sometimes we are asked if the Isthmus popular movement is cultural or political. From the outset, a dividing line is drawn between political and cultural phenomena. Without constructing a model, it should be stated that the Isthmus popular movement is both eminently political and a cultural expression of the Isthmus people.

Istmeño history is a history of struggles against pillage, destruction, and imposition. It is a history of struggle to construct a future as the continuing evolution of millenarian cultures. In any case, the defense of our culture is not a "salvage operation" (we are not flora and fauna becoming extinct), nor does it represent a return to primitivism. The defense of our culture signifies the defense of a way of organizing social relations. This defense is based on the recovery and joint exploitation of our communal resources, on fair interchange of the products of labor, and on control of the negotiating instruments to make the decisions that affect us.

As is the case in the rest of the country, the Isthmus mass media actively promote lifestyles based on competition, individualism, and consumerism. It also defends the interests of those who exploit the people because it makes the existence of *caciques,* the exploitation of labor, and the voracious plundering of merchants appear normal. The mass media unrestrainedly praise the worst actions of the regime and refuse to publicize the problems of the people. Thus, included among COCEI's projects after taking over Juchitán City Hall was the creation of a popular mass medium: Radio Ayuntamiento Popular (RAP).

The task was not at all easy in the beginning. We had only a few general guidelines, little technical experience, and the generous counsel of those who work on new radio communication projects. Our scarce assets were soon enriched with donations from people who immediately noticed the difference between RAP and commercial radio: better music without commercials! This was a success, but not the only one; RAP also dealt with the problems of peasants and workers, initiated a new type of news broadcast, and created a children's program. Nevertheless, RAP had the inherent limitations of any new project. There were no precedents, no models to follow, and no previous experience. All we had was our own capacity to conceive of RAP as something other than a product of self-consumption, that is, of programming attuned only to the exclusive tastes of the programmers. It was only this capacity to comprehend RAP, not as a voice that spoke at the people, but as the voice of the people, that made it possible to take a step forward.

A necessary measure to strengthen RAP, then, was to establish a channel for feedback from the people. The first task: to initiate transmissions in Zapotec. This was undertaken not out of anthropological curiosity, but because Zapotec is the language spoken in the majority of the communities around Juchitán. A good percentage of the population is bilingual, but the majority language is Zapotec.

In accordance with our guidelines, we enlarged our record collection to offer new alternatives while also satisfying existing musical tastes. We abandoned commercial music and offered artistic products: we played boleros, but good boleros; *ranchera* music, but good *ranchera* music; rock, but good rock. Moreover, we worked to demystify "Mexican popular music," which is normally viewed as simply *ranchera* music. One of the great advances of RAP was to offer, through its programming, a panorama of popular music of the distinct cultures of Mexico, from Chiapas marimbas and Yucatán *trovas* to *huapangos* and polkas, along with the sounds of many different regions. We viewed the music of Mexico as an artistic expression of its people, not as a commercial product of record companies or radio stations.

With respect to the music of the Isthmus region, we dedicated several programs daily to playing old tapes, interpretations of new artists, new compositions, and songs now forgotten. On RAP the time dedicated to regional music was very important. In terms of musical programming, it is also important to emphasize our "concerts" of so-called "classical music." We played not only "accessible" works, but also Dvorak, Stravinsky, Bartok, Orff, and others that could be considered of limited accessibility to test their acceptance among our listeners. Moreover, we also requested the airing of concerts at 5:30 and 6:00 in the morning, hours when the listeners are peasants.

One of the most ambitious and successful projects of RAP was its programming for children, run by children! This was a product of a kids' radio workshop. Here our channels of feedback were particularly important in stabilizing the quality of programs. This allowed us to transcend the stage at which only some programs were enthusiastically received by child listeners while others were not.

WHAT IS THE MEANING OF POPULAR RADIO? PRECISELY THAT, THE RADIO OF THE PEOPLE

Certain theories conceive of radio as "popular" when it includes some time slots when "the people of the community" come to the broadcast booth to expound on their problems. We consider this a limited concept. We are not against this activity, but it seems that those who aspire to it represent conceptions of radio "from the outside," which try to approach the people by granting them a space. We consider this too limited.

RAP is not a voice that speaks to the people; it is the voice of the people. Was this achieved by chance, by ceding people a space so that they could express themselves? Not at all! RAP became a true popular medium by forming its broadcast team with the people themselves.

Clarification: COCEI is not an organization that succeeded in uniting with the people, COCEI is the organized expression of a popular movement.

If, in the beginning, it was a small and enthusiastic group that succeeded in starting RAP, the station (like COCEI) eventually transformed itself into an expression of popular culture. It was not enough to give radio time "to the people." It was the people of the town—peasant *compañeros,* workers, students, neighborhood residents, merchant *compañeros,* teachers, and fishermen's wives—who made up the RAP staff. Elements of the people and not an elite made RAP work.

COCEI and RAP are the people expressed politically and through radio. All of the broadcasting in Zapotec was carried out by the townspeople: peasant programs by peasants, neighborhood programs by neighborhood residents, and children's programs realized by children. And the workers, peasants, children, and townspeople who made the programs of RAP were people in struggle; they were participants, in their own lives, in political organization.

RAP is the voice of a popular movement; it is popular radio. RAP constitutes a real radio alternative for the people of the Isthmus. And, with all modesty, let it be said: It is an example for other popular radio projects.

AN EXAMPLE, ANOTHER EXPERIENCE

It is necessary to cover many aspects of RAP, but a few examples will suffice: (1) The program "Igudxa" (fertile land), which airs at the hour when peasants prepare to go to their fields, reviews the region's agrarian problems and comments on current events in a colloquial style. (2) In the children's program, kids present poems, stories, and games in Zapotec and Spanish. (3) The newscasts, instead of presenting a disconnected series of events, succeed through interviews, readings from daily papers, opinions, and statements in establishing a global view of regional events. They also provide a critical review of national and international news. (4) Other programs comment on the country's most important labor struggles. (5) The most popular shows feature poetry, folk tales, and Zapotec legends with music and commentary, the latter by the region's most distinguished intellectuals.

The projects were endless. Day by day, the people contributed new ideas: theater programs, adventure novels, novelized accounts of legends, the works of young poets, and bohemian poetry. In short, a thousand and one ideas emerged as possibilities for popular creation. But faced with this wealth of creativity, with the efforts of a people to express themselves, and to have a voice and expand it, the Mexican government gave a dark and gloomy response: It decided to drown out the freshest and most legitimate voice of a people. The government jammed the transmissions of Radio Ayuntamiento Popular.

BUT INTERFERING WITH RAP
CANNOT SILENCE THE PEOPLE

The jamming of RAP only demonstrates the Mexican government's limitations. Since the government is incapable of speaking with the people, it prevents the people from speaking. The same thing occurred with the Ayuntamiento Popular: Since the Mexican government is incapable of resolving the problems of the Isthmus people, it prevents the people themselves from solving them. The same thing occurs in the case of the *ejido* and communal lands authorities. Because the government cannot resolve the agrarian problems of the region, it prevents the people from resolving them. In the end, Radio Ayuntamiento Popular was denied permission to broadcast.

RAP had the same fate as COCEI's government; when the army occupied Juchitán it destroyed our radio installations. Today, the concept of "cultural broadcasting" of private radio in the region consists of beer commercials, announcers' stupid remarks, and appeals for incorporation into the egoistic and consumer life.

Pichancha

Miguel Flores Ramírez

They charged the father of lies
that he should do something to quench the thirst of the dead
which was great and was drying up all of Juchitán's water.
He who invents things for amusement's sake
didn't want to mislead the dead of his village
but he was set on fulfilling his duty.
To this end, he thought up a ceramic pot
full of holes from which the souls drank with ease
of the waters that still remained in the wells.[1]

NOTE

1. *Pichanchas* are perforated clay vessels historically used for washing corn before grinding it into flour. They have been replaced by perforated aluminum buckets and now serve mainly ceremonial functions.

The
Third
Elegy

Víctor de la Cruz

On that day's dawn
when I knew they'd killed you,
brother,
I had a powerful longing to cry.
Who would have armed those outsiders
who murdered you
and those peasants our fellow-villagers
that afternoon on which the earth went dark
the way the light went out of your eyes
never to come back?
Who provoked those mad dogs
to vent their rage on you
brother and fellow-villagers?
You didn't want to drown,
you wanted to go on seeing flowers open
among our people.
All your sufferings ended there
and all your sweetness
and that of those fellow-villagers
like seven lights snuffed out

some night on a dark road.
Right there their days were darkened,
the sky clouded over
like the days when a storm covers us over.
Here from time to time dawn awakes
with the song of birds
over the leaves of the green trees
and you aren't here to hear them.
There are nights when the moon shines
spilling out all its brilliance
as if it were crying of solitude.
I shall cross that great river, brother,
the one you crossed just now,
and we shall meet again
at the feet of the goddess of death.

The Proud
Midwives
of
Juchitán

Shoshana R. Sokoloff

Juchitán is a city remarkable for its maintenance of traditional Zapotec culture, including dress, language, literature, public ceremony, ritual celebration, and an active role for women in the market economy. In most aspects of life, the Isthmus Zapotecs have adapted to change and incorporated outside influences without an accompanying loss of indigenous culture and identity (Rubin 1987). The strength and integrity of the traditional midwifery system in Juchitán, and the loyalty of local people in all social classes to this system in the face of a growing Western medical presence, is an example of this phenomenon. The midwives have incorporated outside medical influences and have adapted their practice to the presence of doctors and hospitals.

As in other societies providing both traditional and Western models of attention to childbirth, the choices women make between doctors and midwives in Juchitán are influenced by the expense and availability of services, the socio-economic and cultural background of the patient's family, and her past experience with each health care system (Kleinman 1980; Young 1981; Sargent 1982; McClain 1975). However, in Juchitán more women continue to choose in favor of midwives. Researchers studying the choices women make between traditional and Western obstetrical care in other communities suggest that the traditional system is slowly being replaced by the Western system: "Regardless of individual motivation, and judging by the decreasing number of *parteras* available for traditional obstetrical services, childbirth at home will eventually disappear or become comparatively infrequent as an alternative to hospitalization" (McClain 1975:45). In Juchitán, however, the traditional midwifery system thrives. There are women in all social classes who choose the care of midwives over doctors, and midwives attend approximately 75 percent of the births. The midwives continue to provide the services they have always provided, but increasingly refer difficult patients to Western doctors. Thus the women of Juchitán benefit from a dynamic referral system that offers them the best of traditional and biomedical worlds.

My observations about the strong midwifery system and its interaction with a growing biomedical presence are based on a ten-month stay in Juchitán in 1985–86. I interviewed women regarding their childbirth experiences, interviewed midwives and doctors, and had the great pleasure of working closely with four midwives. I observed thirty deliveries and more than two hundred patient visits with the different midwives. In addition, I observed ten deliveries and thirty prenatal visits with doctors at the public hospital, and attended a week of classes offered by the social security hospital staff to empirical midwives. I found a thriving referral system in which empirical midwives provide economical, culturally congruent care for the majority of childbearing women and refer patients needing medical or surgical intervention to doctors and hospitals.

The midwifery referral system in Juchitán draws on the strengths of the traditional system and the strengths of the biomedical system, providing excellent health care at a minimum of cost and a minimum of upheaval to local structures and values. Weaknesses in the chain of referral, often at great cost of maternal and child life, are most often due to economic constraints.

Juchitán's midwives are well known and greatly respected, and they stand out among Juchitecas who are themselves impressive for their colorful dress, forthrightness, and relative economic independence. The four midwives with whom I worked closely—Silvia, Joaquina, María, and Juana—represent different class and educational backgrounds; different ages, personalities, and approaches to me and to their patients; and different levels of exposure to Western medicine, but they share a strong sense of responsibility towards their patients. They talk about the demands of the profession and the strain the irregular schedule and responsibility for life and death put on them and on their families. They are proud of their work and the money they earn for it and feel a moral responsibility to attend women who cannot afford to pay.

The literature tends to characterize traditional midwives as elderly and illiterate (McClain 1981:111). In Juchitán, the midwives span the generations and show varied levels of literacy. The pattern among these women, and the midwives before them, seems to be to start young and work until old age. In other communities, the office of the midwife is often socially inherited from a relative who is a midwife or traditional healer and frequently involves divine revelation in the form of dreams or severe illness (Paul and Paul 1975; Cosminsky 1977; McClain 1975). While the midwives of Juchitán cite many reasons for and paths to the practice of their professions, including inborn talent, training by a doctor, and "just happening to be there when needed," the aspect of divine mandate is absent from their descriptions. Whereas in other communities in Mexico and Guatemala, and even in other communities in the Isthmus region of Oaxaca, the role of midwife and faith healer are intertwined (Paul 1978; Paul and Paul 1975; Cosminsky 1977; Wazir-Jahan 1984), in Juchitán they are quite separate. There is an active system of faith healers, both male and female, but these practitioners do not, as a rule, attend deliveries. In Juchitán, the midwife is respected and valued as a specialist, but not as a sacred specialist.

THE MIDWIVES

Silvia

I met Silvia during my first days in Juchitán. I described my research topic to a family in a courtyard and was told that there was a birth taking place next door. I was led in to the adjoining room, where the new mother rested on a wood-slat bed. The seated midwife, Na Silvia,[1] was surrounded by the two grandmothers and a godmother and held a blue, lethargic infant who made occasional weak efforts to cry. Na Silvia patted the infant and gave occasional single breaths of mouth-to-mouth resuscitation while I was introduced to all present. The consensus was that the infant was too premature and would not survive. The grandmothers asked me if I thought that the baby was premature and were very pleased that I concurred with the estimate of the midwife, who "had never been to school and could not read or write, but had learned well from experience."

The following day I visited Na Silvia in her courtyard. She is a weather-worn, businesslike woman in her late sixties. She dresses in simple versions of the traditional clothing and hangs the skirt she is not wearing on the wall of her large, one-room house. She entertained me under the trees in front of her house in a wide circle of daughters and daughters-in-law, who offered occasional translation of Zapotec words while attending to laundry, food, and children, while their husbands drank beer and commented on our discussion.

Na Silvia described the ways in which her attention to delivery differs from that of doctors: They do a two-finger internal exam, and she simply inserts one finger to see if the baby is coming soon. They only prescribe medicines, while she makes use of herbs as a tea to ease the pains of labor, as an enema to speed delivery, and as a salve to give a postpartum massage. Doctors rarely come to the house to stay with a woman who is delivering, and she comes whenever she is called and stays as long as she is needed.

Na Silvia is the most empirical of all the midwives in that she never went to school and attended a government course for midwives only briefly, speaks little Spanish, and learned to attend deliveries from an aged aunt. She is from a family of limited economic means, lives in the house in which she grew up, and supports a large, extended family on her income. Na Silvia says that she enjoys her work, except when it interferes with her participation in the frequent fiestas. She explained that if a woman calls her before a fiesta begins, she will attend the delivery, but if she is already _bien tomada_ (drunk), she sends the woman to another midwife.

Na Silvia agreed to have me accompany her on her visits to newborns and send a messenger to inform me of deliveries. As we walked through the streets, people asked her who the tall white woman was, and she replied, "A doctor from the United States who came to Juchitán to learn to deliver babies." Na Silvia liked people to know that she was teaching the _doctora,_ and she seemed to enjoy having an extra person present to check on the mother or infant while she was resting. She answered my questions willingly, but briefly, and asked me few questions. Na Silvia has changed her practices very little through the years, with the exception of learning to inject pitocin (a synthetic hormone used to stimulate the contractions of labor) "because the women think that is the more modern way." Her involvement with doctors extends only to calling them if there is a problem.

María

María is tall and stately, with light skin, red-brown hair, and high cheek bones, all characteristics attributed to her fisherman father, who came from California to the Isthmus of Tehuantepec to work and fathered three separate families. At forty-three, María is the youngest of the active midwives and has been delivering babies for twenty years. She is the daughter of a well-known Juchiteca midwife, Na Fidelia, who died recently, and her training represents a mix of empirical learning-by-doing, learning from watching an experienced elder, and formal classroom education. Still, she claims that she actually began attending deliveries by accident. She attended her first delivery at the remote rancho by the sea where she lived when she first married "because women gave birth there and there was no one else to help them."

Later, María moved back to Juchitán and worked as an apprentice alongside her mother. At that time she and her mother went to an intensive four-week course for midwives in the state capital. There, says María, she "learned to be afraid." She became aware of all the things that could go wrong in a delivery, and she "never again went to a delivery without a sense of possible calamity." Mother and daughter had been working side by side for a year when there were two deliveries at the same time, and Na Fidelia decided that María was competent to work alone. From that day on, María says, the two midwives were competitors: "When a woman came in the back door, she stayed with me, and when she came in through the front courtyard, my mother attended her."

María attended several government courses, covering topics relating to pregnancy, delivery, and contraception. Although she had only two years of primary school, she knows how to read and write. She is a natural student; she asks and answers questions as if she is the only student, and she easily applies what she has learned to her clinical practice. She made use of my presence to increase her knowledge and add the weight of a foreign, medical opinion to suggestions she made to her patients.

A midwife rarely walks more than a few steps without hearing the ritualized Zapotec greeting, "Where are you going?" (to which she replies, "To burst a piñata!")[2] or being called to see a child who has grown considerably since last meeting. María thanked me for my company on her lonely excursions at all hours of day or night, and she asked me questions concerning etiologies of physiological events and medical problems. She had learned empirically and from a doctor that suctioning the stomach of a newborn is sometimes helpful, and she enlisted my help in securing catheters of the proper size.

With her patients, María took advantage of my presence to broach the subjects she wanted to discuss. To discourage women from following the local custom of complete bed rest following childbirth, María would frequently say to me, in front of a woman who had delivered the day before, "Isn't it true that where you come from women get up and around the next day after giving birth, and even wash themselves, yet they do not get sick?" "It is better," she would add, "to walk around and let the uterus empty itself." A woman gets better faster that way than if she stays flat on her back for a week or two or for the whole traditional forty-day *cuarentena.* To encourage women to breast-feed soon after delivery, rather than substituting oral rehydration formula for two days, as was local custom, she would ask me, "Didn't you say that women nurse right away in the U.S., and they have enough milk?" While bathing a baby boy, María asked me how the cord is cared for in the United States. I replied that the cord is left uncovered to dry up and fall off. "With no *faja* [binding]?" exclaimed the women present. "But doesn't the umbilicus stick out?" In this case, María defended the local practice of binding the umbilicus but offered a more scientific reason for doing so, pointing out that there are fewer flies and less dust in my country. She applied olive oil, alcohol, talc, and cotton to the cord stump and bound the infant tightly with a bandanna to protect him or her from flies and infection.

Joaquina

Doña Joaquina is called "mother of us all" by the various political parties parading past her door. She is a vigorous eighty-one-year-old who has been delivering successive generations in Juchitán for sixty years. She stands out among the midwives in that she was born to an aristocratic Spanish family in a part of the state far from Juchitán, received formal education through secondary school, and learned to attend deliveries from her brother-in-law, a Japanese doctor. She is small, thin, and fair, with fine features, the brown ends of her hair braided with black ribbon and piled on top of her white head, and wears simple, cotton, Western-style dresses that she makes herself from imported fabric—all in sharp contrast to the local Zapotec women, who are large boned, dark, and fat, and wear brightly embroidered *huipiles* over floor-length, flowered polyester skirts.

Although Doña Joaquina prefers to work alone, without assistants, and even banishes the hovering family members from the room until the first cry of the infant is heard, she agreed to allow me to accompany her to deliveries if I was ready and waiting when the call came. We designed a very pleasant system whereby I came to her house every evening at nine o'clock. We lay in our hammocks, chatting, until the clock struck twelve, and then slept until a knock came calling us to a delivery. During these long talks I learned about Joaquina's life and work.

As Doña Joaquina tells her story, it was unhappy circumstance that brought her to Juchitán. At the age of nineteen, her parents put an end to an unsatisfactory courtship by sending Joaquina off to stay with a married sister in Juchitán. There, lovesick and oppressed by the unaccustomed heat, Joaquina "sat in a hammock and cried until her hair fell out." She got up out of her hammock only when her brother-in-law insisted that she assist him with difficult deliveries.

Soon thereafter, although still a *señorita*, Joaquina began to attend deliveries on her own, finding normal deliveries easy compared to the complications to which she was accustomed. Other midwives and doctors started to refer difficult fetal presentations, therapeutic abortions, incomplete abortions, and retained placentas to her. Ten years ago, she attended one day of a government course for midwives and then begged permission not to return, saying that she could not bear to abandon her patients to sit in a classroom and listen to twenty-five-year-old men tell her what she had "known and practiced for sixty years."

Doña Joaquina still manages most complications on her own, and "months go by" between referrals to a doctor. When faced with a difficult presentation, Joaquina gives the patient a choice between remaining with her or going to a hospital. If necessary, she uses forceps, which are "rapid and effective but painful to the mother." She believes that doctors resort too quickly to surgical delivery and frequently raises her long, slender fingers to demonstrate her technique for manually delivering a complicated breech presentation. Despite Doña Joaquina's lack of scientific training, doctors send patients to her and call her for assistance based on the strength of her skill and experience alone. She has been called to assist in the deliveries of the wives of several of the town's doctors.

Doña Joaquina, who speaks an eloquent Spanish but only enough Zapotec to manage a delivery, prides herself on being more refined, "the way her parents brought her up," than the local population. Rejecting local custom, she shuns drinking, dancing, and fiestas. Nonetheless, she considers Juchitán home and dislikes being away from her house or her patients for more than a day or two.

Juana

Na Juana grew up in Juchitán, lives among her relatives, and speaks Zapotec to her patients. As a young woman she worked for a company that trained her as a practical surgical nurse and sent her to the north of Mexico. There she married, had her children (all in the hospital because she "wasn't from there and didn't know the midwives"). She applied her skills to midwifery only when she and her family moved back to Juchitán twenty years ago.

Na Juana is now in her fifties and has a very active midwifery practice. She sees patients at her house from five to eight each evening and included me in these office visits and, often, in supper with her family, both occasionally interrupted by a call to a delivery. Each of Juana's five children was educated through high school and professional school, and most of them have government jobs. They are very proud of their mother's work and pleased with my interest in it.

Juana's patients appear to be more from the middle class than those of the other midwives. More of the women she sees wear Western-style dress, are married to men with government or unionized jobs, and have health insurance. During one prenatal visit the telephone rang and Juana answered. "Are you seeing patients today?" the caller asked. Juana said that she was and hung up, laughing. "Soon they'll be making appointments." Juana works closely with several doctors and believes strongly in referring a patient when there is the slightest risk to mother or child. She keeps careful records of the deliveries she attends. In 1985 she attended 143 deliveries, of which 23 (16 percent) were referred for Caesarean section.

THE WORK OF THE MIDWIFE

Most of the midwives I studied go out to check on new mothers, wash newborn babies,[3] and attend to their personal shopping in the morning, and receive patients at home in the afternoon and evening. Each has a room set up as a *consultorio* with a bed for examining patients [the room usually doubles as sleeping space for family members at night] and a small dispensary equipped with alcohol, syringes, Vick's Vaporub or other ointment for massage, and other basic medications.

Women usually come to the midwife for an examination and massage every month or two during early pregnancy and every two weeks during late pregnancy. At each prenatal visit the midwife asks the woman about her general state of health and any specific symptoms she is experiencing. If necessary, the midwife prescribes vitamins and patent or herbal medications or, occasionally, refers the patient to a doctor. The prenatal visit ends with words of encouragement to rest and eat well and admonitions to avoid emotional upheaval and lifting heavy objects. The midwife's advice is often reinforced by the group of women, many experienced mothers among them, waiting to be examined.

Women also come to the midwife for a variety of other reasons, including menstrual irregularity or abdominal pain, for birth control pills or monthly injections of a contraceptive, and for injections of medications prescribed by doctors or self-prescribed. Parents bring sick infants, young children for injections, and baby girls to have their ears pierced.[4]

The midwives expect to be interrupted at any time by a call to attend a delivery. When the knock comes at her door, she grabs her shawl and her bag and heads off, on foot or by cab, to the house of the patient. There she remains until she has attended the birth of the baby, washed and dressed mother and infant, and established that all is well.

THE MIDWIFE AND LOCAL TRADITIONAL PRACTICES

The midwives are critically tolerant of local traditional practices and folk traditions. They are tolerant and respectful of the customary practices they view as positive or harmless, such as putting binders on the abdomens (to prevent herniation or infection) and cotton in the ears of mother and baby after delivery (to protect against the *aires* that are thought to be dangerous at this vulnerable time), or lighting candles and placing ears of corn on the delivery bed (to distract the *mal ojo*, evil eye). On the other hand, they try to educate women about those practices they view as harmful to mother or baby. For instance, since they know that milk is a good source of the calcium that is needed during pregnancy, they reject the common wisdom that prenatal milk consumption leads to increased bleeding during delivery and encourage women to drink milk and eat cheese during pregnancy. They discourage women from observing the forty-day postpartum prescription against bathing and exercise because they think it is poor hygiene, and they encourage women to breast-feed soon after delivery.

Folk traditions are more evident at midwife-attended deliveries than at doctor-attended deliveries for several reasons: (1) Women who are more imbued with local tradition are more likely to choose a midwife than a doctor as a birth attendant; (2) the midwife is more likely to be a product of local culture and therefore to respect and comply with the carrying out of traditions; and (3) the midwife-attended delivery usually takes place in the patient's home, where family members are present and free to counsel the patient and observe rituals during delivery as they do during pregnancy and the postpartum period.

CHOOSING BETWEEN MIDWIFE AND DOCTOR

Juchitán is a community receptive to Western medicine. There are doctors' offices at every corner, patients in all socioeconomic groups line up to be attended to,[5] and families spend large portions of their incomes on medications. Frequently, several members of the family of a woman who has just given birth at home will have been to see a doctor that week, and, not infrequently, the new mother herself will be planning to consult a doctor about an unrelated problem when she recovers from childbirth. It appears that childbirth is considered a separate area of health care need and that midwives are considered by most women to be the appropriate health care provider for childbirth and related concerns. Of the 338 births registered at the Juchitán Civil Registry during November and December 1985, 72.5 percent were attended by midwives, 23.0 percent by doctors, and 4.5 percent by neither doctor nor midwife.[6]

Many women chose midwives over doctors for economic reasons. A normal delivery attended by a doctor costs up to eight times what a midwife charges, and midwives often modify fees to accommodate the economic level of the family or arrange flexible payment schedules stretching out over months or years.[7] Furthermore, doctor-attended deliveries more frequently end in expensive Caesarean sections.[8] Women also prefer a birth attendant who speaks Zapotec, is female,[9] is known to the family, and is familiar with local customs. Some women believe that midwives are technically superior to doctors, or they fear hospitals.[10] Midwives are also believed to be more personally familiar with the experience of childbirth and to have more compassion for the mother and more respect for the mother's own desires during the delivery process.

Some women believe that, in addition to providing more compassionate care, midwives are also more proficient in their work because of their greater experience. They suggest that "doctors care for all kinds of medical problems, but midwives are specialists in childbirth." Such women love to recount situations in which midwives knew better than doctors. In one frequently cited case, a doctor is called to see a woman who has been in labor for a long time. After examining her, he tells her that it will be several more hours before she delivers. The doctor leaves and the midwife is called. She says, "It won't be long now," and refuses to leave the bedside. Soon thereafter the baby is born. In a second case, a doctor insists that a baby cannot be born normally and that a Caesarean section is necessary. The mother refuses the operation and calls the midwife, who delivers the baby (now a good-sized toddler nursing at the storyteller's breast) without difficulty. In comparing doctors to midwives, one woman observed that "eight years of medical school does not give a young man the good sense of a midwife."

More often than not, women have their own particular favorite midwife to whom they are fiercely loyal. A single midwife commonly attends all the deliveries in a communal living situation, all the children in one family and in subsequent generations. She calls the mothers her *gente* (her people), and the children her sons and daughters. The children, often themselves by now grandparents, in turn call the midwife *tia* or *abuelita,* aunt or grandmother.

Women who choose doctors as birth attendants do so due to lack of experience or bad experience with midwives, convenience, and the belief that doctors are "more modern and technically superior" to midwives. Women who have had difficult deliveries or stillbirths under the care of a midwife sometimes choose a doctor for subsequent deliveries. One woman told me that her last baby died, and she almost lost her life as well, because she delivered at a *rancho* far away from the city and her midwife didn't know how to help her. Now she brings all her daughters and daughters-in-law to the public hospital to deliver. She finds the hospital "más bonito y más seguro," nicer and more secure. Women who did not grow up in Juchitán or who live outside the city limits are less likely to have family or community connections to a certain midwife and turn more readily to the hospital. Others choose private doctors because of the availability of anesthesia during labor and delivery.

Some women draw on aspects of both the midwifery and medical systems. Women with insurance coverage at the hospital sometimes go for prenatal checkups but call a midwife for delivery. Younger women who believe that doctors have more resources in the event of an emergency occasionally see a doctor and a midwife for regular prenatal visits and then call the doctor for delivery to maintain their contact with the family tradition and satisfy their desire for more scientific care.

CONCLUSION

The midwives of Juchitán are a special, richly varied group of women, greatly respected in the community and preferred by most childbearing women to doctors. The midwifery system in Juchitán is not a closed one, dependent on birth, status, or tradition. It is a lucrative and respected secular profession that has been directly affected by Western medical influence. Midwives are secure in their position as health professionals, with primary responsibility for birth-related health care, and they are aware of the resources and limitations of the coexistent medical system. These factors together set the scene for an effective and enduring referral system for perinatal care.

NOTES

1. *Na* is the Zapotec form of address to an adult woman, equivalent to *doña* or *señora* in Spanish.
2. A *piñata* is a papier-mâché animal filled with candy and fruit that is suspended in the air and broken open by blindfolded children at special celebrations.
3. Washing newborns is considered a specialized skill and is reserved for the midwife during the first week of life.
4. Midwives usually pierce the ears of newborn girls with a needle and thread during the first postpartum visit. If a girl is born in the hospital or at home without a midwife, or if the thread falls out, she is brought to the midwife to have her ears pierced.
5. There are several doctors who charge reduced fees for consultation, 300–500 pesos instead of the usual 2,000–4,000 pesos, and they draw a large clientele from people in lower socioeconomic strata.
6. Those listed as "other" in the section of the registration form requesting status of the birth attendant are, to my knowledge, babies who were born at home without an attendant and those who were born on the way to the hospital.
7. The going rate for a delivery and follow-up visits during the first postpartum week was 5,000–6,000 pesos.
8. Caesarian sections cost 90,000–200,000 pesos.
9. There is a strong prejudice against women being examined by men. Of approximately fifty doctors, only three are women.
10. The perceived, and likely real, increase in complication rate at the hospitals as compared to home is probably due to the fact that midwives refer problems to the hospital before, during, and after delivery.

Afterword

In August 1989, COCEI once again contended the Juchitán municipal elections. With the local PRI in considerable disarray and liberal Heladio Ramírez in the governor's seat, COCEI won a majority of the votes, and despite protests mounted by the Juchitán PRI, the results were recognized in Mexico City. The thrill of the victory was soon followed by internal disagreement over the proper strategy to adopt toward state and federal governments. Should COCEI maintain a strict autonomy and cultural localism, insisting on municipal self-determination and control of resources at the risk of another government economic embargo, as in 1981? Should the movement take a more institutional route, like the Popular Socialist Party (PPS), playing the role of loyal government critic in exchange for access to funds and materials with which to improve the lives of its largely impoverished constituency? Or should COCEI engage in strategic negotiation, alternating between cooperation and confrontation with the State according to the needs of the moment? These are, as Semo (1986:21) notes, the three major ideological currents over which the Mexican Left has struggled historically and that, unresolved, have contributed to its fragmentation.

Negotiation is not a new weapon in COCEI's repertoire. But previously the movement's leadership viewed the State as authoritarian and bourgeois and favored the development of an autonomous left political force, thereby rejecting the post-1977 Communist Party (PCM) strategy of eroding the State from within. After the 1989 elections, however, internal disputes developed among COCEI leaders over the best course to pursue. Several members of the directorate, the former mayor among them, wanted to maintain an autonomous stance and a more confrontational relationship with the State, even at the risk of another economic boycott. The newly elected mayor as well as the leader of the peasant sector (a recently elected federal deputy) favored a greater level of cooperation as a means of obtaining development funds.

According to disgruntled militants, the new mayor imposed his policy. They claim that the mayor and his supporters stifled debate over the new strategies and equated disagreement with disloyalty. Dissenters were told to keep their objections to themselves or leave the organization. By the spring of 1990, a small but growing number of seasoned movement activists had become openly critical of the COCEI municipal administration and charged that the leadership was losing touch with the base. They cited ostentatious displays of wealth on the part of several leaders, reports of corruption, and deals cut with PRI. The important Mexico City weekly *Proceso,* a long-time defender of COCEI, even published an article accusing the leadership of misuse of funds, a charge echoed by some alienated militants. Other observers complained that COCEI had pulled its organizers out of Huatulco, the large tourist development between Salina Cruz and Puerto Escondido, in exchange for the Salinas government's confirmation of the Juchitán vote.

Simultaneously, schisms emerged within the Isthmus Zapotec cultural movement, and between COCEI leaders and Zapotec intellectuals. Consequently, Francisco Toledo removed his collection of paintings from the Casa de la Cultura, and Macario Matus resigned as the Casa's director. With the Casa de la Cultura disorganized, and the formerly united Juchiteco poets and painters bickering among themselves, the quality and quantity of local artistic production declined noticeably.

This was not the first time that COCEI members had clashed over strategic choices and policies. But in the past, especially during the heady years of COCEI's first government (1981–83) and the periods of intense repression that preceded and followed it, the political necessity of remaining united in the face of local class enemies, PRI politicians, and government security forces was sufficient to overcome internal differences. Those disagreements that did exist tended to pit middle-level cadres desiring greater power against the five or six main COCEI decision-makers, critical movement intellectuals against political leaders, or *coceístas* from surrounding villages against the central Juchiteco leadership. However, Zapotec ethnic identity and lower class solidarity tended to override differences among COCEI's majority peasant and worker constituency within Juchitán.

In the late 1980s and early 1990s, as the Mexican government granted COCEI greater legitimacy and the threat of violent repression subsided, the political urgency of quickly resolving disputes within the movement gradually decreased. In March 1990, tensions heightened among *coceístas* over the proposed visit of Mexican president Carlos Salinas de Gortari to Juchitán. Who should receive him? How? And on whose account? Although Salinas's fraudulent electoral victory in the 1988 presidential elections was ratified by vote of the PRI majority in the House of Deputies, it was not recognized by the deputies of the PRD (Party of the Democratic Revolution) or by COCEI. Salinas's visit to the Isthmus could thereby be seen as a calculated maneuver designed to bolster his sagging democratic image, further tarnished by violence and accusations of PRI vote fraud in 1990 state elections in Michoacán, Guerrero, and elsewhere.

Many *coceístas* opposed any public association with the Salinas regime, and PRD leaders, including Cuauhtémoc Cárdenas, chastised COCEI for dealing with Salinas. But though association with Salinas might cost COCEI some of its good standing among its allies and supporters on the left, it also held out the possibility for important gains locally. First, the stamp of approval from the president would undermine the Juchitán PRI and weaken its chances in the 1992 municipal elections. Second, a working relationship with the regime was necessary if the COCEI administration was to obtain the funds required to mitigate, if not remedy, poverty and unemployment, as well as deficiencies in health, education, and basic infrastructure that plague the majority of Juchitán's inhabitants. When COCEI took office in December 1989, the municipal treasury was bankrupt (as it had been in 1981). At the beginning of its term, the administration received only the absolute minimum of funds required to keep the town going. Should COCEI bargain away some of its autonomy in exchange for social peace and funding for its cultural programs and economic development? Could the leadership work with state and federal governments without being coopted into serving as a channel for policies opposed to the interests of Juchitán's peasants, workers, and small merchants who compose the bulk of the COCEI constituency? Could, in short, COCEI manage its relationship with the State to achieve its economic and cultural goals without sacrificing its political ones?

Before Salinas's arrival, the COCEI Political Commission undertook some damage control, distributing a document that emphasized that Salinas was to be received in Juchitán not by COCEI but by the municipal administration and the citizenry as a whole, without distinction for party affiliation. Hence, the commission urged COCEI supporters to put aside the COCEI colors, banners, radical slogans, and other features that mark the movement's political and ethnic distinctiveness. An estimated 4,000 people attended Salinas's visit, few of them from the Juchitán PRI (splintered by defeat and infighting into more than a dozen competing factions).

The mayor's remarks illustrate the current COCEI strategy and reiterate many of the points made in the Political Commission position paper. In his public welcome to President Salinas, Mayor Héctor Sánchez said:

> We accept this pact with the government over which you preside, because we be-
> lieve that every municipality, legally constituted, has the constitutional right to
> deal with state and federal governments, in order that they assume their portion
> of the responsibility for the solution of the problems that affect our communities,
> in the context of the sovereignty and autonomy that the constitution confers upon
> them.

He then marked—directly and unambiguously—the difference between COCEI and the Salinas administration:

> On the national scene, Mexicans in the rural areas as well as in the city continue
> to endure misery. With all respect, Mr. President, we have differences of opinion
> concerning the development model that your government has implemented. We
> believe that modernization does not have to be at the cost of the most unpro-
> tected Mexicans. We are disturbed, Mr. President, by the latest events that have
> placed some families in our country in mourning, particularly in Michoacán and
> Guerrero. In the Isthmus region, experience teaches us that there exist forms of
> rationally resolving electoral conflicts among united municipalities.

The mayor ended his speech with an extensive list of requests for development funds with which to pave roads, resolve the land tenure problem in the community's favor, support the Casa de la Cultura, and provide drainage, garbage pickup, schools, and medical facilities. President Salinas responded favorably, promising an ambitious program of infrastructural development.

Such promises have been made and broken many times before, in Juchitán and throughout Mexico. Knowing this, COCEI holds in reserve its trump card of mass mobilization and pressure politics. For its part, the government has an army detachment based in nearby Ixtepec, the same detachment that was mobilized to eject COCEI from the municipal buildings in December 1983. What will ensue in the future is less predictable than ever before, for the Mexican political system is undergoing rapid change and has become "a moving target for analysis" (Cornelius et al. 1989a:1).

If the federal government consistently channels resources into the region—

which will depend to a degree on the success of Salinas's privatization strategy in fostering economic recovery—COCEI and other political parties (mainly PRI) and groups (large merchants and landowners) will undoubtedly struggle over their control. A temporary peace between state and federal governments and COCEI need not extend to the large landowners, merchants, and bureaucrats who dominate the means of production, commercialization, and finance. These last-mentioned groups will mobilize both to protect and to enlarge their access to surplus value generated by peasants and workers. Thus they will oppose all development plans that involve socialization of land and of the means of production and that promote income redistribution. In this they are likely to be supported by the Salinas government, which has pursued with great fervor the reprivatization drive begun during the administration of Salinas's predecessor, Miguel de la Madrid.

As of August 1991, reports from Juchitán indicated that the Salinas government had come through with a significant portion of the funds promised for local development projects. While bulldozers and other heavy machinery labored to pave Juchitán's muddy, irregular streets, apparent calm reigned in the town as the large influx of federal funding, at least temporarily, subdued the hostility of COCEI's traditional enemies among the Juchitán middle and upper classes. At the Casa de la Cultura, the appointment of an energetic new director seemed to be bearing fruit in a renewal of the creative ferment that had previously characterized the institution. Moreover, one observer noted that the COCEI administration was doing a more efficient and fairer job of allocating resources to its diverse Juchiteco constituency than had COCEI leaders during the movement's first term of office. It appears that COCEI's electoral success and ability to secure funding for local economic development are sufficient to overcome personal and ideological conflicts among its constituent groups.

By the end of COCEI mayor Héctor Sánchez's term of office in winter 1992, Juchitán had taken on a new appearance. Formerly known for its treacherous potholes, grubbiness, and poverty, its main streets are now well paved, and major progress has been made in providing potable water, sewage systems, and lighting to the majority of Juchitecos. In fact, this was COCEI's most effective argument in the next round of mayoral elections in November. Not surprisingly, COCEI won those elections also. The new mayor, Oscar Cruz, who directed many of the public works that reshaped Juchitán, is well prepared to continue the economic development of the city. Moreover, COCEI candidates also won mayoral elections in the nearby Zapotec towns of Unión Hidalgo and San Blas Atempa. At least for the time being, COCEI's power in local politics is assured.

Although the long-term future of COCEI cannot be predicted, the materials presented in this volume attest to the tenacity of Juchitecos in combating adversity. Using Isthmus history as a guide, if the movement should at some point break into competing factions or disband, the social struggles and cultural projects that have marked Juchitán will continue in new forms. Even if capitalist development takes greater hold in the Isthmus, weakening the current markers of cultural distinctiveness (e.g., *huipiles,* the *vela* celebrations, and the Zapotec language), "Zapotec," as a deeply felt identity and source of creative expression, is likely to remain a pole of class-based resistance to economic, cultural, and political oppression in the region for a long time to come.

Appendix:
Chronology
of
Isthmus Zapotec
History
and
COCEI History

(approximate dates)

1350	Zapotecs from Highland Oaxaca move into the Isthmus of Tehuantepec
1521	Spanish conquest of Mexico
1529	The Isthmus is incorporated into Cortés's Marquesado del Valle through a decree issued by Charles V
1580	Over the first fifty years of the conquest the population declines by 90 per cent in comparison to preconquest era
1660	Tehuantepec rebellion
1823	The Isthmus of Tehuantepec is incorporated into the state of Oaxaca through a presidential decree
1847–51	Rebellion of Gregorio Meléndez; Governor Benito Juárez burns Juchitán
1866	Zapotec army from Juchitán and San Blas defeats French interventionists supported by Tehuantepec
1889	Inauguration of Juchitán City Hall; Juchitán named a city
1907	Opening of the Trans-Isthmus Railroad; an estimated twenty trains daily carry cargo between the Veracruz coast and Salina Cruz, Oaxaca
1910	Beginning of the Mexican Revolution
1911	Che Gómez independence movement in Juchitán
1914	Opening of the Panama Canal usurps the Trans-Isthmus Railroad; Isthmus economy declines
1931	Roque Robles/Valentín Carrasco revolt in Juchitán crushed by forces of the Oaxaca state government; General Heliodoro Charis takes power

Appendix

1946	Publication of Miguel Covarrubias's *Mexico South: The Isthmus of Tehuantepec*
1952	Construction of the Pan American Highway through the Isthmus; Juchitán begins ascendance as important regional market center
1962	Construction completed on the Benito Juárez Dam; rampant land speculation in irrigated area surrounding Juchitán
1964	General Charis dies
1968	Opposition movement precursor to COCEI, organized by Major Leopoldo de Gyves Pineda
1971–74	Manuel Musalem (Tarú), leader of PPS, governs Juchitán
1973–74	Formation of COCEI
1978	Completion of the Salina Cruz PEMEX oil refinery
1981	COCEI wins election in Juchitán (March)
1983	COCEI impeached by Oaxaca state congress in August and removed from office in December by army and police forces
1986	COCEI participates in coalition government with PRI until 1989 elections
1989	COCEI wins elections in Juchitán, takes power in September
1992	COCEI wins elections in Juchitán, takes power in January 1993

Glossary

aires	air or breezes that are said to provoke physical or spiritual illnesses
amparo	the Mexican equivalent of a writ of habeas corpus
binnigula'sa'	the Zapotec ancestors
binizá	the Zapotec people
cacicazgo	rule by a local political boss
cacique	local political boss
campesino	peasant, rural person
cardenista	supporter of Cuauhtémoc Cárdenas, PRD leader
coceísta	supporter of the COCEI
colono	resident of a neighborhood or outlying area
compañero (-a)	political comrade or ally
comunero	communal landholder
consultorio	doctor's office
corrido	folk ballad
cuarentena	forty-day postpartum quarantine period
cuento	story, folklore
didxazá	the Zapotec language
ejido	government land held corporately by a community and used by individuals through usufruct
ejidatario	holder of an *ejido* grant
el Istmo	the Isthmus of Tehuantepec
encomendero	recipient of a Spanish land grant

Guchachi' Reza	literally "sliced iguana"; the cultural magazine of the Juchiteco intellectuals
guciguié	summer, the rainy season
guendabianni'	intelligence, wisdom, culture
huapango	style of music and dance from Veracruz, Mexico
huaraches	leather sandals worn by Mexican peasants
huipil	loose-fitting blouse worn by many Mexican indigenous women
indigenista	indigenist, concerned with Mexican indigenous people
indio	Indian (often used derogatorily)
Istmeño	native of the Isthmus of Tehuantepec
jefe político	political boss
latifundio	large landed estate
lo juchiteco	Juchiteco identity
lo zapoteco	the essence of being a Zapotec person, Zapotec identity
machos	men
mayordomo (-a)	fiesta sponsor
mestizaje	racial mixing
monte	hills, the bush, mountainous land
neocardenismo	opposition movement led by Cuauhtémoc Cárdenas that revived many of the ideals of his father, Lázaro Cárdenas
Neza	Juchiteco cultural magazine of the 1930s, literally "road" or "path"
Neza Cubi	a Juchiteco cultural magazine of the late 1960s, literally "the new road"
padrino	godfather, ritual parent
paisano	fellow countryman
partera	midwife
pichancha	perforated clay vessel for washing corn kernels
Porfiriato	the period between 1876 and 1911 during which Porfirio Díaz governed Mexico
priísta	supporter of the PRI
ranchera	style of Mexican country music
rancho	ranch
rapto	abduction of a young woman by a young man for sexual purposes and/or marriage
reforma política	political reform
Tehuano	native of Tehuantepec
totopo	crisp, baked tortillas made in the Isthmus of Tehuantepec
trova	folk music
vallistocracia	the Valley of Oaxaca aristocracy
vallisto	native of the Oaxaca Valley (often used derogatorily)
vela	colorful fiestas held in the Isthmus of Tehuantepec
zapatismo	agrarian movement led by Emiliano Zapata during the Mexican Revolution

Works Cited

Alcerregía, Luis G.
1976   "Conferencia sobre la tenencia de la tierra." Ms., Juchitán.

Alvarado, Arturo, ed.
1987   *Electoral Patterns and Perspectives in Mexico.* Monograph Series, no. 22. La Jolla, Calif.: Center for U.S.-Mexican Studies, University of California, San Diego.

Anderson, Thomas
1971   *Matanza.* Lincoln: University of Nebraska Press.

Amnesty International
1986   *Mexico: Human Rights in Rural Areas.* London: Amnesty International Publications.

Archivo General de la Nación
1793   Ramo de Alcabalas, vol. 37, May 7. México.
1952   *El libro de las tasaciones de pueblos de la Nueva España: Siglo XVI.* México.

Aubague, Laurent
1983   "Dominación lingüística y resistencia étnica en el estado de Oaxaca." In *Dominación y resistencia lingüística en Oaxaca,* edited by Laurent Aubague et al. Oaxaca, Mexico.
1985   *Discurso político, utopía y memoria popular en Juchitán.* Oaxaca: UABJO:IIS.

Bailón, Moisés J.

1985   "El desconocimiento del ayuntamiento de la COCEI." *Guchachi' Reza* 23:3–15.

1987   "Coyote atrapa a conejo: poder regional y lucha popular—el desconocimiento del ayuntamiento de Juchitán en 1983." In *Juchitán: limites de una experiencia democrática*, edited by Moisés J. Bailón and Sergio Zermeño. México: UNAM, Instituto de Investigaciones Sociales.

Bañuelos, Marta, ed., et al.

1988   *Juchitán: lucha y poesía.* México: Editorial Extemporáneos.

Barabas, Alicia

1986   "Rebeliones e insurrecciones indígenas en Oaxaca: la trayectoria histórica de la resistencia étnica." In *Etnicidad y pluralismo cultural: la dinámica étnica*, edited by Alicia Barabas and Miguel Bartolomé, pp. 213–56. México: INAH.

Bartolomé, Miguel, and Alicia Barabas

1986   "La pluralidad desigual en Oaxaca." In *Etnicidad y pluralismo cultural: la dinámica étnica en Oaxaca*, edited by Alicia Barabas and Miguel Bartolomé, pp. 13–96. México: INAH.

Bartra, Roger

1977   "The Problem of the Native Peoples and Indigenous Ideology." In *Race and Class in Post-Colonial Society.* Paris: UNESCO.

Berry, Charles R.

1981   *Reform in Oaxaca, 1856–1876.* Lincoln: University of Nebraska Press.

Berthe, Jean-Pierre

1958   "Las minas de oro del Marqués del Valle en Tehuantepec, 1540–1547." *Historia Mexicana* 8 (1): 122–31.

Binford, Leigh

1983   "Agricultural Crises, State Intervention and the Development of Classes in the Isthmus of Tehuantepec, Oaxaca, Mexico." Ph.D. diss., Department of Anthropology, University of Connecticut.

1985   "Political Conflict and Land Tenure in the Mexican Isthmus of Tehuantepec." *Journal of Latin American Studies* 17:179–200.

Boege, Eckart

1988   *Los Mazatecos ante la nación: contradicciones de la identidad étnica en el México actual.* México: Siglo XXI.

Bourgois, Philippe

1985   "Ethnic Minorities." In *Nicaragua: The First Five Years,* edited by Thomas Walker, pp. 201–16. New York: Praeger.

1988   "Conjugated Oppression: Class and Ethnicity among Guaymi and Kuna Banana Workers." *American Ethnologist* 15 (2): 328–48.

Bourque, Susan C., and Kay B. Warren

1989   "Democracy without Peace: The Cultural Politics of Terror in Peru." *Latin American Research Review* 24 (1): 7–33.

Brasseur, Henri
1981   *Viaje a Tehuantepec.* México: SEP (original 1861).
Brockington, Lolita Gutiérrez
1989   *The Leverage of Labor: Managing the Cortés Haciendas in Tehuantepec,*
        1588–1688. Duke, N.C.: Duke University Press.
Browning, David
1971   *El Salvador: Landscape and Society.* Oxford: Oxford University Press.
Burgoa, Francisco de
1934   *Geográfica descripción de la parte septentrional . . . de la América.* 2 vols.
        México (original 1674).
Cabral, Amílcar
1981   *Cultura y liberación nacional.* Vol. 1. México: Escuela Nacional de
        Antropología e Historia.
Campbell, Howard
1989   "La COCEI: cultura y etnicidad politizadas en el Istmo de Tehuantepec."
        Revista Mexicana de Sociología 51 (2): 247–63.
1990   "The COCEI: Culture, Class, and Politicized Ethnicity in the Isthmus of
        Tehuantepec." *Ethnic Groups* 8 (1).
Carmack, Robert, ed.
1988   *Harvest of Violence: The Maya Indians and the Guatemalan Crisis.*
        Norman: University of Oklahoma Press.
Carr, Barry
1986   "The Mexican Left, the Popular Movements, and the Politics of Austerity,
        1982–1985." In *The Mexican Left, the Popular Movements, and the Politics*
        of Austerity, edited by Barry Carr and Ricardo Anzaldúa Montoya, pp.
        1–18. Monograph Series, no. 18. La Jolla, Calif.: Center for U.S.-Mexican
        Studies, University of California, San Diego.
1989   "The Left and Its Potential Role in Political Change." In *Mexico's*
        Alternative Political Futures, edited by Wayne A. Cornelius, Judith
        Gentleman, and Peter Smith, pp. 367–87. Monograph Series, no. 30. La
        Jolla, Calif.: Center for U.S.-Mexican Studies, University of California,
        San Diego.
Chávez, Elías
1983   "Lo que el pueblo gana en las urnas, lo arrebata Vázquez Colmenares."
        Proceso 153 (Aug. 8): 6–10.
Chiñas, Beverly
1973   *The Isthmus Zapotec: Women's Roles in Cultural Context.* New York:
        Holt, Rinehart, Winston.
1983   *The Isthmus Zapotecs: Women's Roles in Cultural Context.* Updated ed.
        Prospect Heights, Ill.: Waveland Press.
Clifford, James
1983   "On Ethnographic Authority." *Representations* 1 (2): 118–46.
1986   "Introduction: Partial Truths." In *Writing Culture: The Poetics and Politics*

    of Ethnography, edited by James Clifford and George Marcus, pp. 1–26.
    Berkeley: University of California Press.

1988   *The Predicament of Culture.* Cambridge, Mass.: Harvard University Press.

Clifford, James, and George Marcus, eds.

1986   *Writing Culture: The Poetics and Politics of Ethnography.* Berkeley:
    University of California Press.

COCEI (Coalición Obrera Campesina Estudiantil del Istmo)

1977   "Alternativas de lucha." Ms., México.

Cockcroft, James

1989   *Neighbors in Turmoil: Latin America.* New York: Harper and Row.

Cohen, Abner

1981   *The Politics of Elite Culture: Explorations in the Dramaturgy of
    Power in a Modern African Society.* Berkeley: University of California
    Press.

Córdova, Juan de

1987a   *Arte del idioma zapoteco.* México: Ediciones Toledo (original 1578).

1987b   *Vocabulario en lengua zapoteca.* México: Ediciones Toledo (original
    1571).

1942   *Vocabulario castellano-zapoteco.* México: Biblioteca Lingüística
    Mexicana, Instituto Nacional de Antropología e Historia, Secretaría de
    Educación Pública.

Cornelius, Wayne A., Judith Gentleman, and Peter H. Smith

1989a   "Overview: The Dynamics of Political Change in Mexico." In *Mexico's
    Alternative Political Futures,* edited by Wayne A. Cornelius, Judith
    Gentleman, and Peter Smith, pp. 1–51. Monograph Series, no. 30. La
    Jolla, Calif.: Center for U.S.- Mexican Studies, University of California,
    San Diego.

Cornelius, Wayne A., Judith Gentleman, and Peter H. Smith, eds.

1989b   *Mexico's Alternative Political Futures.* Monograph Series, no. 30. La Jolla,
    Calif.: Center for U.S.-Mexican Studies, University of California, San
    Diego.

Cosminsky, Sheila

1977   "Childbirth and Midwifery on a Guatemalan Finca." *Medical
    Anthropology* 1 (3).

Covarrubias, Miguel

1946   *Mexico South: The Isthmus of Tehuantepec.* New York: Alfred A. Knopf.

Crapanzano, Vincent

1986   "Hermes' Dilemma: The Masking of Subversion in Ethnographic
    Description." In *Writing Culture: The Poetics and Politics of Ethnography,*
    edited by James Clifford and George Marcus, pp. 51–76. Berkeley:
    University of California Press.

de la Cruz, Víctor

n.d.   "Canciones zapotecas de Tehuantepec." Transcription and editing by de la
    Cruz of *Notes upon the Ethnography of Southern Mexico,* by Frederick

Starr. Proceedings of the Davenport Academy of Sciences, vol. 9, 1901–3. Davenport, Iowa.

1980a   "El idioma como instrumento de opresión y arma de liberación." *Guchachi' Reza* 4:5–7.

1980b   "Entrevista con Andrés Henestrosa." *Guchachi' Reza* 4:14.

1983a   *Corridos del Istmo*. Juchitán, Oaxaca.

1983b   *La flor de la palabra (guie'sti'didxaza)*. Bilingual ed. México: Dirección General de Culturas Populares y Premia Editora.

1983c   *La rebelión de Che Gorio Melendre*. Juchitán: H. Ayuntamiento Popular.

1983d   "Rebeliones indígenas en el Istmo de Tehuantepec." *Cuadernos Políticos* 38:55–71.

1983e   "Las mil caras culturales de la política." *El Buscón* 6:63–67.

1984   "Hermanos o ciudadanos: dos lenguas, dos proyectos políticos en el Istmo." *Guchachi' Reza* 21:18–24.

de la Cruz, Víctor, ed.

1989   *Relatos sobre el General Charis*. México: Dirección General de Culturas Populares and Ediciones Toledo.

Dennis, Phillip A.

1979   "Inter-Village Conflict and the Origin of the State." In *Social, Political and Economic Life in Contemporary Oaxaca*, edited by Aubrey Williams. Publications in Anthropology no. 24. Nashville: Vanderbilt University.

Díaz-Polanco, Héctor

1982   "Indigenismo, Populism, and Marxism." *Latin American Perspectives* 33:42–61.

1985   *La cuestión étnico-nacional*. México: Editorial Linea.

Doniz, Rafael

1983   *H. Ayuntamiento Popular de Juchitán: Fotografías de Rafael Doniz*. Juchitán: H. Ayuntamiento Popular.

Dorsett, James Robert

1975   "Variations in Isthmus Zapotec Kinship and Ecology at Juchitán and Tehuantepec, Oaxaca." Ph.D. diss., Department of Anthropology, Tulane University.

Esparza, Manuel

1987   *Las tierras de los hijos de los pueblos: el distrito de Juchitán en el siglo XIX*. Oaxaca: Archivo General del Estado de Oaxaca.

Fabian, Johannes

1983   *Time and the Other: How Anthropology Makes Its Object*. New York: Columbia University Press.

Faris, James

1990   "A Critical Primer on Anthropology/Photography." Ms., University of Connecticut.

Faris, James, and Harry Walters

1991   "Navaho History: Some Implications of Contrast of Navaho Ceremonial Discourse." *History and Anthropology* 5:1–18.

Finkler, Kaja
1974   *Estudio comparativo de la economía de dos comunidades de México.*
        México: Instituto Nacional Indigenista.
Florescano, Enrique, ed.
1977   "El indígena en la historia de México." *Historia y Sociedad* 15:70–89.
1981   *Fuentes para la historia de la crisis agrícola de 1785–1786.* 2 vols.
        México: Archivo General de la Nación.
Florescano, Enrique, and Isabel Gil, eds.
1973   *Discreciones económicas generales de Nueva España, 1784–1817.*
        México: Instituto Nacional de Antropología e Historia.
Foweraker, Joe
1989   "Popular Movements and the Transformation of the System." In *Mexico's
        Alternative Political Futures,* edited by Wayne A. Cornelius, Judith
        Gentleman, and Peter Smith, pp. 109–29. Monograph Series, no. 30. La
        Jolla, Calif.: Center for U.S.-Mexican Studies, University of California,
        San Diego.
Friedlander, Judith
1975   *Being Indian in Hueyapan: A Study of Forced Identity in Contemporary
        Mexico.* New York: St. Martin's Press.
Friedman, Jonathan
1987   "An Interview with Eric Wolf." *Current Anthropology* 28 (1): 107–18.
Gage, Thomas
1958   *Travels in the New World.* Norman: University of Oklahoma Press
        (original 1648).
García Martínez, Bernardo
1969   *El Marquesado del Valle.* México: El Colegio de México.
Gerhard, Peter
1962   *México en 1742.* México: José Porrúa e Hijos.
Gobierno del Estado de Oaxaca
1980   *Plan estatal de desarrollo, 1980–1986.* Oaxaca.
Gobierno de México
1981   *Ley de reforma agraria.* México.
Gordon, Sarah, ed.
1988   "Feminism and the Critique of Colonial Discourse." *Inscriptions* 3/4.
Gutiérrez, Marco Antonio
1982   "Entrevista inédita con Leopoldo de Gyves Pineda." *Hora Cero,* Mar. 21,
        pp. 7–8.
Gutiérrez, Roberto J.
1981   "Juchitán, municipio comunista." *A: Análisis Histórico y Sociedad
        Mexicana* 2, no. 4 (Sept.-Oct.): 251–80. Universidad Autónoma
        Metropolitana, Azcapotzalco.
Hamnett, Brian R.
1971a   *Politics and Trade in Southern Mexico.* Oxford: Cambridge University.
1971b   "Dye Production, Food Supply, and the Laboring Population of

Oaxaca, 1750–1820." *Hispanic American Historical Review* 51 (1):
51–78.

Heers, Jacques
1961 "La búsqueda de colorantes." *Historia Mexicana* 11 (1): 11–16.

Henestrosa, Andrés
1987 *Los hombres que dispersó la danza.* México: SEP (original 1929).

Hernández E., and J. Córdoba
1982 *La distribución del ingreso en México.* México: Centro de Investigación para la Integración Social.

Hinojosa, Oscar
1984 "La COCEI sigue su camino tras resistir todas las formas de represión." *Proceso* 374 (Jan. 2): 12–15.

Humboldt, Alexander von
1966 *Ensayo político sobre el reino de la Nueva España.* México: Editorial Porrúa (original 1822).

INEGI
1990 *Resultados preliminares. XI Censo General de población y vivienda, 1990.* México: Instituto Nacional de Estadística, Geografía e Informática.

Iturbide, Graciela, and Elena Poniatowska
1989 *Juchitán de las mujeres.* México: Ediciones Toledo.

Iturribarría, Jorge Fernando
1955 *Oaxaca en la historia: de la época precolombiana a los tiempos actuales.* México: Editorial Stylo.

Jhabvala, Firdhaus
1982 *Plan integral del Istmo de Tehuantepec, documento central.* Oaxaca: Gobierno del Estado de Oaxaca, Instituto Tecnológico de Oaxaca, Centro de Graduados e Investigación.

Jiménez, Sotero Constantino
1983 *Foto Estudio Jiménez. Sotero Constantino, fotógrafo de Juchitán.* México: Ediciones Era.

Kahn, Joel
1989 "Culture: Demise or Resurrection?" *Critique of Anthropology* 9 (2): 5–25.

Katz, Friedrich, ed.
1988 *Riot, Rebellion, and Revolution: Rural Social Conflict in Mexico.* Princeton: Princeton University Press.

Kearney, Michael
1989 "Mixtec Political Consciousness: From Passive to Active Resistance." In *Rural Revolt in Mexico and U.S. Intervention,* edited by Daniel Nugent, pp. 113–24. Monograph Series, no. 27. La Jolla, Calif.: Center for U.S.-Mexican Studies, University of California, San Diego.

Keesing, Roger
1987 "Anthropology as Interpretive Quest." *Current Anthropology* 28 (2): 161–69.

1989   "Creating the Past: Custom and Identity in the Contemporary Pacific."
        Contemporary Pacific I (I/2): 19–42.
Kleinman, Arthur
1980   *Patients and Healers in the Context of Culture.* Berkeley: University of
        California Press.
Knight, Alan
1989   "Popular Organizations and Political Transformation: An Historical
        Perspective." Paper delivered at the Fifteenth Congress of the Latin
        American Studies Association, Miami.
León-Portilla, Miguel
1980   "El testimonio de la historia prehispánica en náhuatl." In *Toltecayotl:*
        aspectos de la cultura náhuatl. México: Fondo de Cultura Económica.
Liekens, Enrique
1952   *Los Zapotecos no son Zapotecos sino Zaes: ensayo etimológico de la voz*
        zá. México.
López, Alejandro
n.d.   "La situación agraria en la comunidad de Juchitán." Ms., Juchitán.
López Chiñas, Gabriel
1982   *El Zapoteco y la literatura zapoteca del Istmo de Tehuantepec.* México:
        Talleres Gráficos de México.
López Monjardin, Adriana
1983a   "Una étnia en lucha." *Guchachi' Reza* 17:2–5.
1983b   "Juchitán, las historias de la discordia." *Cuadernos Políticos* 38 (Apr.-
        June): 72–80.
1986   *La lucha por los ayuntamientos, una utopía viable.* México: Siglo XXI.
Marcus, George, and Michael Fischer
1986   *Anthropology as Cultural Critique.* Chicago: University of Chicago Press.
Markman, Peter, and Roberta Markman
1989   *Masks of the Spirit: Image and Metaphor in Mesoamerica.* Berkeley:
        University of California Press.
Martínez López, Felipe
1985   *El crepúsculo del poder: Juchitán, Oaxaca, 1980–1982.* Oaxaca:
        UABJO:IIS.
Mascia-Lees, Frances G., Patricia Sharpe, and Colleen Ballerino Cohen
1989   "The Postmodernist Turn in Anthropology: Cautions from a Feminist
        Perspective." *Signs* 12 (4): 7–33.
Matloff, Judith
1982   "Mexico's Juchitán: A Popular Challenge to PRI." *NACLA* 16 (6): 41–43.
McClain, Carol
1975   "Ethno-Obstetrics in Ajijic." *Anthropological Quarterly* 48:38–56.
1981   "Traditional Midwives and Family Planning: An Assessment of Programs
        and Suggestions for the Future." *Medical Anthropology.*

McGrane, Bernard
1989   *Beyond Anthropology: Society and the Other.* New York: Columbia
        University Press.
Minh-ha, Trinh T.
1987   "Of Other Peoples: Beyond the 'Salvage' Paradigm." In *Discussions in
        Contemporary Culture,* edited by Hal Foster, vol. 1, pp. 138–41. Seattle:
        Bay Press.
Moguel, Reyna
1979   *Regionalizaciones para el estado de Oaxaca: análisis comparativo.*
        Oaxaca: Centro de Sociología de la UABJO.
Molina, Arcadio G.
1894   *La rosa del amor.* San Blas Atempa, Oaxaca: Imprenta del Istmo.
1899   *El jazmín del Istmo: principios generales para aprender a leer
        escribir y hablar la lengua zapoteca.* Oaxaca: Imprenta de San
        German.
Moorhead, Max L.
1949   "Hernan Cortés and the Tehuantepec Passage." *Hispanic American
        Historical Review* 29 (3): 372–76.
Nader, Laura
1969   "The Zapotec of Oaxaca." In *Handbook of Middle American Indians,* vol.
        6, edited by Robert Wauchope and Evon Z. Vogt, pp. 329–59. Austin:
        University of Texas Press.
Neza
1987   México: Ediciones Toledo (originally published 1935–39).
Nugent, Daniel
1987-88 "Mexico's Rural Populations and 'La Crisis.' Economic Crisis or
        Legitimation Crisis? One Anthropological View." *Critique of Anthropology*
        7 (3): 93–112.
Ong, Aihwa
1987   *Spirits of Resistance and Factory Discipline.* Albany: State University of
        New York Press.
Ornelas Esquinca, Marco Antonio
1983   "Juchitán, Ayuntamiento Popular." Thesis, ITAM.
Paul, Lois
1978   "Careers of Midwives in a Mayan Community." In *Women in Ritual and
        Symbolic Roles,* edited by Judith Hoch-Smith and Anita Spring, pp.
        129–49. New York: Plenum Press.
Paul, Lois, and Benjamin Paul
1975   "The Maya Midwife as Sacred Professional." *American Ethnologist* 2 (4):
        707–26.
Paz, Octavio
1984   "El diálogo y el ruido." *Vuelta* 8 (96): 4–7.

Petrich, Blanche
1983   "De Gives: las autoridades de Oaxaca temen un gobierno socialista en el
        Istmo de Tehuantepec." *Unomásuno,* Sept. 9.
Pinney, Christopher
1989   "Representations of India: Normalisation and the 'Other.' " *Pacific
        Viewpoint* 29 (2): 144–62.
Polier, Nicole, and William Roseberry
1989   "Tristes Tropes." *Economy and Society* 18 (2): 245–64.
Prévot-Shapira, Marie-France, and Hélène Rivière d'Arc
1984   "Los Zapotecos, el PRI, y la COCEI: enfrentamientos alrededor de las
        intervenciones del Estado en el Istmo de Tehuantepec." *Guchachi' Reza* 19
        (June): 11–26.
PRI (Partido Revolucionario Institucional)
1988   *Documentos básicos, declaración de principios, programa de acción,
        estatutos.* México: PRI.
Prieto, Alejandro
1884   *Proyectos sobre la colonización del Istmo de Tehuantepec.* México:
        Imprenta de I. Cumplido.
Prieto, Ana María
1986   "Mexico's National *Coordinadoras* in a Context of Economic Crisis." In
        The Mexican Left, the Popular Movements, and the Politics of Austerity,
        edited by Barry Carr and Ricardo Anzaldúa, pp. 75–94. Monograph
        Series, no. 18. La Jolla, Calif.: Center for U.S.-Mexican Studies,
        University of California, San Diego.
Rabinow, Paul
1977   *Reflections on Fieldwork in Morocco.* Berkeley: University of California
        Press.
Ramírez, Ignacio, and Ernesto Reyes
1983   "El ejército y la policía culminaron el plan oficial contra la COCEI."
        Proceso 372 (Dec. 19): 6–11.
Reding, Andrew
1988   "Mexico at a Crossroads: The 1988 Election and Beyond." *World Policy
        Journal* 5 (4): 615–49.
1989   "A Facade of Reform." *World Policy Journal* 6 (4): 685–729.
Reina, Leticia
1980   *Las rebeliones campesinas en México, 1819–1906.* México: Siglo
        XXI.
Reyes Osorio, Sergio, et al.
1974   *Estructura agraria y desarrollo agrícola en México.* México: Fondo de
        Cultura Económica.
Reynoso, Carlos, ed.
1991   *El surgimiento de la antropología posmoderna.* México: Ed. Gedisa.

Richardson, W. H.
1988   *Mexico through Russian Eyes, 1806–1940.* Pittsburgh: University of
        Pittsburgh.

Rodríguez, Francisco
1984   "Pemex en Salina Cruz: especifidades de la inmigración y el empleo." In
        El puerto industrial de Salina Cruz, Oaxaca, pp. 94–120. México:
        Instituto de Geografía UNAM and Centro de Investigaciones y
        Documentación de América Latina.

Rojas, Basilio
1964   *La rebelión de Tehuantepec.* México.

Rorty, Richard
1980   *Philosophy and the Mirror of Nature.* Oxford: Blackwell.

Rosaldo, Renato
1986   "From the Door of His Tent: The Fieldworker and the Inquisitor." In
        Writing Culture: The Poetics and Politics of Ethnography, edited by James
        Clifford and George Marcus, pp. 77–97. Berkeley: University of
        California Press.

Royce, Anya Peterson
1975   *Prestigio y afiliación en una comunidad urbana: Juchitán, Oaxaca.*
        México: Instituto Nacional Indigenista.

1982   *Ethnic Identity: Strategies of Diversity.* Bloomington: University of
        Indiana Press.

Rubin, Jeffrey W.
1987   "State Policies, Leftist Oppositions, and Municipal Elections: The Case of
        the COCEI of Juchitán." In *Electoral Patterns and Perspectives in Mexico,*
        pp. 127–60. Monograph Series, no. 22. La Jolla, Calif.: Center for U.S.-
        Mexican Studies, University of California, San Diego.

Russell, Bertrand
1971   *La perspectiva científica.* Barcelona: Ediciones Ariel.

Sahagún, Bernadino de
1979   *Historia general de las cosas de Nueva España.* Edited by Angel María
        Garibay K. México: Editorial Porrúa.

Said, Edward
1978   *Orientalism.* New York: Pantheon.

Salomon, Frank
1987   "Ancestors, Grave Robbers, and the Possible Antecedents of Cañari 'Inca-
        Ism.' " *Etnologiska Studier* 38:207–32. Goteborgs Ethnographic Museum,
        Sweden.

Sangren, Steven
1988   "Rhetoric and the Authority of Ethnography: 'Postmodernism' and
        the Social Reproduction of Texts." *Current Anthropology* 29 (1):
        405–24.

Santana, R.
1981   "El caso de Ecuarunari." *Nariz del Diablo* 2 (7): 30–38. Quito, Ecuador.

Sargent, Carol F.
1982   *The Cultural Context of Therapeutic Choice: Obstetrical Decisions among the Bariba of Benin.* Boston: D. Reidel.

Schryer, Fran
1990   *Ethnicity and Class Conflict in Rural Mexico.* Princeton: Princeton University Press.

Scott, James
1985   *Weapons of the Weak.* New Haven: Yale University Press.

Sembane, Ousamane
1970   *God's Bits of Wood.* Garden City, New York: Doubleday Anchor.

Semo, Enrique
1986   "The Mexican Left and the Economic Crisis." In *The Mexican Left, the Popular Movements, and the Politics of Austerity,* edited by Barry Carr and Ricardo Anzaldúa, pp. 19–32. Monograph Series, no. 18. La Jolla, Calif.: Center for U.S.-Mexican Studies, University of California, San Diego.

Simon, Jean-Marie
1987   *Guatemala: Eternal Spring, Eternal Tyranny.* New York: W. W. Norton.

Smith, Robert S.
1959   "Indigo Production and Trade in Colonial Guatemala." *Hispanic American Historical Review* 39 (3): 181–211.

Spivak, Gayatri Chakravorty
1990   *The Post-Colonial Critic: Interviews, Strategies, Dialogues.* London: Routledge.

Spores, Ronald
1965   "The Zapotec and Mixtec at Spanish Contact." In *Handbook of Middle American Indians,* vol. 3, pp. 962–87. Austin: University of Texas Press.

Stavenhagen, Rodolfo
1970   "Classes, Colonialism and Acculturation." In *Masses in Latin America,* edited by Irving Louis Horowitz, pp. 235–88. New York: Oxford University Press.

1975   *Social Classes in Agrarian Societies.* New York: Doubleday.

1980   *Problemas étnicos y campesinos.* México: INI.

Stephen, Lynn
1988   "Culture as a Resource: Four Cases of Self-Managed Indigenous Craft Production." Ms.

Stern, Steve, ed.
1987   *Resistance, Rebellion, and Consciousness in the Andean Peasant World, Eighteenth to Twentieth Centuries.* Madison: University of Wisconsin Press.

Stoler, Ann

1984   *Capitalism and Confrontation in Sumatra's Plantation Belt, 1875–1975.*
        New Haven: Yale University Press.

Street, Susan

1989   "The Role of Social Movements in the Analysis of Sociopolitical Change
        in Mexico." Paper delivered at the Fifteenth International Congress of the
        Latin American Studies Association, Miami.

Taller de Investigación Sociológica, UNAM

1984   "Juchitán: el fin de la ilusión." In *Oaxaca, una lucha reciente: 1960–83,*
        edited by René Bustamante et al., pp. 308–417. México: Ediciones Nueva
        Sociología.

Thompson, J. Eric, ed.

1958   *Thomas Gage's Travels in the New World.* Norman: University of
        Oklahoma Press.

Toledo, Francisco

1986   *Toledo: lo que el viento a Juárez.* México: Ediciones Era.

Toledo, Francisco, and Víctor de la Cruz

1983   "Entrevista a Daniel López Nelio." *Guchachi' Reza* 17:19–25.

Torres de Laguna, Juan

1928   "Descripción de Tehuantepec." *Revista Mexicana de Estudios Históricos,*
        apéndice 2, pp. 196–270.

1983   *Descripción de Tehuantepec.* Juchitán, Oaxaca (original 1580).

Tutino, John

1978   "Indian Rebellion in the Isthmus of Tehuantepec: A Sociohistorical
        Perspective." Proceedings of the 42d International Conference of
        Americanists, 7 (3): 197–214. Paris.

1980   "Rebeliones indígenas en Tehuantepec." *Cuadernos Políticos* 24 (Apr.-
        June): 89–101.

1981   "Rebelión indígena en Tehuantepec." *Guchachi' Reza* 7:3–16.

Tyler, Stephen

1987a   *The Unspeakable: Discourse, Dialogue, and Rhetoric in the Postmodern
        World.* Madison: University of Wisconsin Press.

1987b   "Still RAYTING: Response to Scholte." *Critique of Anthropology* 7 (1):
        49–51.

UNAM and Casa de la Cultura, Juchitán

1986   *Modelo pedagógico de diálogo cultural y alfabetización. Para la
        población de Juchitán y el Istmo de Tehuantepec.* México: UNAM:IIA and
        Casa de la Cultura, Juchitán, Oaxaca.

Vansina, Jan

1985   *Oral Tradition as History.* Madison: University of Wisconsin Press.

Varese, Stefano

1988   "Multi-Ethnicity and Hegemonic Construction: Indian Projects and the

Future." In *Ethnicities and Nations,* edited by Francisco Bellizi, pp. 57–77. Austin: University of Texas Press.

Vargas Llosa, Mario

1983   "Historia de una matanza." *Vuelta* 81 (Aug.): 4–15.

Vásquez de Espinosa, Antonio

1966   *Description of the Indies, c. 1620.* Translated by Charles Upson Clark. Washington, D.C.: Smithsonian Institution.

Walicki, Andrzej

1970   "Rusia." In *Populismo: sus significados y características nacionales,* edited by Ghita Ionescu and Ernest Gellner. Buenos Aires: Amorrortu Editores. Published in English as *Populism: Its Meanings and National Characteristics.* London, 1969.

Warman, Arturo

1972   *Los campesinos, hijos predilectos del régimen.* México: Nuestro Tiempo.

1976   *Y venimos a contradecir: los campesinos de Morelos y el Estado nacional.* México: Ediciones de a la Casa Chata.

1983   "El futuro del Istmo y la Presa Juárez." *Guchachi' Reza* 15:2–4.

Wazir-Jahan, Karim

1984   "Malay Midwives and Witches." *Social Science and Medicine* 18 (2): 159–66.

Whitecotton, Joseph

1984   *The Zapotecs: Princes, Priests, and Peasants.* Norman: University of Oklahoma Press.

Wolf, Eric

1957   "Closed Corporate Communities in Mesoamerica and Central Java." *Southwestern Journal of Anthropology* 13:1–18.

Young, James C.

1981   *Medical Choices in a Mexican Village.* New Brunswick, N.J.: Rutgers University Press.

Zeitlin, Judith Frances

1978   "Community Distribution and Local Economy in the Southern Isthmus of Tehuantepec: An Archaeological and Ethnohistorical Investigation." Ph.D. diss., Department of Anthropology, Yale University.

1989   "Ranchers and Indians on the Southern Isthmus of Tehuantepec: Economic Change and Indigenous Survival in Colonial Mexico." *Hispanic American Historical Review* 69 (1): 23–60.

Zermeño, Sergio

1984   "Sombra y vacío: adiós al 68?" *Nexos* 7, no. 81 (Sept.).

Source Notes

All of the poems and one song were translated from Spanish by Nathaniel Tarn. Several of the poems originally appeared in the *Taos Review* 1 (1989). Cynthia Steele translated "Juchitán, a Town of Women" from the Spanish original. Leigh Binford translated the articles "Indigenous Peoples' History (by Whom and for Whom?)" and "Juchitán: Histories of Discord." Howard Campbell translated all the other materials that originally appeared in Spanish.

PART ONE. HISTORIES OF CONFLICT, STRUGGLE, AND MOBILIZATION IN THE ISTHMUS OF TEHUANTEPEC

Víctor de la Cruz, "Indigenous Peoples' History (by Whom and for Whom?)," translation of "Historia de los pueblos indios (por quién y para quién?)," *Guchachi' Reza* 20 (Sept. 1984): 3–7.

Andrés Henestrosa, "The Foundation of Juchitán," translation of "La fundación de Juchitán," *Guchachi' Reza* 10:2, n.d.

John Tutino, "Ethnic Resistance: Juchitán in Mexican History," revised and expanded version of "Indian Rebellion at the Isthmus of Tehuantepec: A Socio-Historical Perspective," Proceedings of the 42d International Congress of Americanists, vol. 3 (Paris, 1978), pp. 197–214.

Tomás Ruiz, "A New Corrido for Che Gómez," translation of "Nuevo Corrido de Che Gómez," *Guchachi' Reza* 9 (Dec. 1981): 15.

Adriana López Monjardin, "Juchitán: Histories of Discord," translation of

"Juchitán: las historias de la discordia," *Cuadernos Políticos* 38 (Oct.–Dec. 1983): 72–80.

"Memories of Anastasia Martínez," translation of "Recuerdos de Anastasia Martínez," *Guchachi' Reza* 23 (June 1985): 19–21.

Leigh Binford, "Irrigation, Land Tenure, and Class Struggle in Juchitán, Oaxaca," revised version of "Political Conflict and Land Tenure in the Mexican Isthmus of Tehuantepec," *Journal of Latin American Studies* 17, no. 1 (1985): 179–200.

Arturo Warman, "The Future of the Isthmus and the Juárez Dam," translation of "El futuro del Istmo y la Presa Juárez," *Guchachi' Reza* 15 (June 1983): 2–4.

Gabriel López Chiñas, "The One Who Rode Duarte's Horse," translation of "El que montó el caballo de Duarte," in *La flor de la palabra,* ed. Víctor de la Cruz (México: Premia Editora, 1983), pp. 64–67.

PART TWO. REPRESENTATIONS OF THE JUCHITECOS BY THEMSELVES AND OTHERS

Víctor de la Cruz, "Who Are We? What Is Our Name?" translation of "Quiénes somos? Cual es nuestro nombre?" *La flor de la palabra,* ed. Víctor de la Cruz (México: Premia Editora, 1983), pp. 80–83.

G. F. Von Tempsky, "A German Traveler's Observations in Juchitán," in *Mitla: A Narrative of Incidents and Personal Adventures on a Journey in Mexico, Guatemala and Salvador in the Years 1853 to 1855 with Observations on the Modes of Life in Those Countries,* ed. J. S. Bell (London: Longman, Brown, Green, Longmans & Roberts, 1858), pp. 281–87.

"The Juchitecos as Seen by Benito Juárez," translation of excerpts from "Los Juchitecos vistos por Benito Juárez," a speech delivered by Governor Benito Juárez at the opening of the ninth period of sessions of the Oaxaca State Congress, July 2, 1850, *Guchachi' Reza* 8:7–9, n.d.

Macario Matus, "Juchitán Political Moments," translation of "Momentos políticos de Juchitán," *Hora Cero,* May 25, 1981.

Andrés Henestrosa, "The Forms of Sexual Life in Juchitán," translation of "Las formas de la vida sexual en Juchitán," *Guchachi' Reza* 22 (Mar. 1985): 3–5, originally published in *Revista de Ciencias Sociales* 3 (Oct. 1930).

Elena Poniatowska, "Juchitán, a Town of Women," translation of excerpts from "El hombre del pito dulce," introductory essay to *Juchitán de las mujeres,* by Graciela Iturbide and Elena Poniatowska (México: Ediciones Toledo, 1989), pp. 13–17.

Obdulia Ruiz Campbell, "Representations of Isthmus Women: A Zapotec Woman's Point of View," previously unpublished.

Víctor de la Cruz, "Social Scientists Confronted with Juchitán (Incidents of an Unequal Relationship)," translation of "Los científicos frente a Juchitán (incidentes de una relación desigual)," *Guchachi' Reza* 19 (June 1984): 8–10.

PART THREE. COCEI: ISTHMUS ZAPOTEC POLITICAL RADICALISM

Macario Matus, "My Companions Have Died," translation of "Han muerto mis compañeros," in *La flor de la palabra,* ed. Víctor de la Cruz (México: Premia Editora, 1983), p. 77.

Jeffrey W. Rubin, "The COCEI against the State: A Political History of Juchitán." A longer version of this article appeared under the title "State Policies, Leftist Oppositions, and Municipal Elections: The Case of the COCEI in Juchitán," in *Electoral Patterns and Perspectives in Mexico,* ed. Arturo Alvarado, Monograph Series, no. 22 (San Diego: Center for U.S.-Mexican Studies, 1987), pp. 127–60.

Marta Bañuelos, comp., "Testimonies of COCEI Women," translation of interviews with COCEI women conducted by Bañuelos, which appear in her article "Ellas no son diferentes, protesta, exige, la mujer de Juchitán," in *Juchitán: lucha y poesía,* ed. Marta Bañuelos et al. (México: Editorial Extemporáneos, 1988), pp. 27–33. The original Spanish headings were chosen by Bañuelos.

"Inaugural Speech of Leopoldo de Gyves de la Cruz as Mayor of Juchitán (March 10, 1981)," translation of "Discurso pronunciado por Leopoldo de Gyves de la Cruz en la toma de posesión el 10 de marzo de 1981," *Guchachi' Reza* 9:10–11, n.d.

COCEI, "Alternatives for Struggle: The Context of the COCEI Alternative," translation of "Alternativas de lucha: la COCEI su alternativa en este contexto," in *COCEI: alternativa de organización y lucha para los pueblos del Istmo,* Memoria del Primer Congreso Nacional sobre Problemas Agrarios (México: Universidad Autónoma de Guerrero, 1983). This political pamphlet was presented by COCEI representatives in Chilpancingo, Guerrero, in 1982.

Sergio Zermeño, "COCEI: Narodniks of Southern Mexico?" translation of excerpts from "Juchitán: la cólera del régimen. Crónica y análisis de una lucha social," in *Juchitán: limites de una experiencia democrática,* Cuadernos de Investigación Social 15 (México: UNAM-IIS, 1987), pp. 65–97.

Macario Matus, "Naked Speech," translation of "Palabra desnuda," in *Juchitán: lucha y poesia* (México: Editorial Extemporáneos, 1988), p. 61.

Alejandro Cruz, "A Birth in the Mountains," translation of "Parto en las montañas," *Guchachi' Reza* 17 (Dec. 1983): 6.

PART FOUR. *GUENDABIAANI':* THE POLITICS OF CULTURE IN JUCHITÁN

Gabriel López Chiñas, "The Zapotec Language," translation of "El Zapoteco," in *La flor de la palabra,* ed. Víctor de la Cruz (México: Premia Editora, 1983), pp. 68–69.

Howard Campbell, "Class Struggle, Ethnopolitics, and Cultural Revivalism in

Juchitán," revised version of "The COCEI: Culture, Class, and Politicized Ethnicity in the Isthmus of Tehuantepec," *Ethnic Groups* 8 (1990): 1.

"Interview with Daniel López Nelio," translation of excerpts from "Entrevista a Daniel López Nelio," by Francisco Toledo and Víctor de la Cruz, *Guchachi' Reza* 17 (Dec. 1983): 19–25. The interviewer's comments and López Nelio's references to them have been omitted.

Víctor de la Cruz, "Rain," translation of "Lluvia," in *En torno a las islas del mar océano,* by Víctor de la Cruz (Juchitán, 1983), p. 61.

Enedino Jiménez, "The Sun," translation of "Gubidxa: el sol," *Guchachi' Reza* 18 (Mar. 1984): 10.

Víctor de la Cruz, "Brothers or Citizens: Two Languages, Two Political Projects in the Isthmus," translation of "Hermanos o ciudadanos: dos lenguas, dos proyectos políticos en el Istmo," *Guchachi' Reza* 21 (Dec. 1984): 18–24.

Andrés Henestrosa, "The Bell," translation of "La campana," *Guchachi' Reza,* n.d., originally published in *Los hombres que dispersó la danza* (México: SEP, 1987, original 1929).

Macario Matus, recorder, "Trapped Lightning," translation of "El rayo atrapado," *Guchachi' Reza* 6:15, n.d.

Manuel M. Matus, "The Tales of Moonje'," translation of "Las historias de Moonje'," *Guchachi' Reza* 24 (Sept. 1985): 3–4.

Manuel López Mateos, "When Radio Became the Voice of the People," translation of "Una experiencia: cuando la voz de la radio es la voz del pueblo," in *Juchitán: lucha y poesía,* ed. Marta Bañuelos et al. (México: Editorial Extemporáneos, 1988), pp. 17–18.

Miguel Flores Ramírez, "Pichancha," translation of poem of same name, *Guchachi' Reza* 24 (Sept. 1985): 2.

Víctor de la Cruz, "The Third Elegy," translation of "La tercera elegía," in *En torno a las islas del mar oceano,* by Víctor de la Cruz (Juchitán, 1983), p. 61.

Shoshana R. Sokoloff, "The Proud Midwives of Juchitán," previously unpublished.

Contributors

Marta Bañuelos is professor of political science at the Universidad Autónoma Metropolitana-Iztapalapa in Mexico City. She has written a number of articles on the struggles of Mexican workers in the magazine *La Situación de las Luchas de los Trabajadores,* published by Taller de Investigación Obrera and the Universidad Autónoma Chapingo of Mexico.

Alicia Barabas is an anthropologist affiliated with the Instituto Nacional de Antropología e Historia in Oaxaca, Oaxaca. She coedited *Etnicidad y pluralismo cultural: la dinámica étnica en Oaxaca* (INAH, 1986) and coauthored *Tierra de la palabra* (INAH, 1982) with Miguel Bartolomé, and has written many articles and several books.

Miguel Bartolomé is an anthropologist affiliated with the Instituto Nacional de Antropología e Historia in Oaxaca, Oaxaca. He coedited *Etnicidad y pluralismo cultural: la dinámica étnica en Oaxaca* (INAH, 1986) and coauthored *Tierra de la palabra* (INAH, 1982), and has written many articles and several books.

Leigh Binford is associate professor of anthropology at the University of Connecticut. He has conducted fieldwork in Oaxaca since 1980 and is coauthor with Scott Cook of *Obliging Need: Rural Petty Industry in Mexican Capitalism* (University of Texas Press, 1990).

Howard Campbell is assistant professor of anthropology at the University of Texas at El Paso. Campbell has conducted research in the Isthmus since 1981 and in 1990 completed his Ph.D. thesis, "Zapotec Ethnic Politics and the Politics of Culture in Juchitán, Oaxaca (1350–1990)," at the University of Wisconsin-Madison.

Alejandro Cruz was a talented young poet and COCEI activist who was killed by members of the Isthmus PRI in Tehuantepec, Oaxaca, in 1987.

Leopoldo de Gyves de la Cruz is a COCEI leader who served as mayor of Juchitán from 1981 to 1983 and federal deputy from 1986 to 1989.

Víctor de la Cruz, besides being the author of many books of poetry, has also written widely on Isthmus Zapotec history, language, and customs, and COCEI politics. He is the editor of *Guchachi' Reza* and is also currently employed as an anthropologist with CIESAS-Oaxaca. In the past he was director of the Juchitán Casa de la Cultura.

Miguel Flores Ramírez is married to a Juchiteca and is an aficionado of Isthmus Zapotec culture.

Andrés Henestrosa of Juchitán has been an influential writer, journalist, and politician in Mexico for sixty years. Among his many writings is the well-known *Los hombres que dispersó la danza*.

Graciela Iturbide is one of Latin America's finest photographers. She has been the recipient of a Guggenheim Foundation fellowship, and her work has been displayed in prominent galleries in Mexico City, Paris, and elsewhere and reproduced in many books and magazines in Mexico and the United States.

Enedino Jiménez is a leader of the opposition teacher's union in Oaxaca, a COCEI activist, and the author of many poems.

Gabriel López Chiñas authored numerous books including *Vinnigulasa, Guendaxheela (el casamiento),* and *El Zapoteco y la literatura zapoteca del Istmo de Tehuantepec*. He was also a professor of Spanish literature at the National Autonomous University of Mexico (UNAM), and, for a short time, director of the university's radio station. López Chiñas died in 1983.

Manuel López Mateos is an editor for Addison-Wesley publishers in Mexico. In 1983 López Mateos directed Radio Ayuntamiento Popular, COCEI's Juchitán-based radio station.

Adriana López Monjardin is a journalist and anthropologist employed by the National Institute of Anthropology and History in Mexico City. She is the author of *La lucha por los ayuntamientos: una utopía viable* (Siglo XXI, 1986).

Daniel López Nelio is one of the founders of COCEI, the leader of the COCEI peasant sector, and a former federal deputy in the Mexican Congress.

Anastasia Martínez is a Zapotec woman from Juchitán, Oaxaca.

Macario Matus is the author of numerous poems and essays and directed the Casa de la Cultura in Juchitán from 1979 to 1989. Currently he works as a journalist for several major Mexican newspapers and lives in Mexico City.

Manuel M. Matus is a writer, folklorist, and researcher in the Instituto de Investigaciones de Humanidades in Oaxaca, Oaxaca.

Elena Poniatowska is one of Mexico's best-known contemporary writers. Among her many books is *La noche de Tlatelolco*.

Jeffrey W. Rubin is assistant professor of political science at Amherst College. Rubin conducted research in Juchitán in 1985 and 1986, and is the author of several articles and a Ph.D. dissertation (Harvard University, 1991) on COCEI.

Tomás Ruiz lives in the first ward of Juchitán, Oaxaca.

Obdulia Ruiz Campbell is a native of San Blas Atempa, Oaxaca, and a student at the University of Texas at El Paso.

Shoshana R. Sokoloff is a medical doctor who graduated from Harvard Medical School and carried out her thesis among Zapotec midwives in Juchitán.

Nathaniel Tarn (née Michael Mendelson) is the author of more than twenty books of poetry and has translated Neruda, Vallejo, and other Latin American writers into English. He holds a Ph.D. in anthropology from the University of Chicago.

Francisco Toledo is one of Mexico's best-known modern artists. In addition to his many art exhibitions in New York, Paris, Tokyo, Mexico City, and elsewhere, Toledo's work has been presented in numerous books, including *Toledo: lo que el viento a Juárez* (México: Ediciones Era, 1986).

John Tutino is a professor of history at Boston College. Among his many publications on Mexican history is *From Insurrection to Revolution in Mexico: Social Bases of Agrarian Violence, 1750–1940* (Princeton University Press, 1987).

G. F. Von Tempsky was a German explorer who wrote a chronicle of his nineteenth-century travels through Mexico and Central America.

Arturo Warman is a Mexican anthropologist specializing in peasant studies. He is particularly known for *Los campesinos: hijos predilectos del régimen* and *Y venimos a contradecir: los campesinos de Morelos y el estado nacional*, the latter published by Johns Hopkins Press as *We Come to Object: The Peasants of Morelos and the National State*. He recently served as director of the National Indigenist Institute.

Sergio Zermeño is the author of several important books on Mexican politics, including one on the 1968 student movement (*México: una democracia utópica*, Siglo XXI, 1980). He is currently a researcher at the Instituto de Investigaciones Sociales of the National Autonomous University of Mexico in Mexico City.

Index

A

Abduction, 130–31, 139–40
Agrarian question, 91, 95–96, 201
Agrarian Reform Ministry, 153, 161, 180
Agriculture: changes in, 159–60,
    233–34; climatic limits to, 87–88,
    101–2; in colonial period, 48, 51–52;
    future, 105–6; in Isthmus of Tehuan-
    tepec, 6, 104
Alburquerque, Bernardo de, 126
Alfa-Omega Project, 198–200
Altamirano, Teodoro, 26, 73–78, 182
Alvarez Bravo, Lola, 224
Alvaro Obregón colony, 75, 161
Ancestors, 32–34
Anthropology, xiii, 10–14, 20n2
Art, 223
Artists, 280
Asunción Ixtaltepec. *See* Ixtaltepec
Avellán, Juan de, 49–50
Aztecs, 44–45, 125, 215

B

Benito Juárez Dam, 7, 15, 70, 89, 101–6,
    159, 233
Bresson, Henri Cartier, 224
Burgoa, Francisco, 32–33, 35–36
Bustillo, Mario, 163

C

Capitalism: development of, 69; and land
    tenure, 102; penetration of Isthmus by,
    16
Cárdenas, Cuauhtémoc, 2, 18n1, 217,
    281
Cárdenas, Lázaro, 159
Carrasco, Valentín, 183
Casa de la Cultura, 222–25, 245, 280,
    282–83
Castillo, Heberto, 18n1, 218
Charis, Heliodoro, 7, 26, 60, 74–77, 81–
    82, 159
Charis, Javier, 74, 170

Charles IV, 126

Cheguigo, 63

Chicapa del Castro, 91

Childbirth, 275, 277n7, 277n8

Chontal Maya, 43, 219

Class: and education, 186–87; and ethnic identity, 174n6, 213, 217, 229n7, 231n19; structure, 218; struggle, 218. *See also* COCEI

Cloth, 52–55, 68

COCEI: accomplishments, 105, 157, 163–64; alliances, 157, 162, 164; analyses, 17–18, 18n8, 167–68, 175n16, 191–202, 280; appeal, 95, 167–68, 219; and capitalism, 16; and Central America, 165; characteristics, 4; class composition, 16, 95, 221, 229n7; debates within, 279–81; demands, 14, 127, 190, 282; and ethnic conflict, 16, 235; and ethnic identity, 16, 161, 214, 216, 280; and ethnopolitics, xiv–xv, 215; future, 152, 200–202; goals, 228; history, xviii, 1–3, 7–8, 17, 127, 147–49, 150, 157–58, 160–62, 196–97, 202, 245; ideology, 151–52, 183–84, 185–90, 215–16; and land, 94–95, 160–61; leadership, 220; limits to expansion, 219; and new social movements, 14–18; political activity, 170–71, 216–17; and political reform, 194; and popular radio, 17, 261–62; and populism, 152, 193–94; publications, 226; relations with Mexican government, 194–95, 197–98, 279–84; repression of, 97, 128, 149, 150–51, 153, 162, 169–70, 177–82; and Sendero Luminoso, 196–97; strategy and tactics, 161–66, 199, 279–81; structure, 179, 220–21; studies of, 19n6; women's roles in, 150–51, 178–82, 226–27; and Zapotec culture, 3, 221–26, 234–35; and Zapotec history, 127. *See also* Culture; Elections; Institutional

Revolutionary Party; Isthmus of Tehuantepec; Isthmus Zapotec Culture; Juchitán; Kinship; Mexican government; Politics; Radio; Representation; Social and economic development; Tehuantepec

Cochineal, 51–53

Cocijo, 42

Colonialism: accommodation to, 50; economy, 47–48; impact of, 32–34, 45–47; and Juchitán, 244; and language, 242–43; and trade, 51

Comitancillo, 219

Commerce: in colonial era, 51; and trade, 68; women's roles in, 134, 137, 178–79

Communal land: 27, 88, 90, 102–3, 159, 245

Conflict, 54–55

Constantino Jiménez, Sotero, 224–25

Corn, 48, 88, 104, 159–60, 234

Cortés, Hernando, 6, 45, 47

Cortés, Juan. *See* Cosijopi

Cosijoeza, 207

Cosijopi, 45, 47

Covarrubias, Miguel, 9, 145, 222

Creative and resistant adaptation, 53, 56

Credit, 95, 164

Cruz, Alejandro, 153, 205, 225

Cruz, Oscar, 283

Cruz, Víctor de la, xi, xix–xx, 29–37, 79n7, 114–15, 117–18, 143–46, 209, 222, 225, 237–38, 241–48, 265

Cultural revival, 230n14

D

Díaz, Felix, 81, 84

Díaz Ordaz, Gustavo, 72, 92–96, 103

Díaz, Porfirio, 60, 110, 126

Disease, 8–9, 46–47, 58

Doctors, 275

Dominicans, 46–49

Doniz, Rafael, 224, 226

E

Echeverría, Francisco Javier, 55, 72
Echeverría, Luis, 151, 188
Economic development: competing versions of, 165; failures, 101–6; and political struggle, 105–6. *See also* Isthmus of Tehuantepec; Isthmus Zapotec culture; Juchitán
Economy: decline of, 49–50, 53; gender relations in, 134; precolonial, 43; and Spanish colonialism, 45
Education, 179, 269–73
Eisenstein, Sergei, 135, 224
Ejido Emiliano Zapata, 75
Ejidos, 27, 90–92, 97n2, 98n6, 98–99n10, 99n11, 99–100n13, 161, 189, 218
Elections: annulment of, 171; COCEI participation, 1–2, 97, 148–50, 157–58, 162, 164, 198; fraud in, 162, 168, 171, 200, 281; in Juchitán, 166, 169–71, 175n15, 279; national, 148–49; political importance of, 168
Elites: colonial, 53–55; influence of, 70–71; and Mexican state, 53, 55; and modernization, 71; opposition to COCEI, 164–65, 166–67; precolonial, 42
Encomienda, 45
Espinal, 91, 96, 97n1
Ethnic identity: and capitalist development, 69–70; future, 284; in Juchitán, 174n6; in Mexico, 41; and peasant identities, 59; and political discourse, 214; pride in, 141; and resistance, 58–60; uses of, 214–15. *See also* COCEI; Institutional Revolutionary Party
Ethnicity: and class, 213, 228; and class consciousness in Juchitán, 161; and economy in Mexico, 41; and political discourse, 71
Ethnographic writing, 10–14, 20n14

F

Family relations, 140–41, 179
Federal Irrigation District No. 19, 7, 70, 89
Fiestas, 135, 139, 216–17, 220–21
Flores Ramírez, Miguel, 263

G

Gender relations, 112–14, 115n2, 129–31, 227, 231n18. See also *Guchachi' Reza;* Women
Gómez, Che. *See* Gómez, José F.
Gómez, José F., 26, 63, 72–73, 75, 78, 81–83, 126–27, 183, 229n7, 256
Gorio Melendre, Che. *See* Gregorio Meléndez, José
Gregorio Meléndez, José, 25, 56–58, 73, 78, 110, 120–21, 126, 245
Guchachi' Reza, 3–4, 10, 12–14, 17, 208–9, 225–26, 230n4, 234, 245, 247
Guergue, José Joaquin, 54, 57
Guiengola, 43, 50–51
Gurrión, Adolfo C., 127
Gyves, Alexandre de, 119
Gyves de la Cruz, Leopoldo [Polín] de, 76, 183–84, 198–99, 220
Gyves Pineda, Leopoldo de, 128, 133, 178

H

Haciendas Marquesanas, 47–48, 53–54, 57
Henestrosa, Andrés, 3, 73, 112, 129–31, 208, 222, 224, 243
History: discourses of, 65–79, 112; of Juchitán, 39–40; and mythology, 29, 31–37; struggles over, 26–27, 73; study of, 23–24. *See also* COCEI; Indigenous people; Isthmus Zapotec language; Juchitán
Homosexuality, 230n9
Huatulco, 219, 280
Huave, 43, 45, 48, 55, 125, 219, 250–51

Hughes, Langston, 224
Huilotepec, 57
Humboldt, Alexander von, 53

I

Idle Lands Law, 70, 79n4, 189
Indigenous people: exploitation of,
241–42; and history, 29, 30–37; resistance, xvii–xix
Indigo, 51–53
Industry, 6, 18
Institutional Revolutionary Party (PRI):
and COCEI, 1–2, 177–82; constituency, 71; corruption in, 163; electoral
fraud, 281; and ethnic identity, 74–77,
218; ideology, 71, internal conflicts,
163, 170; in Mexico, 147–49; and modernization, 194, 246–47; and national
culture, 217; peasant support for, 218;
reform of, 170–71, 175n14; and Zapotec language, 246–47. *See also* Politics
Iribarren Sierra, Carlos, 244
Irrigation: impact of, 159–60; and land
conflict, 89–91; limits 52, 70, 93; peasant access, 97–98n3
Isthmus of Tehuantepec: agriculture, 88,
101; beauty of, 9; and capitalist development, 233; climate, 8, 87–88, 101;
COCEI analyses of, 188–90; colonial
economy, 45, 50; commercial development, 51; description, 87–88; economic development, 160, 174n4;
education, 185–87; infrastructure, 8;
location, 4–6, 18n4; map, 5; physical
geography, 6; population, 6; social
problems, 186–87; strategic importance, 200; and Valley of Oaxaca, 43
Isthmus Zapotec: alliances, 6–7; and
Christianity, 46; colonial economy, 6;
conquest and colonization of, 6–7; cultural traditions, 44; disease, 8–9; domestic relations, 139; economy, 8,
233–34; origins, 6, 42–44, 125; outsiders' views of, 9; population, 9; and
poverty, 9; rebellions, 7; resistance, 44,
233–34; study of, 8; survival of identity, 174n6; and trade, 43–44
Isthmus Zapotec culture: absence of cultural divisions, 59–60; and class,
229n6; and COCEI, 208–10, 220–21;
and death, 230n12; defense, 235, 259;
and economic development, 193–94;
maintenance of, 45, 180, 267; and preference for midwives, 275; and politics
59, 201–2, 207–10, 216–17; regional influence, 230n10; and resistance, 49;
threats to, 233–34; transformation of,
210
Isthmus Zapotec language: and COCEI,
209, 220, 222–23; and history, 235,
256; incidence, 180; metaphoric use,
35–36; in Oaxaca, 4, 18n3; and politics, 229–30n9, 245; and popular government, 246; PRI uses of, 169; and
radio, 260–61; and resistance, 222–23;
and social relations, 248; Spanish influence on, 228–29n3, 245; survival
of, 185, 237–38. *See also* Tehuantepec
Ixtaltepec, 57, 97n1
Ixtepec, 84, 219
Iturbide, Graciela, 224

J

Jalapa del Marqués, 90, 219
Javier Echeverría, Francisco, 55, 57
Jiménez, Albino, 81–83
Jiménez, Enedino, 209, 225, 239
Jiménez Girón, Eustaquio, 244
Jiménez, Juan, 244
José López Portillo Sugar Mill, 70, 94
Juárez, Benito, 56–58, 67, 74, 79n3,
110–11, 123–24, 126
Juárez Maza, Benito, 126–27
Juchitán: analysis of politics in, 168; and
Central American revolution, 199–
200; development plans for, 172; economic and social relations, 69–70,

159–60, 283; economy, 6; founding, 39–40; history, 15, 67, 151, 158–59; and Isthmus Zapotec culture, 59–60; literary movement, 225–26; location, 4; merchants, 68; and Mexican government 169, 171–72; migration from, 159; physical geography, 6; political struggles, 70, 76–77, 104–5, 164–65, 194–95; popular government, 157, 162–65, 197–202; population, 4, 18n2, 229n5; PRI political strategies'in, 163; relations with San Blas Atempa, 19n6; and social scientists, 143–46; and Third World revolution, 17; uniqueness, 41–42; and Zapotec resistance, 54, 60

Juchitecos: characterization, 41; and identity, 41, 75, 174n6, 180; and independence movements, 7; rebellions, 84–85; relations with Oaxacan government, 123–24, 133–35; representations, 3, 119–20, 123–24; response to capitalist expansion, 68; uniqueness, 25–26, 41–42

K

Kinship, 74–75, 221
Kolko, Berenice, 224

L

Land: access to, 88, 187; and agrarian bureaucracy, 95–96; availability, 88–89; concentration, 70, 72, 76, 89–90, 102, 159–60; conflict over, 48, 54, 56–57, 67, 97n1; distribution, 48, 77–78, 161; expropriation, 102; invasion, 95, 99–100n13; and politics in Juchitán, 201, 218; speculation 7, 89–90

Land tenure: changes in, 174n3, conflict over definitions, 90–97; forms, 89–90, 102, 189; peasant views, 98n6; and political conflict, 91–97; transformations of, 102–3

La Ventosa, 91

Liekens Cerqueda, Enrique, 243, 245
Livestock raising, 6, 45, 47–49, 54
López Chiñas, Gabriel, 3, 208, 211, 243
López Chiñas, Jeremías, 243
López Mateos, Adolfo, 98n6
López Mateos, Manuel, 90, 208
López Miro, Genaro, 243
López Nelio, Daniel, 111, 127, 208, 213, 220
López Portillo, José, 151, 162–63, 188–89

M

Maqueo, Esteban, 54, 57
Madrid, Miguel de la, 96, 163, 166, 283
Marquesado del Valle de Oaxaca, 45, 47
Marriage, 130–31, 139–41
Martínez, Felipe, 171, 230n11
Mass media, 259–60, 262
Mata, Juan de, 126
Matus, Macario, 3, 79n7, 112, 155, 203, 209, 222–23, 226, 280
Matus, Oscar, 127
Merchant capital, 88
Mexican Communist Party (PCM), 1, 18n1, 127, 164, 173–74n1, 198–99, 279–80
Mexican government: national politics, 166; political strategies, 281; relationship to COCEI, 175n17; and repression, 168
Mexican Revolution, 81–85
Mexican Socialist Party (PMS), 18n1, 218
Meyer, Pedro, 224
Midwives, 267–77
Missionaries, 32, 46, 125–26
Mitla, 44, 51
Mixe, 219
Mixtecs, 43, 125, 214
Modernization, 71
Modotti, Tina, 224
Molina, Arcadio, 243–44
Monte Albán, 42–43, 51, 207

Mulattoes, 49–50, 52
Musalem, Manuel, 7, 73, 159
Music, 260–61

N

National Front against Repression, 17,
   21n20
National Plan of Ayala Coordinating
   Committee, 17, 21n20
"New social movements," 14–17
New Society of Juchiteco Students, 243,
   245
Neza, 3, 17, 208, 230n4, 243, 245
Neza Cubi, 3, 73, 79n7, 208, 230n14
Niltepec, 97n1

O

Oaxaca: anthropology in, 19n8; income
   of residents, 19n9; indigenous groups,
   4; major cities, 6; state investment, 9;
   political reform, 163; politics, 163,
   166
Obregón, Alvaro, 74

P

Pan American Highway, 8, 88, 159, 172
Patronage, 165, 218
Peasants: and COCEI, 164; in colonial
   period, 52; differentiation, 16, 68; economic situation, 187; ideology and politics, 59; payment of tribute, 45–47;
   political identification, 217–18; and
   popular radio, 261–62; preconquest
   economy, 42–43; and Sendero Luminoso, 186–87; and social science, xvii;
   subsistence production, 52
Photography, 224–25
Pineda Henestrosa, Víctor, 128, 154,
   178–80, 218, 229n9
Pineda, Jesús, 171
Pineda, Rosendo, 60
Pitao Cozipi, 42
Poetry, 225
Political conflict, 43

Political reform, 173, 194–95
Politics: and art 223–24; and COCEI,
   195; and historical discourse, 71–73;
   and Institutional Revolutionary Party,
   218, 241, 246–47; and popular culture, 226; and social science, 143–46;
   and writing, 13–14. *See also* Isthmus
   Zapotec culture; Isthmus Zapotec language; Mexican government; Representation
Popular histories, 249–51, 253, 255–57
Population: decline, 146–47; ethnic composition, 51; growth, 51, 54
Populism, 191–93
Postmodernism, 10–12, 19n10, 19–
   20n11, 20–21n17
Popular Socialist Party (PPS), 159,
   173–74n1
Prieto, Alejandro, 88

R

Radio, 14, 180, 209, 234, 260–62
Ramírez, Heladio, 97, 171, 173, 230n11,
   279
Rasgado, Federico, 76–77
Rebellion: in Juchitán, 15, 25–26, 78–
   79n3; in Latin America, xvii; against
   Oaxacan government, 55–58; against
   Spanish, 7, 25, 49–50, 126
Reciprocal exchange, 221, 230n13
Representation: and anthropology, 10–
   12, 20n12; and COCEI, 4; and colo-
   nial discourse, 109; of gender
   relations, 112–14; and *Guchachi'*
   Reza, 13; and Isthmus Zapotec, 13,
   109–10; of Juchitecos, 111–14; and
   politics, 12–14; and power relations,
   12, 20n15, 20n16, 20–21n17; and
   writing, 13
Repression: of COCEI by PRI, 153,
   165–66; in colonial period, 126; by
   Mexican workers, 187, 189; of Radio
   Ayuntamiento Popular, 262. *See also*
   COCEI

Resistance: changes in, 50–51; in colonial period, 49–50; and culture, xix; of Juchitecos to Oaxacan government, 123–24; representation of, xix–xx; as response to repression, 231n9
Resistant accommodation, 53, 60
Reyes Cabrera, Manuel, 244
Robles, Roque, 183
Romero, Juana C., 115
Russell, Bertrand, 31

S

Saints, 84
Saint Vincent, 39–40, 84–85, 125–26, 135, 249–51
Salina Cruz: COCEI influence, 219; economy, 18n5; industry, 8, 18n5, 159; and irrigation, 70; migration to, 9
Salinas de Gortari, Carlos, 96, 175n17, 229–30n9, 281–82
Salt, 43, 48, 55–57, 68
San Blas Atempa, 19n6, 57, 90, 93, 219, 283
Sánchez, Héctor, 127, 175n17, 212, 220, 282–83
San Dionisio del Mar, 97n1
Santa María Xadani. *See* Xadani
Slavery, 45, 48–49
Social movements, 195–96
Spanish conquest, 6, 45, 125
Spanish language, 247–48

T

Taru. *See* Musalem, Manuel
Tehuantepec: alliance with Aztecs, 44; gender relations, 139–40; and indigo production, 49–52; and Isthmus Zapotec language, 244; lack of COCEI influence, 219; political decline, 47; population, 54; rebellion, 89; relations with Juchitán, 57–58; and San Blas Atempa, 19n6
Toledo, Francisco, 3, 17, 208–9, 222–25, 228–29n3, 280

Toltecs, 125
Trade, 48–49, 55
Trans-Isthmus Railroad, 88, 102, 159, 198
Tribute, 43, 45, 47, 49–50, 88–89, 126

U

Unified Socialist Party of Mexico (PSUM), 18n1, 164, 170, 173–74n1, 175n11
Usury, 88, 103

V

Vásquez Colmenares, Pedro, 74–75, 163, 197
Violence, 166–67, 221
Virginity, 130–31, 139–40

W

Women: domestic relations, 140–41; in Juchitán history, 60n1; and leadership in COCEI, 220; and midwifery, 267–77; representations of, 133–35, 138–39; and repression, 227; roles, 137–41; status, 41, 112–13; testimonies, 178–82, 250. *See also* COCEI
Workers, 127, 162, 164

X

Xadani, 91, 219, 247

Y

Yodo, Víctor. *See* Pineda Henestrosa, Víctor

Z

Zaachila, 34, 43–44, 51, 125
Zapotec Christianity, 46
Zapotecs: arrival in Isthmus, 6; conquest and colonization, 6–7; relations with Aztecs, 7, 44; struggles, 125–27
Zoque, 43, 45, 219